Cosmic Healing Code:

365 Powerful Techniques to Awaken Divine Energy

Through Numerology, Astrology, Reiki, Crystals &

Chakra Mastery for Mind-Body-Spirit Alignment

By The Peaceful Shaman

This book is a work of nonfiction. While every effort has been made to ensure accuracy, the content is intended for educational and informational purposes only and should not be considered a substitute for professional medical, psychological, or legal advice. Always consult a qualified professional regarding personal health or spiritual practices.

Published by The Peaceful Shaman

Front Matter

This book is dedicated to the radiant souls who dare to embark on a journey of self-discovery and healing. It is for those who yearn to unlock their inner wisdom, to embrace their authentic selves, and to live a life brimming with purpose, joy, and profound connection. This dedication extends to the courageous hearts who seek to transcend limitations, to heal emotional wounds, and to cultivate a deep and abiding sense of peace within. It is a testament to the unwavering belief in the innate capacity of each individual to heal and thrive, to tap into their limitless potential, and to create a life that aligns with their truest aspirations. This work is a beacon of hope for those who feel lost or overwhelmed, a gentle guide for those seeking clarity and direction, and a powerful tool for those ready to embrace the transformative power of holistic wellness. May these pages serve as a catalyst for your personal growth, a source of inspiration on your unique path, and a reminder of the incredible strength and resilience that resides within you. May this journey of self-discovery lead you to a deeper understanding of your connection to the universe, empowering you to live a life that resonates with your soul's truest calling. To those who seek wholeness, to those who embrace change, to those who believe in the power of healing—this book is for you. It is a testament to the boundless potential of the human spirit, a celebration of resilience, and an unwavering affirmation of the transformative power of self-love and self-compassion. May it illuminate your path, guide your steps, and inspire you to embrace the extraordinary journey of cosmic healing. May the energy of this book resonate deep within your being, awakening your innate ability to heal, grow, and evolve into the most vibrant and authentic expression of yourself.

Table of Contents

Chapter 1: Embracing Your Cosmic Journey

Our bodies are not merely physical vessels; they are intricate, vibrant expressions of energy, constantly interacting with the universe's subtle currents. Imagine an invisible, shimmering field surrounding you, pulsating with light and information – this is your aura, your energetic signature. Within this aura, energy flows through pathways called meridians, much like rivers flowing across a landscape. These meridians connect to energy centers within your body known as chakras, swirling vortexes of energy that influence your physical, emotional, and spiritual well-being. Understanding this energetic blueprint is the key to unlocking a life of vibrant health and profound inner peace.

This year-long journey, a cosmic dance of self-discovery and healing, begins with recognizing this fundamental truth: you are inherently capable of healing yourself. This isn't a magical claim, but a recognition of your body's innate wisdom and resilience. Just as a seed contains the blueprint for a magnificent tree, your body holds the blueprint for its own restoration and evolution. Energy healing isn't about fixing something broken; it's about nurturing the inherent power within you to flourish.

Think of your energy field as an intricate tapestry, woven with threads of light and shadow. When these threads are aligned and flowing harmoniously, you experience a sense of balance, vitality, and joy. However, life's stresses, traumas, and negative thought patterns can disrupt this flow, creating imbalances that manifest as physical ailments, emotional turmoil, and mental fog. Perhaps you experience chronic headaches, unexplained fatigue, or persistent anxiety. These might not be isolated symptoms but reflections of energetic blockages, whispers from your body urging you to pay attention.

The chakras, those vibrant energy centers, are particularly susceptible to these imbalances. Each chakra governs specific aspects of your being: the root chakra anchors you to the earth, providing a sense of security and stability; the sacral chakra fuels your creativity and emotional expression; the solar plexus chakra empowers you with self-confidence; the heart chakra opens your capacity for love and compassion; the throat chakra empowers clear communication; the third eye chakra enhances intuition and insight; and the crown chakra connects you to your higher purpose and spiritual essence.

When a chakra is blocked or imbalanced, it can *disrupt the flow of energy* throughout your entire system, leading to a cascade of effects. For instance, a blocked root chakra can manifest as feelings of insecurity and anxiety, potentially leading to physical problems like digestive issues or back pain. A blocked heart chakra might express itself through relationship difficulties or an inability to forgive. By learning to understand and balance your chakras, you're not just treating symptoms; you're addressing the root cause of your energetic imbalances.

The meridians, those energetic pathways, are equally crucial to your well-being. They act like a complex network of rivers, carrying energy throughout your body. When these meridians are blocked, energy stagnates, creating further imbalances. Techniques like acupuncture and acupressure work by stimulating these meridians, restoring the flow of energy and promoting healing.

Your **aura**, that luminous energy field, acts as a protective shield, constantly interacting with the energies around you. It reflects your emotional state, your beliefs, and your overall energetic health. A vibrant, strong aura indicates a robust energy field, capable of resisting negative influences and promoting well-being. A weak or depleted aura, however, might leave you feeling vulnerable and susceptible to illness or negativity. Strengthening your aura is a crucial aspect of cultivating overall energetic health.

Learning to perceive and work with these energetic components is not as mystical as it sounds. It's a matter of developing your awareness and honing your intuition. Throughout this journey, we'll explore various techniques to strengthen your energetic body, including meditation, visualization, crystal healing, and energy work. These practices are not merely esoteric exercises; they are powerful tools for self-healing and personal transformation. Imagine yourself as a skilled artisan, carefully weaving and mending the threads of your energetic tapestry. You are not a passive recipient of your energy; you are its active creator and conductor. Through conscious effort and dedicated practice, you can learn to identify energy blockages, clear stagnant energy, and cultivate a vibrant, harmonious flow.

This is not a journey of quick fixes, but a process of mindful self-discovery. It's about cultivating a deeper understanding of your energetic landscape, nurturing your inner wisdom, and empowering yourself to create the life you truly desire. The process involves cultivating self-awareness, recognizing your patterns and habitual responses, and ultimately transforming them to nurture your well-being.

Take a moment now to connect with your body. Close your eyes and gently bring your awareness to the sensations within. Notice the rhythm of your breath, the subtle pulsations of your heart, the gentle flow of energy coursing through your veins. This is your energetic blueprint, a living testament to your inherent capacity for healing and growth. The journey begins with this fundamental awareness.

Consider this: your thoughts, beliefs, and emotions are not just intangible concepts; they are powerful energy forces shaping your reality. A negative thought pattern can create a ripple effect throughout your energy field, leading to imbalances and disharmony. Conversely, positive thoughts and affirmations can create a powerful surge of energy, promoting healing and well-being. Cultivating a positive mindset is not merely about feeling good; it's about harnessing the power of your thoughts to create positive change.

This concept isn't about forcing positivity, but about consciously choosing thoughts that serve your well-being. It's about recognizing when negative thought patterns arise and gently redirecting them towards more constructive avenues. Through practices like meditation and affirmations, you'll learn to cultivate a more positive internal landscape, fostering a vibrant and harmonious energy flow. This internal shift can then positively impact your external reality.

The power of intention is equally crucial. By setting clear intentions and visualizing desired outcomes, you're actively shaping your energy field and attracting positive experiences. This isn't about wishing for things passively; it's about aligning your energy with your goals, creating a resonant frequency that draws them to you. This involves setting realistic goals and working towards them with focused energy and determination.

Gratitude also plays a vital role. When you practice gratitude, you shift your focus from what's lacking to what you already possess. This simple act of appreciation creates a powerful energetic uplift, attracting more positive experiences into your life. By actively cultivating gratitude, you not only enhance your emotional well-being, but also amplify your capacity to attract abundance and positivity.

Throughout this year, we'll explore various techniques to develop these skills, from guided meditations to practical exercises in visualization and affirmation. We'll learn to create a sacred space, a sanctuary where you can connect with your inner wisdom and nurture your energetic body. We'll learn how to cleanse and purify your energy field, removing stagnant energy and opening yourself to a more vibrant flow. The tools and techniques we'll explore are not merely esoteric practices; they are practical pathways to a healthier, happier, and more fulfilling life.

This is your journey, your unique and personal voyage of self-discovery. Embrace the process, be patient with yourself, and remember that healing is not a destination but a continuous unfolding. Trust in your inherent capacity for healing and allow yourself to be guided by your inner wisdom. The universe is conspiring with you, eager to support your transformation. Let the journey begin. The universe operates on the principle of resonance. Like tuning forks vibrating at the same frequency, our intentions, when aligned with our deepest desires, create a powerful energetic signal that attracts corresponding experiences into our lives. This is the essence of manifestation – not a magical trick, but a fundamental law of energetic interaction. Your thoughts, beliefs, and emotions are not passive observers; they are active participants in shaping your reality. Every thought you think, every emotion you feel, sends out a vibrational frequency that interacts with the universe's subtle energies.

Think of your mind as a powerful radio transmitter. When you consistently broadcast negative thoughts – doubts, fears, anxieties – you're tuning into a frequency that attracts more of the same. You might find yourself experiencing setbacks, disappointments, and challenges, reinforcing the belief that you're not capable of achieving your goals. This is not a matter of blame or judgment, but a recognition of the energetic principle at play. Your energy is broadcasting a signal, and the universe is responding accordingly.

However, the beauty of this energetic principle lies in its malleability. Just as you can change the station on your radio, you can consciously shift your mental frequency to attract more positive experiences. By cultivating a positive mindset, setting clear intentions, and visualizing desired outcomes, you're reprogramming your energetic transmitter, sending out a signal that attracts abundance, joy, and fulfillment. This isn't about suppressing negative emotions or pretending everything is perfect; it's about consciously choosing thoughts that serve your highest good.

Let's explore the practical application of intention setting. The process begins with clarity. What is it that you truly desire? Don't just focus on the outcome; consider the underlying feelings and emotions associated with achieving your goal. If you desire financial abundance, for instance, what does that feeling of abundance feel like? Does it involve a sense of security, freedom, or generosity? Imagine yourself already experiencing these feelings. Feel the joy, the gratitude, the sense of ease.

Once you've clearly defined your desired outcome and associated feelings, visualize yourself already possessing it. Engage all your senses. See yourself living in your dream home, feeling the sun on your skin, smelling the fresh air. Hear the laughter of loved ones, taste the delicious food, feel the soft texture of your clothes. The more vividly you can visualize it, the stronger the energetic signal you'll send out into the universe.

Affirmations are another powerful tool for aligning your energy with your intentions. Affirmations are positive statements that you repeat regularly, reinforcing your desired reality. They're not about self-deception; they're about consciously reprogramming your subconscious mind, replacing limiting beliefs with empowering ones. For example, instead of saying, "I'm struggling financially," you might affirm, "I am attracting abundance and prosperity into my life." Repeat these affirmations daily, feeling the truth of the words resonate within you.

Visualization and affirmations are most effective when combined with *action*. Intention setting isn't about passively wishing for things; it's about actively working towards your goals. If your intention is to improve your health, you might incorporate regular exercise, healthy eating, and stress-reducing practices into your life. If your intention is to find a fulfilling career, you might research different opportunities, network with professionals, and update your resume. Your actions provide the energetic momentum that amplifies your intentions, drawing your desired outcome closer.

Consider the story of Sarah, a talented artist struggling with self-doubt. She longed to have her artwork exhibited in a prestigious gallery, but fear held her back. Through daily meditation and visualization, she practiced seeing herself confidently presenting her work in the gallery, feeling the joy and satisfaction of recognition. She affirmed her creative talent and worthiness, repeating phrases such as, "My art is beautiful and inspiring," and, "I am a successful and confident artist." She also took proactive steps, researching galleries, preparing a high-quality portfolio, and submitting her work. Within months, she received an invitation to exhibit her work, a direct result of her focused intentions and consistent actions.

The power of gratitude is often underestimated in the manifestation process. When you focus on what you're grateful for, you shift your energy from lack to abundance. Gratitude creates a positive feedback loop, attracting more positive experiences into your life. It's not about ignoring challenges; it's about acknowledging the good in your life, even amidst difficulties. Keep a gratitude journal, listing things you're thankful for each day, however small. This simple practice can significantly shift your energetic vibration, making you more receptive to positive opportunities.

Remember, manifestation is a process, not an event. It requires *consistency, patience, and a willingness to trust the universe's guidance.* There will be times when you doubt yourself, when you face setbacks or challenges. During these times, remember the power of your intentions. Reaffirm your commitment to your goals, visualize your desired outcome, and continue practicing gratitude. Your persistence will eventually bear fruit, drawing your desires into your reality.

The journey of manifestation is also deeply intertwined with the chakra system. Each chakra resonates with specific intentions and desires. For example, working with the root chakra can help manifest feelings of security and stability. The sacral chakra supports creativity and abundance. The solar plexus chakra empowers self-confidence and personal achievement. The heart chakra opens the path to love and fulfilling relationships. The throat chakra facilitates clear communication and self-expression. The third eye chakra enhances intuition and spiritual insight, while the crown chakra connects you to your higher purpose and spiritual essence.

By working with each chakra individually, through meditation, crystal healing, and other techniques, you can amplify your intention-setting practices. For instance, if you're aiming for a career change, focusing on your throat chakra can help you clearly articulate your aspirations and communicate effectively with potential employers. If you're seeking a loving relationship, focusing on your heart chakra can open you to compassion, vulnerability, and authentic connection. Integrating these chakra-specific practices into your manifestation journey can amplify your results, allowing you to tap into the full spectrum of your energetic potential.

The process of manifestation is not just about achieving external goals; it's also about cultivating inner harmony and well-being. When you align your intentions with your soul's purpose, you not only achieve your desires, but you also experience a profound sense of fulfillment and inner peace. This integration of external achievement and inner harmony is the ultimate expression of a life lived in alignment with your true self.

Remember, you are not alone on this journey. The universe supports your aspirations. Trust in your innate ability to manifest your dreams, and allow the power of intention to guide you toward a life of abundance, joy, and profound fulfillment. Embrace the process, be patient with yourself, and celebrate every step of your progress. The journey itself is a testament to your growth, a testament to your power to shape your reality through the conscious application of intention.The universe whispers secrets to those who learn to listen. It speaks not in booming pronouncements but in the subtle stirrings of intuition, the quiet nudges of your inner voice. Connecting with your inner wisdom is the key to unlocking your true potential, to navigating life's complexities with grace and purpose, and to aligning yourself with the cosmic flow. This isn't about seeking grand revelations or mystical experiences; it's about cultivating a deep, abiding connection with the wellspring of knowledge that resides within you.

This journey of self-discovery begins with introspection, a deliberate turning inward to explore the landscapes of your own mind and heart. Journaling is a powerful tool for this process. Grab a notebook, a pen, and a quiet space. Don't overthink it; simply allow your thoughts and feelings to flow onto the page. Write about your dreams, your fears, your aspirations, your daily experiences. Don't censor yourself; let the words emerge unfiltered. This is a space for honesty, a sanctuary for your unedited thoughts and emotions. Over time, patterns will emerge, revealing hidden beliefs, unconscious biases, and recurring themes in your life.

Consider this exercise: Spend ten minutes each morning writing down three things you are grateful for. This seemingly simple practice has profound effects. It shifts your focus from lack to abundance, cultivating a positive emotional state and priming your mind for receiving the universe's blessings. It's not just about listing material possessions, but also about acknowledging the less tangible gifts: the warmth of the sun, a kind gesture from a stranger, the love of a pet, your own good health. The more consistently you practice this, the more attuned you become to the positive aspects of your life, developing a heightened sense of appreciation for both the big and small things.

Meditation is another invaluable tool for connecting with your inner wisdom. It's not about emptying your mind, which is nearly impossible, but about observing your thoughts and emotions without judgment. Find a comfortable position, either sitting or lying down, and close your eyes. Focus on your breath, the gentle rise and fall of your chest or abdomen. When your mind wanders, as it inevitably will, simply acknowledge the thought without getting caught up in it. Gently guide your attention back to your breath.

Here's a guided meditation to help you connect with your inner wisdom:
Find a quiet space where you can relax without interruption. Sit comfortably with your spine straight, but not rigid. Close your eyes gently.
Begin by focusing on your breath. Notice the sensation of the air entering and leaving your body. Feel the rise and fall of your chest or abdomen. Inhale deeply, filling your lungs with fresh air, and exhale slowly, releasing any tension or stress.
Now, imagine a soft, warm light emanating from within your heart center. This light represents your inner wisdom, your connection to the universe. Allow this light to expand, filling your entire being with warmth, peace, and clarity.
As you breathe, visualize this light illuminating the corners of your mind, dissolving any

negativity, fear, or doubt. Let go of any worries or anxieties that are weighing you down. Release them into the light, allowing it to transform them into positive energy.

Now, ask yourself a question. It could be something specific, like "What is the best path forward for me in this situation?" or something more general, like "What is my true purpose in life?" Listen quietly within. The answer may not come immediately, but allow yourself to be open to the subtle whispers of your intuition. Don't strive for a definitive answer; simply allow the question to resonate within you.

Continue to focus on your breath and the warm light within your heart. Allow your mind to rest, to settle, to be still. Simply be present in this moment, connected to the boundless wisdom that resides within you.

When you are ready, gently bring your awareness back to your surroundings. Open your eyes slowly, taking a few moments to integrate the experience.

Mindfulness, the practice of being fully present in the moment, is another pathway to inner wisdom. It involves paying attention to your senses, your thoughts, and your emotions without judgment. Simple activities, like eating a meal slowly and deliberately, savoring each bite, or taking a walk in nature, noticing the sounds, smells, and sights around you, can enhance your mindfulness practice. These moments of quiet observation create space for your inner wisdom to emerge. The everyday activities become gateways to deeper awareness and self-understanding. Through mindful practices, the routine tasks of daily life transform into profound moments of connection with yourself and the universe.

Listening to your intuition is crucial. Intuition is that inner knowing, that gut feeling that often guides you in the right direction. It's not always clear or loud; sometimes it's a subtle whisper, a hunch, a feeling in your gut. Learn to recognize these subtle signals. When faced with a decision, take some time to quiet your mind and listen to your inner voice. What does your intuition tell you? Trust your instincts; they are often far wiser than your intellect.

Connecting with your inner wisdom is not a destination, but an ongoing process. It's a continuous exploration of self, a journey of unveiling the depths of your being. Through consistent practices of journaling, meditation, and mindfulness, you will develop a profound connection with the wellspring of knowledge that resides within. This connection empowers you to make informed choices, navigate challenges with grace, and create a life aligned with your soul's purpose. Embrace this journey; it is a path towards greater self-awareness, personal fulfillment, and a deeper connection to the universe. Remember, the answers you seek are not out there, but within you, waiting to be discovered. The more you practice these techniques, the louder and clearer your inner wisdom will become, guiding you toward a life of greater purpose and fulfillment.Our journey of self-discovery deepens now, moving beyond the realm of introspection and mindfulness to explore the intricate energy system that governs our physical, emotional, and spiritual well-being: the chakras. Imagine your body not just as a physical vessel, but as a radiant field of energy, a vibrant tapestry woven with threads of light and life force. This energy flows through seven primary energy centers, known as chakras, each resonating with a specific frequency and influencing different aspects of our lives. Understanding these energy centers is crucial to achieving holistic balance and unlocking your full potential.

The word "*chakra*" originates from Sanskrit, meaning "wheel" or "spinning disc." This aptly describes the dynamic nature of these energy vortices, constantly spinning and radiating energy throughout our being. They are not merely hypothetical concepts; their presence is felt, their influence is undeniable. A subtle shift in the energy of a chakra can manifest as a physical ailment, an emotional imbalance, or a mental block. Conversely, a balanced chakra system radiates vitality, clarity, and a deep sense of inner peace.

Let's embark on a journey to meet each of these vital energy centers, starting with the root chakra, the foundation upon which our entire energetic structure is built. This chakra, located at the base of the spine, is associated with the color red and governs our sense of security, grounding, and stability. When balanced, the root chakra provides a feeling of safety and belonging, fostering resilience and a sense of being firmly planted in the world. An imbalanced root chakra, however, can manifest as feelings of fear, anxiety, insecurity, and instability. Physical symptoms might include digestive problems, lower back pain, and problems with the legs and feet. Crystals associated with the root chakra, such as red jasper and garnet, can help to restore balance and enhance its energy flow. A simple exercise to connect with your root chakra is to stand barefoot on the earth, feeling the connection between your body and the ground, consciously drawing up the earth's energy into your body. Visualize the energy swirling in a vibrant red color. Spend a few moments appreciating this grounding sensation.

Moving upwards, we encounter the ***sacral chakra***, located just below the navel. This chakra is associated with the color orange and governs creativity, sexuality, pleasure, and emotional expression. A balanced sacral chakra fosters emotional fluidity, creativity, and healthy relationships. Imbalances can manifest as emotional blocks, sexual dysfunction, lack of creativity, and difficulty expressing emotions. Physical symptoms may include reproductive issues, lower abdominal pain, and urinary tract problems. Crystals like carnelian and orange calcite can help to restore balance and promote healthy energy flow in the sacral chakra. To connect with your sacral chakra, imagine a warm, pulsating orange light flowing through your lower abdomen. Visualize the energy flowing freely, creating a sense of ease and openness. Allow yourself to feel the warmth and energy, embracing creativity and emotional expression. Next, we encounter the solar plexus chakra, situated in the upper abdomen. This chakra is associated with the color yellow and governs personal power, self-esteem, and self-confidence. A balanced solar plexus chakra fosters confidence, self-worth, and the ability to assert oneself effectively. Imbalances can manifest as low self-esteem, feelings of inadequacy, and difficulty setting boundaries. Physical symptoms may include digestive problems, ulcers, and stomach aches. Crystals such as yellow calcite and citrine can assist in balancing this chakra. An exercise to connect with your solar plexus chakra involves visualizing a bright yellow light in your upper abdomen, radiating outwards. Feel the warmth and energy, recognizing your inner strength and power. Affirmations such as "I am powerful," "I am confident," and "I am worthy" can enhance the effects of this practice.

The **heart chakra**, situated in the center of the chest, is associated with the color green and governs love, compassion, forgiveness, and connection. This chakra is the bridge between the lower three chakras, which are focused on the physical and emotional aspects of being, and the upper three chakras, which deal with the mental and spiritual aspects. A balanced heart chakra fosters empathy, compassion, and healthy relationships. Imbalances can manifest as feelings of loneliness, isolation, resentment, and difficulty loving oneself or others. Physical symptoms may include heart problems, chest pains, and respiratory issues. Crystals like rose quartz and emerald can aid in balancing this chakra, facilitating emotional healing and fostering a sense of connection. A powerful exercise is to visualize a vibrant green light radiating from your heart center, expanding outwards to encompass all beings. Feel the warmth and love, and send out feelings of compassion and understanding.

The **throat chakra**, located in the throat area, is associated with the color blue and governs communication, self-expression, and truth. A balanced throat chakra allows for clear and honest communication, both verbally and non-verbally. Imbalances can manifest as difficulty expressing oneself, feeling unheard or misunderstood, or withholding the truth. Physical symptoms might include throat problems, neck pain, and thyroid issues. Crystals such as blue lapis lazuli and turquoise can facilitate clear communication and support the throat chakra's energy. A simple exercise is to visualize a brilliant blue light in your throat area, feeling a sense of ease and openness as you express yourself freely.

The **third eye chakra**, situated in the center of the forehead between the eyebrows, is associated with the color indigo and governs intuition, insight, wisdom, and psychic abilities. A balanced third eye chakra fosters heightened intuition, clarity of thought, and a strong connection to one's inner wisdom. Imbalances can manifest as confusion, lack of clarity, difficulty focusing, and suppressed intuition. Physical symptoms may include headaches, eye problems, and sinus issues. Crystals like amethyst and sodalite can support the third eye chakra's function. To connect with this chakra, visualize a deep indigo light pulsating in your forehead, enhancing your intuitive abilities and expanding your awareness.

Finally, we reach the **crown chakra**, located at the top of the head, associated with the color violet and governing spiritual connection, enlightenment, and higher consciousness. This chakra connects us to the divine, fostering a sense of unity and oneness with the universe. A balanced crown chakra allows for profound spiritual experiences, a strong sense of purpose, and a deep connection to something greater than oneself. Imbalances can manifest as feelings of disconnection, lack of purpose, and a sense of being lost or unfulfilled. Physical symptoms may include headaches, insomnia, and neurological issues. Crystals like clear quartz and amethyst can aid in enhancing the crown chakra's energy. Connect with this chakra by visualizing a brilliant violet light radiating from the top of your head, connecting you to the universe's boundless energy and wisdom.

Throughout this journey of exploring the seven chakras, remember that these energy centers are *interconnected*. An imbalance in one chakra can affect the others, creating a ripple effect throughout the entire system. The key to holistic wellness lies in recognizing and addressing these imbalances, restoring the flow of energy and bringing your entire being into harmony. The practices and exercises described here are merely a starting point. As you become more attuned to your energy system, you will discover even deeper ways to nurture and balance your chakras, enhancing your physical, emotional, and spiritual well-being, and ultimately strengthening your connection to the cosmic flow. The path towards self-discovery and holistic healing is a continuous journey, and this exploration of the chakras marks a significant step forward in your transformative experience. Embrace this newfound knowledge and watch as your energy, your life, and your understanding of yourself transform. The universe awaits, ready to support you in this profound exploration of your inner self.Now that we've embarked on a journey into the depths of your inner energy system, understanding the intricate dance of your seven chakras, it's time to create a sanctuary – a sacred space – where you can nurture this energy, heal imbalances, and deepen your connection to the cosmic flow. This space isn't merely a physical location; it's a vibrational resonance, a haven of tranquility where your energy can freely expand and your spirit can soar. Think of it as a personal energy amplifier, a place designed to amplify your intentions and facilitate profound healing.

The preparation of this space is as crucial as the healing practices themselves. The environment significantly impacts the effectiveness of any energy work. A cluttered, chaotic space reflects a cluttered, chaotic mind, hindering the flow of energy and preventing deep relaxation. Conversely, a clean, peaceful, and intentionally organized space creates a harmonious environment that supports healing and self-discovery. Begin by decluttering your chosen space – this could be a corner of your bedroom, a quiet nook in your living room, or even a dedicated meditation room. Remove anything that evokes negative feelings or represents stagnant energy – broken objects, things you no longer use, or items that simply weigh you down emotionally. The goal is to create a sense of spaciousness, both physically and energetically.

Cleanliness is paramount. A thorough physical cleaning is essential. Wiping surfaces, dusting, vacuuming, and airing out the space removes not only physical dust but also energetic residue. Imagine the energy in your space as a delicate tapestry; dust particles represent accumulated negativity, hindering the free flow of positive energy. By cleaning, you're preparing a blank canvas upon which you can weave a new, vibrant energy pattern. This isn't simply about tidiness; it's about creating a sacred container for your healing journey. Use natural cleaning products whenever possible, avoiding harsh chemicals that can disrupt the delicate energy balance. The scent of lavender, chamomile, or sandalwood can further enhance the tranquility of your space, creating a calming and inviting atmosphere.

Once the physical cleansing is complete, it's time to address the energetic cleansing. This is where you actively clear the space of any lingering negative energies, residual emotions, or unwanted vibrations. One of the most effective methods is smudging – a centuries-old practice of burning sacred herbs, such as sage, palo santo, or cedar, to purify and cleanse the energy of a space. As the smoke wafts through your space, visualize it dissolving negativity, removing stagnant energy, and replacing it with a fresh, clean, positive vibration. Intention is key here; clearly state your intention to cleanse the space, to remove negativity, and to create a sanctuary for healing and self-discovery.

Alternatively, sound healing can be equally effective in cleansing your sacred space. The vibrations of singing bowls, chimes, or even your own voice can dislodge stagnant energy and restore balance. Allow the resonant sounds to fill the space, visualizing them washing away negativity and infusing the space with positive, healing vibrations. The act of creating sound itself can be a powerful form of intention-setting, aligning your energy with the purpose of your sacred space. Experiment with different sounds and frequencies, finding those that resonate most deeply with you and your healing journey.

Now, it's time to imbue your sacred space with positive energy. Creating an altar is a powerful way to personalize your space and focus your intentions. Choose a surface – a small table, a shelf, or even a windowsill – and arrange meaningful objects that resonate with your healing journey. Crystals, of course, play a vital role. Select crystals that correspond to the chakras you wish to focus on or crystals that simply bring you a sense of peace and tranquility. Rose quartz for love, amethyst for spiritual awareness, clear quartz for amplification – the possibilities are endless.

Beyond crystals, incorporate objects that hold personal significance. A photograph of a loved one, a cherished piece of artwork, a feather representing freedom, a small plant symbolizing growth – each item should evoke positive emotions and strengthen your connection to your intention. Consider adding candles to represent light and intention, incense to enhance the atmosphere, or a small bowl of water to symbolize purity and cleansing. As you arrange these items, feel the energy shifting in your space, transforming it into a vibrant vortex of positive energy.

Visualizations and affirmations further amplify the transformative power of your sacred space. As you sit in your prepared space, visualize a radiant white light filling every corner, cleansing and purifying the environment. Imagine this light dissolving any remaining negativity, creating a protective shield of positive energy around the space. Affirm your intentions, stating clearly and confidently the purpose of this space: "This is my sacred space, a haven of healing and self-discovery. Here, I embrace my inner peace, connect with my higher self, and manifest my deepest desires." Repeat these affirmations, allowing them to permeate your being and infuse your space with their potent energy.

The creation of your sacred space is a continuous process, an evolving reflection of your inner journey. As you progress on your path of self-discovery, you may adjust the objects on your altar, add new elements, or modify the practices you use to cleanse and energize the space. Embrace the fluidity of this process, trusting your intuition to guide you in creating a truly unique and deeply personal sanctuary for your healing journey. This space becomes your sanctuary, a place where you can consistently connect with your inner wisdom, embrace your true self, and embark on profound healing with confidence and clarity. Your cosmic journey begins here, in this carefully curated space designed to amplify your innate healing abilities and connect you deeply to the universe's boundless energy. ***This is not just a room; it is your gateway to transformation.***

Chapter 2: Mastering Your Chakras

Now, as we journey deeper into the landscape of your inner self, we arrive at the foundation— the *Muladhara*, or **root chakra**. This vibrant crimson energy center resides at the base of your spine, anchoring you to the earth and providing a sense of grounding, stability, and security. Imagine it as the sturdy bedrock upon which your entire energetic structure rests. A balanced root chakra is the cornerstone of holistic well-being, providing a sense of safety, confidence, and resilience in the face of life's challenges.

When the root chakra is functioning optimally, you experience a profound connection to the earth, feeling safe, secure, and confident in your ability to navigate life's ups and downs. You feel a sense of belonging, rootedness, and a deep trust in the universe's benevolent support. Your physical body feels strong and vital, your finances are stable, and your overall sense of well-being radiates outwards. You feel grounded and present, able to manage stress effectively and maintain a healthy sense of self-worth.

However, when this foundational chakra is imbalanced, the consequences can be far-reaching. A blocked or underactive root chakra manifests as feelings of insecurity, anxiety, fear, and a lack of stability in various aspects of life. This imbalance can lead to financial instability, difficulty establishing healthy relationships, and a pervasive sense of unease or even panic. Physical manifestations can include digestive problems, lower back pain, immune deficiencies, and a general feeling of being ungrounded or "spaced out." You might find yourself constantly seeking external validation or clinging to possessions for a sense of security.

One common manifestation of a weakened root chakra is **financial insecurity**. This isn't simply about having enough money; it's about a deep-seated feeling of lack and scarcity. Individuals with an imbalanced root chakra often struggle with money management, feeling perpetually stressed about finances regardless of their actual financial situation. They may overspend, hoard, or engage in impulsive financial decisions driven by fear and insecurity. This fear isn't necessarily rational; it stems from a deeper sense of instability and a lack of trust in their ability to provide for themselves.

Another area affected by a weakened root chakra is **relationships**. Feeling insecure and ungrounded translates into difficulty forming and maintaining healthy connections. Individuals may struggle with intimacy, fear abandonment, or constantly seek reassurance from others. Their relationships may be marked by codependency, control issues, or a pervasive lack of trust. This stems from a lack of self-trust and a deep-seated belief that they are inherently unworthy of love and belonging.

Restoring balance to the root chakra is a journey of self-discovery and self-acceptance. It involves nurturing a sense of safety, security, and self-worth, which allows you to connect more deeply with your innate strength and resilience. This involves several key practices, including grounding meditations, visualization techniques, and crystal healing.

Grounding meditations are a powerful tool for connecting to the earth's energy and restoring a sense of stability. Find a quiet space where you can sit or lie down comfortably. Close your eyes and focus on your breath, feeling the rhythm of your inhale and exhale. Visualize roots extending from your base chakra down into the earth, anchoring you firmly to the ground. Feel the earth's energy rising up through your roots, filling you with a sense of stability and support. Imagine the earth's grounding energy soothing your anxieties and filling you with a sense of peace and security. Spend a few minutes focusing on this connection, allowing the earth's energy to nourish and revitalize you. Repeat this meditation daily, even for just a few minutes, to maintain a strong connection to your root chakra.

Visualization techniques can further enhance the grounding process. Imagine a vibrant red light emanating from your root chakra, expanding outward like a warm embrace. Visualize this energy filling your entire body, providing you with strength, stability, and resilience. Imagine yourself as a strong, resilient tree, deeply rooted in the earth, unyielding to the winds of change. Feel the strength of your roots, the stability of your trunk, and the unwavering resilience of your branches. These visualizations will help to reinforce your sense of security and empower you to face life's challenges with greater confidence.

Crystal healing can also be incredibly beneficial in balancing the root chakra. *Red Jasper*, in particular, is a powerful grounding stone that promotes stability and security. Hold the Red Jasper in your hand during your meditation or keep it near your root chakra throughout the day. Allow its energy to soothe your anxieties and enhance your sense of connection to the earth. Other crystals associated with the root chakra include *Garnet, Black Tourmaline, and Hematite*, each offering unique properties that can support grounding and stability.

Beyond these practices, consider making **changes to your lifestyle** that support root chakra balance. *Prioritize healthy eating habits*, focusing on grounding foods like root vegetables and whole grains. *Engage in regular physical activity*, such as walking, hiking, or gardening, to further strengthen your connection to the earth. *Spend time in nature*, allowing the natural world to nourish your soul and restore your sense of connection. Remember, this is a holistic journey encompassing mind, body, and spirit; physical practices complement and strengthen your energy work.

Let's consider a real-life example: Sarah, a successful businesswoman, was constantly overwhelmed by anxiety and a nagging sense of insecurity, despite her professional achievements. She felt a deep-seated fear of failure, always striving for more, never feeling quite enough. Through energy healing sessions focusing on her root chakra and incorporating grounding meditations and Red Jasper, Sarah began to reconnect with her inner strength and resilience. She began to recognize her self-worth, independent of external validation. Her anxiety lessened, replaced by a sense of calm confidence. She learned to trust in her ability to navigate life's challenges, leading to improved relationships and a more balanced approach to her work and life. Her financial anxieties eased as she established healthy financial habits grounded in self-trust and confidence rather than fear.

Another example is Mark: a struggling musician who constantly doubted his abilities and felt insecure about his prospects. He spent years feeling disconnected from his passion and suffered from chronic back pain. Through incorporating grounding exercises, sound healing using resonant tones targeted to the root chakra, and consciously spending time in nature, Mark reconnected with his creative energy. He found a new sense of stability, both personally and professionally. His back pain gradually subsided as he addressed the energetic imbalances at the root of his physical discomfort. His newfound sense of grounding fueled his creativity and confidence, leading to new opportunities and a more fulfilling life.

Remember, balancing your root chakra is a journey of self-discovery, not a destination. It's a process of ongoing exploration and self-nurturing. Be patient with yourself, trusting in your innate ability to heal and grow. Embrace the practices we've discussed, and allow them to guide you toward a deeper sense of grounding, stability, and security, empowering you to build a strong foundation for a life filled with joy, confidence, and inner peace. As you cultivate a strong and balanced root chakra, you'll find that every other aspect of your life blossoms and flourishes, reflecting the strength and security of your energetic foundation. This journey is a testament to your inherent resilience and the power of self-healing, allowing you to connect with the earth's energy and build a life filled with confidence and unwavering self-belief. Each day, as you engage in these practices, you deepen your connection to the earth, enhancing your ability to weather life's storms and embrace its gifts with newfound strength and clarity. The journey to a balanced root chakra is a journey to a more grounded, secure, and empowered you. Having established a firm foundation with the root chakra, we now ascend to the sacral chakra, Svadhisthana, a swirling vortex of vibrant orange energy nestled just below your navel. This energetic center is the wellspring of your creativity, your capacity for pleasure, and your ability to express your emotions freely and authentically. Unlike the grounding energy of the root chakra, the sacral chakra pulsates with a fluid, dynamic energy, a vibrant current that flows through your life, fueling your passions and inspiring your creativity. It's the seat of your sensuality, your emotional fluidity, and your connection to the joy and pleasure inherent in life.

A balanced sacral chakra allows you to move through life with *grace and fluidity*, embracing change with ease and navigating emotional landscapes with resilience. You express your feelings openly and honestly, without fear of judgment or reprisal. Your creativity flows effortlessly, inspiring you to create and innovate in all aspects of your life. You are comfortable with intimacy and embrace healthy relationships filled with passion and connection. Your sexual energy is healthy and balanced, enhancing your sense of self and your capacity for connection with others.

Imagine a river flowing freely, its waters clear and vibrant. This is the image of a balanced sacral chakra: a smooth, unimpeded flow of creative energy, emotional expression, and sensual pleasure. You feel alive, energized, and connected to the joy of being. You experience a sense of abundance and fulfillment in all areas of your life, including your relationships, creative pursuits, and even your finances – the sacral chakra influences your ability to receive and manifest abundance. You are not only creating but also attracting the resources and opportunities you need to nourish your life's passions.

However, when the sacral chakra is blocked or imbalanced, the consequences can be profound and far-reaching. The free-flowing river becomes stagnant, its waters murky and choked with debris. This manifests as a range of emotional and physical challenges. You may find yourself struggling with low self-esteem, feeling inadequate or unworthy of love and happiness. Your creativity may feel stifled, replaced by feelings of inertia and lack of inspiration. You might experience difficulties in your intimate relationships, struggling to form deep connections or to express your needs and desires openly.

One of the most common manifestations of an imbalanced sacral chakra is a *suppressed capacity for pleasure*. This isn't simply about sexual pleasure; it encompasses all forms of joy and fulfillment, from the simple pleasure of a warm bath to the ecstatic joy of creative expression. Individuals with a blocked sacral chakra often feel disconnected from their bodies and their senses. They may struggle to experience pleasure or find themselves constantly seeking external validation to fill an inner void. This can manifest as addictive behaviors, compulsive shopping, or other forms of self-sabotage designed to fill the void left by the lack of inner joy.

Another significant consequence of an imbalanced sacral chakra is *emotional stagnation*. This manifests as difficulty processing emotions, leading to emotional repression, suppression, or outbursts of uncontrolled anger, sadness, or fear. The inability to freely express emotions leads to pent-up energy, creating blockages in the flow of life force. This emotional repression can manifest physically as digestive issues, reproductive problems, or even chronic pain, indicating a profound imbalance in the energetic flow of the body. Restoring balance to the sacral chakra involves a multifaceted approach, engaging the mind, body, and spirit. It's a journey of self-discovery, of reconnecting with your inner joy, and reclaiming your ability to experience and express your emotions authentically. This healing journey requires gentle self-compassion and the willingness to explore your emotional landscape with honesty and grace.

Creative expression is paramount in balancing the sacral chakra. Engage in activities that bring you joy and allow your creativity to flow freely. This could be anything from painting and dancing to writing poetry or playing music. The key is to engage in activities that ignite your passion and allow you to express yourself without self-judgment or inhibitions. Let your creativity flow, whether it's writing a song, painting a picture, dancing to your favorite music, or crafting with your hands, tap into the joy of creating something from nothing.

Mindful movement is another powerful tool for harmonizing the sacral chakra. Practices such as yoga, tai chi, and qigong promote fluidity and energy flow throughout the body. These practices encourage gentle movement and deep breathing, helping to release blockages and restore the natural flow of energy. Dancing, particularly free-form dance, can be incredibly cathartic, allowing you to express emotions through movement. Feeling your body move, letting go of inhibitions, allows you to free trapped emotional energy.

Crystal healing can also be extremely beneficial. Carnelian, with its vibrant orange hue, is a particularly potent stone for the sacral chakra. Its energy promotes creativity, vitality, and emotional balance. Holding Carnelian, meditating with it, or wearing it as jewelry can help to activate and balance the sacral chakra. Other crystals associated with this chakra include orange calcite, sunstone, and amber, each possessing unique properties that support emotional healing and creative expression.

Embracing healthy sexuality is an essential aspect of sacral chakra balance. This involves cultivating a positive and healthy relationship with your own body and sexuality. It's about embracing your sensuality and exploring your desires in a safe and consensual manner. This is not about promoting promiscuity, but about fostering a healthy respect for your body and its needs, whether you are partnered or single. A healthy relationship with your sexuality is fundamental to a well-balanced sacral chakra. It is an aspect of life-force energy that needs to be acknowledged, appreciated, and treated with respect.

Beyond these practices, consider **nurturing your emotional intelligence**. This involves developing your ability to identify, understand, and manage your emotions effectively. Engage in practices such as journaling, meditation, or emotional processing with a therapist to develop self-awareness and emotional regulation. Learning to recognize and process emotions rather than repress or avoid them is key to unlocking the flow of creative energy and the joy of life.

Let's consider the example of Emily: a talented writer who struggled with writer's block and low self-esteem. She felt unable to express her creativity and doubted her ability to connect with others deeply. Through regular creative journaling, mindful movement, and working with Carnelian, Emily began to reconnect with her inner joy and release her creative block.

She found newfound confidence in expressing her emotions and forming authentic connections with others. Her writing flourished, and her life took on a new vibrancy.

Another example is David: a successful businessman who felt emotionally numb and disconnected from his inner self. He found himself in a stagnant relationship and felt unable to experience true joy or intimacy. Through a holistic healing approach encompassing energy work focused on his sacral chakra, creative dance therapy, and using orange calcite meditation, David began to feel more comfortable expressing his feelings, which improved his relationships and allowed him to experience authentic joy and connection. His career also experienced a breakthrough as he embraced a more creative approach to problem-solving and leadership.

The path to a balanced sacral chakra is a journey of *self-discovery* and *self-acceptance*. It's about embracing your creativity, nurturing your emotional intelligence, and allowing yourself to experience the full spectrum of human experience, including pleasure, joy, and even pain. As you cultivate a balanced sacral chakra, you'll find that your life is filled with passion, creativity, and authentic connection, allowing you to live a richer and more fulfilling life. Embrace this journey of self-discovery, and allow your inner light to shine brightly.Now, we ascend to the solar plexus chakra, Manipura, a radiant sun of golden energy residing in the area of your abdomen, just above your navel. This powerful energy center is the seat of your personal power, self-esteem, and self-confidence. Unlike the fluid energy of the sacral chakra, Manipura radiates a strong, assertive energy, a fiery core that fuels your ambition, drive, and willpower. It's the engine room of your being, propelling you forward with determination and purpose. A balanced solar plexus chakra empowers you to take control of your life, to pursue your goals with unwavering conviction, and to navigate challenges with resilience and strength.

Imagine a sun blazing brightly, its golden rays radiating warmth and energy. This is the image of a balanced **solar plexus chakra**: *a powerful, radiant energy that fuels your actions and* *empowers you to achieve your full potential.* You feel confident, assertive, and capable of overcoming any obstacle. You have a strong sense of self, knowing your worth and standing firmly in your truth. You are not afraid to express your opinions, set boundaries, and pursue your dreams with unwavering determination. You are self-reliant, resourceful, and capable of taking charge of your life, making confident decisions and acting on them.

This chakra governs your *willpower, your ability to manifest your desires, and your sense of personal authority.* It's the energy center that allows you to take initiative, to stand up for yourself, and to claim your place in the world. It is also deeply connected to your digestive system, reflecting your ability to process and assimilate experiences and information. However, when the solar plexus chakra is blocked or imbalanced, the consequences can be significant and far-reaching. The radiant sun dims, its light obscured by clouds of doubt and fear. This manifests as a range of emotional and physical challenges, primarily centered around a diminished sense of self-worth and personal power. You might experience low self-esteem, feeling inadequate, unworthy, or powerless in the face of life's challenges. You may struggle to assert yourself, fearing conflict or criticism. You might find yourself constantly seeking external validation, relying on others for approval and direction rather than trusting your own inner guidance. Your ambition may be stifled, replaced by feelings of apathy, procrastination, and self-doubt.

The physical manifestations of an imbalanced solar plexus chakra often involve the *digestive system.* This is because the chakra governs the processing and assimilation of both physical and emotional nourishment. Issues like indigestion, irritable bowel syndrome (IBS), ulcers, and other digestive problems can indicate a blockage or imbalance in Manipura. Chronic fatigue, low energy levels, and a general sense of being overwhelmed can also be indicative of an underactive or blocked solar plexus chakra. This is because the chakra is responsible for providing the energy to power through daily tasks and manage stress.

Individuals with an imbalanced solar plexus chakra may struggle with *setting boundaries, saying no to others, or expressing their needs clearly*. They might feel responsible for the feelings and needs of others, often at the expense of their own well-being. This can lead to feelings of resentment, burnout, and a diminished sense of self. They might also struggle with decision-making, feeling paralyzed by fear of making the wrong choice. This stems from a lack of self-trust and confidence in their own inner wisdom.

Another common manifestation is a tendency towards *people-pleasing*. Individuals struggling with a blocked Manipura will often prioritize the needs and desires of others above their own, fearing rejection or disapproval. This can lead to a feeling of being overwhelmed and taken advantage of, further depleting their already weakened sense of personal power. They may feel incapable of setting boundaries, leaving themselves vulnerable to exploitation and emotional exhaustion.

Restoring balance to the solar plexus chakra involves **reclaiming your personal power and nurturing your self-esteem**. It's a journey of self-discovery, of identifying and challenging limiting beliefs, and developing a strong sense of self-worth. This requires courage, self-compassion, and a willingness to step outside your comfort zone.

One of the most effective ways to strengthen your solar plexus chakra is to *engage in activities that foster self-empowerment*. This could include setting clear goals and taking concrete steps towards achieving them. It involves celebrating your accomplishments, both big and small, and recognizing your strengths and capabilities. It's about acknowledging your value and worth, regardless of external validation or approval. This self-affirmation is a crucial step in strengthening your connection to your inner power.

Assertiveness training is another powerful tool for balancing Manipura. This involves learning to express your needs and opinions clearly and respectfully, even when it means saying no to others. It is about establishing healthy boundaries and protecting your energy from those who drain or deplete you. Assertiveness training teaches you how to communicate effectively without aggression, allowing you to stand up for yourself without compromising your relationships.

Setting boundaries is crucial for reclaiming your personal power. This involves learning to say no to requests that overextend you, to prioritize your own needs, and to protect your energy from those who demand more than you can give. It involves creating a shield around your personal space, allowing you to nurture your own well-being without feeling guilty or selfish. This can be a challenging process, but it is essential for cultivating a strong and healthy solar plexus chakra.

Yellow Calcite is a powerful crystal for the solar plexus chakra, radiating warmth and energy that promotes self-confidence and personal power. Its vibrant yellow hue mirrors the sun-like energy of Manipura, enhancing its radiance and promoting a sense of inner strength and resilience. Holding yellow calcite, meditating with it, or wearing it as jewelry can help to activate and balance this important energy center, dissolving blockages and restoring the flow of energy. It is a powerful tool for boosting self-esteem and fostering a feeling of self-worth. Other crystals associated with the solar plexus chakra include tiger's eye, sunstone, and citrine, each contributing unique properties to support personal power and self-empowerment.

Incorporating practices that *cultivate self-awareness* is vital for healing the solar plexus chakra. Journaling is a valuable tool for identifying and releasing limiting beliefs and self-doubt. Meditation helps to quiet the mind and connect with your inner strength and wisdom. Yoga and other forms of mindful movement can help to release emotional blockages and improve energy flow throughout the body. These practices help to increase self-awareness and facilitate healing on a deep level.

Consider the example of Sarah: a talented artist who suffered from crippling self-doubt. She constantly sought external validation for her work and struggled to assert herself in her professional life. Through regular self-affirmations, assertiveness training, and working with yellow calcite, Sarah began to cultivate a stronger sense of self-worth and confidence. She started to set boundaries with clients, increasing her self-respect and enabling her to create art without fear of criticism. She learned to trust her inner guidance, recognizing her talent and worth. Her self-belief blossomed, leading to professional success and personal fulfillment.

Another example is Mark: a man who spent years people-pleasing at his job, feeling exhausted and taken advantage of. He felt powerless to express his own needs and opinions, leading to low self-esteem and a sense of being undervalued. Through assertiveness training, boundary-setting exercises, and meditation with tiger's eye, Mark began to reclaim his personal power. He learned to say no to unreasonable demands, to prioritize his own well-being, and to express his opinions with confidence. His workplace relationships improved, his stress levels decreased, and his self-esteem soared. He discovered a newfound sense of personal fulfillment and clarity in his career path.

The journey to a balanced solar plexus chakra is a process of *self-discovery* and *self-acceptance*. It's about *embracing your strengths, challenging your limitations, and developing a profound sense of self-worth*. As you cultivate a balanced Manipura, you'll find that your life is filled with purpose, confidence, and a powerful sense of self-empowerment, enabling you to navigate challenges with resilience and create the life you truly desire. Embrace this powerful journey, and allow your inner radiance to shine brightly. This journey of self-discovery will lead you to a more fulfilling and empowered existence. Now, let's journey to the heart of your being – the Anahata, or heart chakra. Situated in the center of your chest, this vibrant green energy center is the wellspring of love, compassion, and forgiveness. It's the bridge connecting your lower chakras, rooted in the physical and emotional realms, with your higher chakras, realms of spiritual connection and wisdom. Anahata is the energetic hub where the lower and upper energies meet and harmonize, creating a powerful symphony of balance and well-being. A healthy, open heart chakra allows love to flow freely, both to and from you, fostering deep, fulfilling relationships and a profound sense of connection with yourself and the world around you.

Imagine a radiant emerald green light emanating from your chest, pulsating with warmth and unconditional love. This is the essence of a balanced Anahata. You feel deeply connected to others, capable of empathy, compassion, and profound love. You experience joy in relationships, both romantic and platonic. You express your emotions openly and honestly, without fear of vulnerability. You forgive easily, letting go of resentment and anger, freeing yourself from the weight of past hurts. You radiate kindness and understanding, embracing both your strengths and imperfections with acceptance and self-compassion. Your self-love is unwavering, a foundation of strength and resilience that allows you to navigate life's challenges with grace and equanimity.

This chakra is not just about romantic love; it encompasses *all forms of love*: the love for family, friends, pets, and even for yourself. It's about the capacity to connect with others on a deeply emotional level, to understand and share their experiences, and to offer support and compassion without judgment. It is about self-love, understanding, and acceptance of who you are, flaws and all. A balanced heart chakra nurtures healthy relationships, built on trust, mutual respect, and genuine connection. It enables you to set healthy boundaries, to love yourself enough to protect your energy and well-being from those who would seek to drain or deplete it. It's the energy of acceptance and forgiveness, both of others and of yourself.

However, when the heart chakra is blocked or imbalanced, its radiant green light dims, casting shadows on your emotional and relational landscape. The *energy flow becomes constricted, hindering your ability to give and receive love, creating emotional distress, and impacting your relationships*. This imbalance can manifest in various ways, often *impacting your ability to form and maintain healthy relationships*. You might find yourself struggling with feelings of loneliness, isolation, or a deep sense of disconnection from others. You might struggle to trust others, fearing betrayal or rejection, leading to emotional guardedness and a reluctance to open yourself up to intimacy. You might experience difficulty expressing your emotions, either bottling them up or erupting in anger or resentment.

The consequences of an imbalanced Anahata extend beyond relationship challenges. You may experience *emotional pain*, such as sadness, grief, or despair, often stemming from unresolved issues or past traumas. You might find it difficult to forgive yourself or others, carrying the weight of guilt, resentment, or anger. This emotional baggage can manifest physically as chest pains, breathing difficulties, or heart-related issues, reflecting the chakra's position at the heart of your being. A lack of self-love can manifest as low self-esteem, self-criticism, and a tendency towards self-sabotage. You might be overly critical of yourself and others, struggling to see the good in yourself or in those around you.

One common manifestation is a tendency toward *codependency*, where your sense of self-worth is inextricably linked to the validation of others. You might find yourself constantly seeking external approval, sacrificing your own needs and desires to please others, fearing rejection or abandonment. This pattern often stems from a deep-seated insecurity and lack of self-love. You might find yourself drawn to relationships that are emotionally draining or abusive, reflecting a deep-seated need for validation and a lack of self-respect. You may struggle to establish healthy boundaries in your relationships, allowing others to overstep your limits and deplete your energy.

Another indication of an imbalanced heart chakra is *difficulty expressing emotions*. You may suppress your feelings, believing it's "weak" to express vulnerability. This emotional repression can lead to feelings of resentment, anger, or bitterness, often manifesting as physical symptoms like chest pains or digestive problems. You might struggle to communicate openly and honestly in your relationships, fearing judgment or rejection. This emotional suppression can create distance and prevent the formation of deep, meaningful connections.

Restoring balance to your heart chakra involves *cultivating self-love, practicing forgiveness, and nurturing healthy relationships*. It's a journey of emotional healing, of releasing past hurts, and of opening your heart to the possibility of love and connection. This journey requires self-compassion, courage, and a willingness to confront your emotional wounds.

One of the most potent practices for healing the heart chakra is **loving-kindness meditation**. This involves cultivating feelings of compassion and goodwill, first towards yourself and then towards others, extending outwards to friends, family, even strangers. By sending loving intentions to those you meet and know, you begin to soften your heart and open to compassion, even for those who may have hurt you in the past. Repeat phrases such as "May I be filled with loving-kindness," "May I be happy," "May I be healthy," and "May I live with ease". Then, extend these phrases to others, first those close to you, and eventually expanding to encompass everyone.

Forgiveness, both of yourself and others, is another crucial aspect of healing the heart chakra. Holding onto resentment and anger only perpetuates emotional suffering. Forgiveness is not condoning the actions of others but rather releasing yourself from the burden of negativity. This may involve journaling, meditation, or engaging in therapeutic practices to process and release past trauma. The process may involve expressing your emotions, writing letters (that you don't need to send) which might help with processing and releasing stored emotions.

Nurturing healthy relationships is essential for a balanced heart chakra. This involves surrounding yourself with supportive, loving people who uplift and inspire you. It also means setting healthy boundaries, prioritizing your own well-being, and choosing relationships that nourish your soul, rather than those that drain your energy. Learning to say "no" to requests that compromise your well-being is a sign of self-respect and setting a healthy boundary. Green Aventurine is a powerful crystal for the heart chakra, its vibrant green hue mirroring the chakra's energy. Holding or wearing Aventurine can help to activate and balance the heart chakra, promoting feelings of love, compassion, and forgiveness. Other heart chakra crystals include rose quartz, emerald, and jade, each offering unique properties to support emotional healing and relationship harmony. Use these stones in meditation, carry them with you, or incorporate them into your living space to enhance the flow of energy.

Practicing self-care is crucial for healing the heart chakra. This means prioritizing activities that nurture your physical, emotional, and spiritual well-being. This could involve engaging in activities you enjoy, spending time in nature, practicing yoga or meditation, or simply taking time to relax and recharge. Self-care practices create a space for self-reflection and emotional processing, clearing the path towards self-compassion and acceptance. The more you practice self-care, the more you will begin to understand and love your true self.

Consider the story of Elena: a woman who carried the weight of years of emotional neglect and resentment. She struggled to trust others, fearing intimacy and vulnerability. Through loving-kindness meditation, forgiveness exercises, and working with rose quartz, Elena began to heal her heart chakra. She learned to forgive those who had hurt her, to embrace her own self-worth, and to open her heart to new relationships. She discovered a deep sense of self-love and acceptance, allowing her to form healthy, fulfilling relationships that brought joy and emotional stability into her life.

Another example is David: a man who always prioritized the needs of others, neglecting his own well-being. He suffered from low self-esteem and a constant feeling of being unappreciated. Through self-compassion practices, boundary-setting exercises, and working with green Aventurine, David began to cultivate a stronger sense of self-love and respect. He learned to prioritize his own needs, to say no to demands that overextended him, and to cultivate relationships that nurtured his emotional health. He found he attracted more balanced relationships and felt fulfilled and empowered.

Healing the heart chakra is a journey of *self-discovery and emotional growth*. It's a process of releasing past hurts, cultivating self-love, and opening your heart to the possibility of love, compassion, and forgiveness. As you nurture your Anahata, you'll find that your relationships deepen, your emotional well-being improves, and your life is filled with a profound sense of connection and peace. Embrace this journey, allowing your heart to open to the boundless love that awaits you. The path to a balanced heart chakra is a journey of self-discovery that leads to a more fulfilling and emotionally resonant life.Now, let's ascend to the throat chakra, Vishuddha, the vibrant turquoise jewel of self-expression. Nestled at the base of your throat, this energy center governs your ability to communicate your truth authentically and to receive the truth of others with openness and clarity. It is the bridge between your heart's wisdom and the world, the conduit through which your inner voice finds its expression. A healthy, open Vishuddha allows for clear, confident communication, honest self-expression, and a receptive ear to the world around you. Imagine a brilliant turquoise light emanating from your throat, a vibrant hum of energy resonating with truth and authenticity. This is the essence of a balanced Vishuddha.

In this state of balance, your voice rings true, both literally and figuratively. You speak your mind with clarity and confidence, expressing your thoughts and feelings with ease and grace. You are a powerful listener, capable of truly hearing what others are saying, both verbally and nonverbally, and you respond with empathy and understanding. You feel a deep connection to your inner voice, your intuition, and you trust your own truth. You are not afraid to express your creative gifts, whether it's through singing, writing, painting, or any other form of artistic expression. Your communication style is clear, confident, and resonant. You easily connect with others on an intellectual and emotional level, building strong and fulfilling relationships based on open and honest communication. Your life is vibrant with creativity and self-expression, your truth shining brightly for all to see. You are able to articulate your needs effectively, assert your boundaries with grace and confidence, and express your desires freely. You enjoy active listening, fully engaging with those you are communicating with rather than just passively waiting for your turn to speak.

But what happens when the vibrant turquoise of Vishuddha dims? When the flow of energy becomes constricted or blocked, the consequences can be far-reaching, profoundly impacting your relationships, your sense of self, and even your physical health. An imbalanced throat chakra manifests in many ways, often hindering your ability to communicate effectively. You might struggle with expressing your needs and desires, feeling unheard or misunderstood, leaving you feeling frustrated and alone. You might be overly critical of yourself or fear judgment, leading to self-censorship and a reluctance to share your thoughts or feelings.

One common manifestation of an imbalanced Vishuddha is *difficulty in communicating effectively*. You might find yourself struggling to articulate your ideas clearly, mumbling, stammering, or experiencing writer's block. This can affect your relationships, preventing you from expressing your needs or concerns to those closest to you. It can also hinder your professional life, impacting your ability to present ideas, negotiate effectively, or give presentations with confidence. Your communication can become strained or unclear, creating misunderstanding and conflict. This is often compounded by a fear of rejection or judgment, silencing your voice and inhibiting your authentic self-expression. You might find yourself holding back your true feelings, resulting in resentment, frustration, and emotional distress.

Beyond verbal communication, an imbalanced Vishuddha can impact *creative expression*. If your throat chakra is blocked, you may find yourself creatively stifled. You might lose your passion for hobbies you once loved, experience writer's block or artist's block, or find it difficult to express yourself artistically in any medium. This creative stagnation can lead to feelings of dissatisfaction, unfulfillment, and a sense of being disconnected from your passions.

Furthermore, an imbalanced throat chakra can *manifest physically*, often as throat problems. Recurring sore throats, hoarseness, laryngitis, or even thyroid issues can all be linked to a blocked or imbalanced Vishuddha. These physical symptoms serve as an alert, highlighting the need to address the underlying energetic imbalance and restore harmony to the chakra.

Emotional suppression often accompanies an imbalanced throat chakra. You might be accustomed to bottling up your feelings, believing that expressing your emotions is weak or inappropriate. This emotional repression can manifest as feelings of resentment, anger, or anxiety, often leading to physical symptoms like headaches, jaw pain, or digestive issues. This pattern can strain relationships, as the inability to openly communicate emotions creates distance and misunderstanding. It can also manifest as gossip or passive-aggressive behavior, indirect ways of expressing suppressed emotions.

Another key indicator is a *tendency towards people-pleasing*. The fear of speaking your truth or upsetting others leads you to sacrifice your own needs and desires. This can manifest in difficulty setting boundaries, often leading to feelings of overwhelm and resentment.
The path to restoring balance to your throat chakra begins with a commitment to self-expression and authentic communication. This involves cultivating courage and self-trust, allowing your true voice to emerge.

Vocal exercises are a potent tool for activating the throat chakra. Humming, chanting, and singing can help to release blockages and promote a free flow of energy. Start by humming softly, gradually increasing the volume and pitch. Try different tones and sounds, noticing how your body responds. Chanting mantras, especially those related to communication and self-expression, can also be highly effective. Consider incorporating singing, either in a choir, karaoke or even alone in the shower to liberate your voice and unlock its power. Experimenting with vocalizations is vital. Speak your truth, slowly and thoughtfully, to yourself if needed.

Journaling provides a safe space to explore your thoughts and feelings, a powerful way to unlock your authentic voice. Write freely, allowing your emotions to flow onto the page. Don't censor yourself; just let the words come out naturally. This may reveal hidden emotions and underlying issues impacting communication.

Affirmations, positive statements repeated regularly, can help to reprogram your subconscious mind and cultivate self-belief. Choose affirmations related to communication, self-expression, and self-worth. Repeat them to yourself several times daily, visualizing yourself communicating with confidence and clarity. Examples include, "I speak my truth with courage and clarity," "I am a powerful and effective communicator," "I am confident in expressing my needs and desires."

Crystals can amplify the energy of Vishuddha, helping to open and balance this important chakra. *Blue Lace Agate*, with its calming blue hues, is a particularly powerful stone for enhancing communication and self-expression. Hold it during meditation, wear it as jewelry, or place it on your throat chakra to activate its energy. Other beneficial crystals include aquamarine, sodalite, and turquoise, each offering its unique properties to support balanced communication.

Remember the story of Sarah: a young woman who struggled with stage fright and self-doubt. She found it challenging to speak up in meetings and often felt unheard. Through regular vocal exercises, journal writing, affirmations, and working with blue lace agate, Sarah began to cultivate a stronger sense of self-belief and courage. Her communication improved, both personally and professionally. She found herself confidently expressing her thoughts and opinions, commanding respect and building strong connections.

Another example is David: a man who was always afraid of public speaking. This anxiety stemmed from a past experience of ridicule, leaving him feeling vulnerable. Using guided meditation combined with crystal healing, particularly turquoise and sodalite, he was able to revisit past experiences and address limiting beliefs. With consistent work on affirmations and vocal exercises, he gradually overcame his fear and now enjoys public speaking.

The path to a balanced throat chakra is a journey of self-discovery, a process of embracing your *authentic voice and expressing your truth with confidence and clarity*. As you cultivate this energy center, you will find your communication improves, your self-esteem grows, and your life becomes more fulfilling and expressive. **Embrace this journey, allowing your true voice to shine. The rewards are immeasurable.**

Chapter 3: Harnessing the Power of Astrology

The celestial dance of the sun, moon, and planets at the moment of your birth weaves a unique tapestry, a cosmic blueprint that shapes your personality, your strengths, and the challenges you navigate in life. This is the essence of **astrology**, a timeless practice offering profound insights into the energetic patterns that influence your being. Understanding your astrological sign—the position of the sun at your birth—is a crucial step in this journey of self-discovery and holistic well-being.

Each of the twelve zodiac signs represents a distinct energetic signature, a vibrational frequency that permeates your life. These signs are not merely labels but potent symbols reflecting archetypal energies that interact with your chakra system, influencing your emotional landscape, your relationships, and your overall health.

Let's embark on a celestial journey, exploring the twelve zodiac signs and their impact on your energy flow. We will delve into the unique characteristics, strengths, and potential challenges associated with each sign, offering practical exercises to help you integrate these astrological insights into your holistic wellness practice.

Aries (March 21 – April 19): The Fiery Pioneer

Aries, ruled by the planet Mars, is the first sign of the zodiac, embodying the energy of initiation, action, and courage. Arians are known for their dynamism, their pioneering spirit, and their unwavering drive. Their energy is like a wildfire, burning brightly with passion and enthusiasm. They are natural leaders, unafraid to take risks and forge their own path. However, this intense energy can sometimes manifest as impulsiveness, impatience, and a tendency to become easily frustrated.

Exercise: To harness the Aries energy, take a moment each morning to set a clear intention for the day. Focus on one specific action you want to accomplish, and commit to taking the first step towards achieving it. This will help you channel your fiery energy into productive action.

Taurus (April 20 – May 20): The Earthy Grounder

Taurus, governed by Venus, is an earth sign grounded in the senses and material world. Taureans are known for their practicality, their love of comfort and beauty, and their unwavering determination. They possess a strong sense of stability and are remarkably resilient. Yet, this steadfastness can sometimes lead to stubbornness, possessiveness, and a reluctance to embrace change.

Exercise: Connect with nature. Spend time outdoors, feeling the earth beneath your feet and breathing in the fresh air. This will help you ground your energy and cultivate a sense of stability and calm. Engage your senses—taste, smell, touch—to connect with the richness of your surroundings.

Gemini (May 21 – June 20): The Airy Communicator

Gemini, ruled by Mercury, is an air sign characterized by its intellectual curiosity, adaptability, and vibrant communication skills. Geminis are quick-witted, versatile, and effortlessly connect with others. Their minds are always buzzing with ideas, making them naturally engaging conversationalists. However, this mental agility can sometimes lead to scattered energy, superficiality, and an inability to focus on one task for an extended period.

Exercise: Engage in activities that stimulate your mind—reading, writing, learning a new language. This will help you channel your intellectual energy into constructive pursuits. Practice mindful breathing to help you ground your scattered energy and enhance your focus.

Cancer (June 21 – July 22): The Watery Nurturer

Cancer, governed by the moon, is a water sign deeply connected to emotions, intuition, and family. Cancers are nurturing, empathetic, and highly sensitive individuals. They create safe and comforting environments for themselves and those they care about. However, their emotional depth can also make them vulnerable to mood swings, clinginess, and a tendency to overthink.

Exercise: Practice self-compassion. Acknowledge and accept your emotions without judgment. Engage in self-care practices that nourish your emotional well-being, such as journaling, meditation, or spending time in nature.

Leo (July 23 – August 22): The Fiery Leader

Leo, ruled by the sun, is a fire sign radiating warmth, generosity, and confidence. Leos are natural leaders, charismatic, and full of life. They shine brightly, inspiring others with their enthusiasm and creativity. Yet, their strong ego can sometimes lead to arrogance, a need for constant attention, and a tendency to be overly dramatic.

Exercise: Practice acts of kindness and generosity. Sharing your gifts and talents with others will help you connect with your inner radiance and cultivate a sense of purpose. Reflect on your strengths and accomplishments to boost self-esteem, without losing sight of your vulnerabilities.

Virgo (August 23 – September 22): The Earthy Analyst

Virgo, ruled by Mercury, is an earth sign known for its practicality, attention to detail, and analytical mind. Virgos are meticulous, organized, and always strive for perfection. They are highly capable and dependable. However, this meticulous nature can sometimes lead to overthinking, criticism of oneself and others, and a tendency to become overly critical.

Exercise: Practice mindfulness. Pay attention to the present moment without judgment. This will help you calm your mind and appreciate the details of your life without getting lost in analysis. Learn to accept imperfections—both in yourself and the world around you.

Libra (September 23 – October 22): The Airy Diplomat

Libra, governed by Venus, is an air sign characterized by its diplomacy, harmony-seeking nature, and love of beauty. Libras are graceful, charming, and always strive for balance and fairness. They are natural peacemakers, often acting as mediators in conflicts. However, this desire for harmony can sometimes lead to indecisiveness, people-pleasing, and a tendency to avoid conflict.

Exercise: Practice assertiveness. Learn to express your needs and opinions without compromising your values or the needs of others. Cultivate your sense of self-worth, recognizing that your needs are just as important as anyone else's.

Scorpio (October 23 – November 21): The Watery Transformer

Scorpio, ruled by Pluto and Mars, is a water sign known for its intensity, depth, and transformative power. Scorpios are passionate, resourceful, and possess an uncanny ability to see through illusions. They are highly intuitive and intensely loyal. However, this intensity can sometimes manifest as possessiveness, jealousy, and a tendency to hold onto grudges.

Exercise: Practice self-awareness. Explore your emotions and shadow self without judgment. Embrace your transformative power to heal past wounds and emerge stronger from challenges. Engage in shadow work to address limiting beliefs.

Sagittarius (November 22 – December 21): The Fiery Explorer

Sagittarius, ruled by Jupiter, is a fire sign characterized by its optimism, adventurous spirit, and love of knowledge. Sagittarians are expansive, philosophical, and always seeking new experiences. They are open-minded and embrace diversity. However, their quest for knowledge can sometimes lead to restlessness, impulsiveness, and a tendency to be overly blunt.

Exercise: Cultivate gratitude. Appreciate the richness of your life and all the experiences you've encountered. Practice mindfulness to stay grounded in the present moment, while still maintaining your adventurous spirit.

Capricorn (December 22 – January 19): The Earthy Achiever

Capricorn, ruled by Saturn, is an earth sign known for its ambition, discipline, and practicality. Capricorns are highly driven, focused, and dedicated to achieving their goals. They are responsible, reliable, and possess a strong work ethic. However, this ambition can sometimes lead to overworking, a fear of failure, and a tendency to be overly serious.

Exercise: Practice self-care. Prioritize activities that bring you joy and relaxation. This will help you maintain balance and avoid burnout. Learn to celebrate your accomplishments without becoming overly consumed by your ambition.

Aquarius (January 20 – February 18): The Airy Humanitarian

Aquarius, ruled by Uranus and Saturn, is an air sign characterized by its independence, originality, and humanitarian spirit. Aquarians are innovative, progressive, and deeply committed to social justice. They are unconventional thinkers, unafraid to challenge norms. However, this independent spirit can sometimes lead to detachment, rebellion, and a tendency to be emotionally distant.

Exercise: Connect with your community. Contribute your time and talents to causes you care about. This will help you connect with others and cultivate a sense of belonging. Practice empathy, connecting with the emotions of others.

Pisces (February 19 – March 20): The Watery Mystic

Pisces, ruled by Neptune and Jupiter, is a water sign deeply connected to intuition, spirituality, and compassion. Pisceans are imaginative, empathetic, and possess a profound understanding of the human condition. They are artistic, intuitive, and deeply compassionate. However, their heightened sensitivity can sometimes lead to escapism, a tendency to be overly idealistic, and difficulty setting boundaries.

Exercise: Practice grounding techniques. Connect with the earth, through walks in nature or engaging in physical activities. This will help you stay grounded and manage your heightened sensitivity. Develop healthy boundaries, protecting your energy from those who may drain it.

Understanding your astrological sign is a journey of self-discovery, a process of becoming more aware of your inherent strengths and potential challenges. By integrating these insights into your holistic wellness practice, you can harness the unique energetic patterns that shape your life, creating a path toward greater self-awareness, emotional balance, and overall well-being. Remember, astrology is a tool for self-understanding, not a rigid system of prediction. Use these insights to empower yourself and navigate your life with greater clarity and purpose. Embrace the wisdom of the cosmos, and allow it to guide you on your unique journey.Beyond the sun sign, the intricate dance of planetary relationships—the astrological aspects—adds another layer of complexity and depth to our energetic landscape. These aspects, formed by the angles between planets in our birth charts, reveal dynamic interactions that profoundly influence our moods, relationships, and overall well-being. They are not static pronouncements but rather energetic currents that ebb and flow, impacting us throughout our lives. Understanding these aspects is key to harnessing the full power of astrology for holistic healing.

Consider the **conjunction**, a powerful alignment where planets sit close together, within a few degrees of each other. This aspect *intensifies the energies of both planets involved, creating a potent blend of their influences.* For example, a Sun-Mars conjunction might indicate a highly driven and assertive individual, brimming with energy and initiative. However, this intense combination can also lead to impulsiveness and a tendency to overextend oneself. The key lies in harnessing this potent energy, channeling it into productive pursuits rather than letting it manifest as aggression or frustration. Mindfulness practices, coupled with conscious self-regulation, become essential tools for navigating the intensity of a conjunction.

The **opposition**, a 180-degree angle between two planets, represents a *dynamic tension, a push and pull of opposing energies.* This aspect highlights areas of conflict or imbalance that require attention. For instance, a Sun-Saturn opposition might indicate a struggle between personal ambition and feelings of limitation. The individual may experience internal conflict between their desire for success and self-doubt. Working with this opposition involves identifying the root cause of the conflict and finding a balance between the opposing forces. This could involve setting realistic goals, fostering self-compassion, and seeking support to navigate challenges.

The **trine**, a harmonious 120-degree angle, *signifies ease and flow.* Planets in trine *support and enhance each other, creating a sense of natural harmony.* A trine between Venus and Jupiter, for instance, could indicate a fortunate individual with a natural talent for attracting abundance and experiencing joy in life. However, even harmonious aspects require conscious effort to maintain balance. An overreliance on the ease and flow of a trine might lead to complacency and a lack of drive to overcome challenges. Regular self-reflection and the proactive pursuit of personal growth are crucial to prevent this.

The **square**, a challenging 90-degree angle, *creates friction and tension, highlighting areas that require growth and adaptation.* A square between Mars and Pluto, for example, could suggest an individual prone to intense emotions and power struggles. This aspect requires careful navigation, as it can lead to conflict and feelings of frustration. The key lies in understanding the underlying tension and developing strategies for constructive expression of energy. This could involve engaging in activities that channel aggressive impulses, such as physical exercise or creative pursuits, and practicing emotional regulation techniques. Beyond these fundamental aspects, numerous other planetary relationships exist, each with its unique energetic signature. The **sextile**, a 60-degree angle, *fosters opportunity and ease of collaboration*, while the **quincunx**, a 150-degree angle, *presents challenges requiring adjustment and adaptability.* Each aspect demands attention and understanding, providing insights into the nuances of our energetic landscape.

Let's explore some practical examples to illustrate how these aspects manifest in everyday life. Imagine an individual with a strong Sun-Jupiter conjunction. This combination often signifies optimism, expansiveness, and a generous spirit. However, if unchecked, it could lead to overindulgence, both materially and emotionally. This person might need to practice moderation, cultivating self-discipline to avoid excesses and maintain balance. Regular meditation or grounding practices could help them manage their expansive energy, channeling it into productive activities rather than impulsive actions.

Alternatively, consider someone with a Mars-Saturn square. This aspect frequently reveals a struggle between ambition and self-doubt, leading to feelings of frustration and self-criticism. This individual might find it challenging to take initiative, constantly second-guessing themselves. To work with this aspect, they might benefit from setting small, achievable goals and celebrating each accomplishment. Self-compassion and positive affirmations become essential tools in overcoming self-doubt and cultivating self-belief.

The influence of astrological aspects extends beyond individual personalities, impacting relationships as well. A harmonious aspect between the Venus of one partner and the Mars of the other often suggests a strong attraction and passionate connection. However, even harmonious aspects require nurturing. Open communication and mutual respect are vital to sustain the relationship. Conversely, a challenging aspect between planetary placements might highlight potential areas of conflict, requiring conscious effort to resolve differences and build a stronger connection. *Understanding these aspects within the relational dynamic can help partners navigate challenges and strengthen their bond.*

Working with the energetic influences of astrological aspects involves a multi-faceted approach. **Self-awareness** is paramount. Recognizing the patterns and tendencies associated with these aspects allows us to anticipate challenges and develop strategies for constructive responses. Mindfulness practices, such as meditation and deep breathing, can help regulate emotions and channel energy in productive ways. Energy healing modalities, like Reiki, can further enhance our capacity to work with the energetic currents revealed through astrological aspects, restoring balance and fostering healing.

Crystal healing also plays a crucial role in this process. Certain crystals resonate with specific planetary energies, helping to amplify positive aspects and mitigate challenging ones. For instance, *carnelian*, associated with Mars, can help channel assertive energy constructively, while amethyst, linked to Jupiter, can promote optimism and abundance. Integrating crystal healing into our daily routines can amplify the positive effects of harmonious aspects and support us in navigating challenging ones.

In conclusion, while our sun sign provides a foundational understanding of our energetic blueprint, the intricate web of astrological aspects adds another layer of richness and complexity. By understanding the dynamic interplay of planetary energies, we gain profound insights into our personalities, relationships, and overall well-being. Harnessing this knowledge through self-awareness, energy healing, and crystal work empowers us to navigate life's challenges with greater clarity, grace, and resilience, ultimately fostering a more balanced and fulfilling existence. The cosmos provides a map; we are the navigators of our own unique journey. Embrace the wisdom of the stars, and allow it to guide you towards wholeness and harmony.The birth chart, a celestial snapshot of the planetary positions at the moment of our birth, provides a foundational understanding of our inherent energetic patterns. However, the universe is dynamic, not static. Planets are constantly moving, creating a continuous flow of energetic influences known as astrological transits. These transits act as temporary overlays on our birth chart, highlighting specific areas of our lives that are ripe for growth, change, or challenge. Understanding these transits is akin to receiving ongoing celestial guidance, enabling us to navigate the ebb and flow of life with greater awareness and grace.

Transits are not predictions of fate but rather *energetic opportunities*. They offer a glimpse into the prevailing cosmic currents that influence our emotional state, relationships, and overall well-being. A challenging transit doesn't mean disaster is imminent; rather, it signals a period of growth and transformation. It's an invitation to confront limiting beliefs, break free from old patterns, and embrace the evolution of our consciousness. Conversely, a harmonious transit doesn't guarantee effortless bliss; it presents an opportunity to amplify positive energies and manifest desired outcomes through conscious intention and action.

Let's consider the influence of the major planets on our daily lives during transit. When transiting Jupiter, the planet of expansion and abundance, moves through a particular house in our birth chart, it typically indicates a period of growth and opportunity in that area of life. For example, if Jupiter transits the fifth house (creativity, romance, children), we might experience increased creativity, a blossoming romance, or the arrival of a child. This transit encourages us to embrace expansion and seize opportunities for self-expression and joy. However, the potential for overindulgence exists. The key is to consciously channel Jupiter's expansive energy into purposeful activities rather than becoming complacent or excessively self-indulgent.

Conversely, a transiting Saturn, the planet of discipline and structure, often brings periods of challenge and responsibility. When Saturn transits a house in our birth chart, it highlights areas where we need to develop greater discipline, maturity, and responsibility. For instance, if Saturn transits the tenth house (career, public image), we might face obstacles in our professional life, demanding greater focus and perseverance. While this period may feel restrictive, it's an opportunity to develop resilience, self-discipline, and a strong work ethic, eventually leading to long-term stability and success.

Transiting Mars, the planet of action and energy, infuses our lives with dynamism and drive. During a Mars transit, we might experience an increase in assertiveness, motivation, and energy levels. However, this can also lead to impulsiveness and potential conflict if we don't channel this heightened energy constructively. Engaging in physical activity, creative expression, or other healthy outlets helps to manage Mars' intense energy effectively. Meditation and mindfulness techniques are crucial for maintaining inner peace amidst increased activity levels.

Venus, the planet of love, beauty, and harmony, brings periods of enhanced creativity, connection, and appreciation for life's pleasures during its transit. Relationships often flourish during a Venus transit, as this period fosters understanding, harmony, and mutual appreciation. However, an overreliance on external validation or a tendency towards self-indulgence could arise. Mindful self-reflection ensures that we maintain balance between healthy pleasures and inner peace.

The influence of Uranus, Neptune, and Pluto during their transits is significantly different, given their longer orbital periods. These outer planets introduce profound shifts and transformations, often impacting society at large alongside individual lives. Uranus, associated with rebellion and innovation, introduces unexpected change and challenges established structures. Neptune, connected to intuition and spirituality, fosters a deeper connection to the self and the universe, potentially causing confusion or heightened sensitivity. Pluto, the planet of transformation and power, initiates intense periods of change, often involving significant emotional upheaval, but leading to profound personal growth. Navigating these transits effectively requires a holistic approach that blends astrological understanding with self-awareness and mindful practices. By monitoring planetary movements and their influence on our birth charts, we can anticipate periods of heightened challenge or opportunity. This anticipatory awareness allows us to develop strategies for self-care and self-regulation during these periods. For instance, during a challenging transit, it might be crucial to prioritize self-compassion, mindfulness practices, and self-soothing techniques. Conversely, during a harmonious transit, we can harness the favorable energies through setting intentions, manifesting goals, and engaging in activities that support our overall well-being.

Reiki, a gentle yet powerful energy healing modality, proves especially helpful in navigating the energetic shifts brought about by transits. Regular Reiki sessions can assist in restoring energetic balance, clearing blocks, and promoting emotional regulation. *By harmonizing our energy field*, Reiki helps us navigate challenging transits with greater ease and resilience. Crystal healing further complements this approach. Different crystals resonate with various planetary energies, enabling us to leverage their supportive vibrations during transits. For example, amethyst is associated with Jupiter's energy and can promote spiritual growth, optimism, and abundance during periods of Jupiter transit. Carnelian, associated with Mars, can provide the extra boost of energy and courage during a Mars transit. Choosing crystals that complement the current transit can create a powerful synergy, amplifying positive energies and mitigating challenges.

Numerology also plays a vital role. By calculating our daily, weekly, or monthly numerological numbers based on specific dates, we can gain further insight into the energetic influences of these periods. These numerical vibrations often align with astrological transits, deepening our understanding of the prevailing energies. Combining both astrological and numerological interpretations can provide a holistic view and offer valuable insights into challenges and opportunities.

Our journey through life is a continuous dance with the cosmic currents. Astrological transits provide a roadmap, not a rigid schedule. They offer insights into the energetic tides that influence our emotions, relationships, and experiences. By understanding these transits and employing self-care practices, Reiki, crystal healing, and numerological awareness, we gain the power to navigate these shifts with grace, resilience, and a profound sense of self-awareness. We move from being passive recipients of cosmic influences to conscious co-creators of our own destinies. The journey of self-discovery is not a solitary pursuit; it is a partnership with the cosmos itself. Embrace the wisdom of the stars, listen to your intuition, and allow the universe to guide you on your unique path of healing and growth. The celestial dance awaits, and you are ready to lead the way. The universe whispers secrets through the celestial dance of planets, and astrology offers a language to decipher these cosmic messages. While planetary transits illuminate the energetic currents influencing our lives, a deeper dive into our birth charts reveals a tapestry of innate strengths, challenges, and karmic patterns. This self-knowledge, gleaned from the astrological blueprint of our existence, forms the bedrock for profound self-understanding and personal growth.

Your birth chart, a celestial snapshot taken at the precise moment of your arrival into this world, acts as a personalized roadmap to your soul's journey. Each planet's placement within the twelve houses and its relationship to other planets reveals facets of your personality, potential, and life path. Understanding these placements isn't about labeling yourself or becoming defined by astrological interpretations. Rather, it's about gaining a deeper awareness of your inherent strengths, weaknesses, and recurring themes in your life. For example, the position of the Sun sign, often perceived as the most prominent astrological influence, reveals your core identity, your natural expression, and the essence of your being. But this is merely one thread in the rich tapestry of your astrological map. The Moon, representing your emotional world, reveals your subconscious patterns, reactions, and emotional needs. Understanding your Moon sign helps you to navigate your emotional landscape with more compassion and self-awareness, recognizing the triggers and patterns that might otherwise lead to reactivity.

Mercury, the planet of communication and intellect, illuminates your communication style, mental processes, and how you process information. Is your communication direct and assertive, or more subtle and nuanced? Understanding your Mercury placement helps you to refine your communication skills, fostering clearer and more effective interactions with others.

Venus, the planet of love and beauty, reveals your values, preferences, and approach to relationships. Do you prioritize harmony and diplomacy, or are you more passionate and expressive in your connections? Understanding your Venus placement can illuminate your relationship patterns and guide you towards healthier, more fulfilling partnerships.

Mars, the planet of action and energy, highlights your drive, ambition, and assertive nature. Are you a fiery, impulsive individual, or more measured and strategic in your actions? Recognizing your Mars energy helps you channel your motivation constructively, avoiding impulsive reactions and harnessing your drive for positive outcomes.

Jupiter, the planet of expansion and abundance, reveals areas where you experience growth, opportunity, and good fortune. Understanding your Jupiter placement helps you identify areas where you can cultivate optimism, seize opportunities, and attract abundance into your life.

Saturn, the planet of discipline and structure, highlights areas requiring maturity, responsibility, and perseverance. Recognizing the lessons associated with your Saturn placement helps you to develop resilience, cultivate self-discipline, and embrace challenges as opportunities for growth.

Uranus, Neptune, and Pluto, the outer planets, signify transformative energies that introduce profound shifts and awakenings. These transits often manifest in societal changes as well as personal upheavals, prompting deep introspection and recalibration of life paths.

Beyond the planetary placements, the aspects formed between planets reveal the dynamic interplay between different energies in your birth chart. Harmonious aspects indicate supportive energies, while challenging aspects represent areas requiring greater self-awareness and potential conflict resolution. These aspects are not static; they are dynamic interactions that create tension and resolution throughout your life journey. Understanding your entire birth chart, however, is just the beginning. It's not a static prophecy, but a dynamic blueprint evolving with your life experiences. Astrology offers a framework for understanding your innate predispositions, but it's your choices, actions, and consciousness that shape your destiny. You are not a victim of your planetary placements; you are the master of your own narrative.

Astrological insights can be powerful tools for self-discovery, *but they are not definitive pronouncements*. It's crucial to approach astrological interpretations with a sense of discernment and avoid rigid adherence to predictions. Instead, use these insights as a springboard for self-reflection, empowering you to make conscious choices aligned with your true nature.

For instance, if your astrological chart suggests a propensity for conflict in relationships, this **isn't a condemnation of your relationship abilities** but rather an *invitation to understand your triggers and communicate your needs more effectively*. By acknowledging these potential challenges, you can cultivate self-awareness and develop strategies for navigating relationship dynamics with greater grace and maturity.

Similarly, if your chart highlights a strong creative drive, this **isn't simply a validation of existing talents**, but a call to action. It's *a gentle nudge to embrace your creative potential, nurturing your artistic expression and allowing your creativity to blossom.*

Integrating astrological insights into your daily life involves more than just reading your horoscope. It's about *understanding the underlying energies that shape your experiences*. It requires active engagement – introspection, journaling, meditation, and conscious decision-making. This is where the holistic practices we've discussed previously, like Reiki, crystal healing, and numerology, become invaluable allies. They help you work with the cosmic energies, balancing your energy system, enhancing your intuition, and aligning your actions with your astrologically revealed potential.

Imagine using crystal healing to amplify the positive energies highlighted in your birth chart. For example, if your chart suggests a strong connection to the element of water, you might incorporate crystals like Aquamarine or Lapis Lazuli to enhance your emotional intuition and empathy. If your chart shows a preponderance of fire signs, crystals like Carnelian or Sunstone might provide extra energy and drive to pursue your goals.

Numerology can further refine your understanding by adding a numerical layer to the astrological interpretation. By combining both systems, you can gain a deeper understanding of the energetic patterns influencing your life.

Reiki, as we've discussed, harmonizes the energetic flow within your body, clearing blockages and aligning your energy centers. Regular Reiki sessions can help you to effectively navigate challenging astrological periods and capitalize on the positive energies highlighted in your chart. This holistic approach fosters balance and harmony, allowing you to live in alignment with the wisdom of the stars.

Ultimately, astrology is not a tool for predicting the future, but rather **a compass guiding you on your path of self-discovery**. It illuminates your strengths, weaknesses, and potential for growth, empowering you to make informed choices that align with your truest self. This is a journey of self-awareness, an ongoing conversation between you and the cosmos, a partnership that empowers you to create a life that is authentic, fulfilling, and aligned with your soul's purpose. It's about embracing the wisdom of the stars and using that wisdom to illuminate your own unique path towards holistic well-being. The universe is vast and mysterious, but your own inner wisdom is even more powerful. Let astrology be your guide, but let your intuition be your compass. The journey awaits.The celestial dance of planets, as revealed through astrology, doesn't exist in isolation. It's intricately woven into the fabric of our energetic being, influencing the flow of energy within our chakra system and impacting our overall well-being. This is where the profound synergy between astrology and energy healing modalities truly shines. By understanding the energetic signatures of planetary placements and transits, we can refine and enhance our energy healing practices, creating a more potent and personalized approach to holistic wellness.

Imagine your birth chart as a vibrant, pulsating energy field, with each planet radiating its unique frequency. The Sun, the radiant heart of your chart, dictates your core essence and vitality. Understanding your Sun sign's elemental nature (fire, earth, air, or water) allows you to choose crystals that resonate with its energy. For example, a fiery Aries Sun might benefit from the invigorating energy of *Carnelian*, while an earthy Taurus Sun might find solace and grounding with a *Rose Quartz*.

The *Moon*, representing your emotional landscape, reveals your subconscious patterns and reactions. Its placement in a particular sign and house indicates the nature of your emotional responses and the areas where you might experience emotional blockages. Understanding this can guide the selection of crystals that support emotional healing. For instance, a Moon in Cancer, known for its sensitivity, might find comfort and emotional balance with Moonstone, while a Moon in Scorpio, often associated with intensity, might benefit from the transformative energy of Black Tourmaline.

Mercury, governing communication and intellect, reveals your mental processes and how you interact with the world. Its placement can indicate areas where energetic blockages might manifest as mental clutter or communication difficulties. Crystals like Clear Quartz, known for its clarity and amplification properties, can be invaluable in enhancing mental clarity and improving communication.

Venus, the planet of love and beauty, reflects your values, relationships, and sense of harmony. Its placement can illuminate where imbalances might occur in your relationships or your approach to self-love. Rose Quartz, a stone of unconditional love, is a powerful ally for healing emotional wounds and fostering harmonious relationships, particularly for those with a Venus in a challenging aspect.

Mars, the planet of action and energy, illuminates your drive, ambition, and assertiveness. Its placement reveals potential areas of frustration or blocked energy if your actions are stifled or your passions are ignored. Crystals like Red Jasper can enhance motivation and overcome inertia, particularly helpful for those with Mars in a challenging position.

Jupiter, the planet of expansion and abundance, points to areas of growth, opportunity, and good fortune. Working with crystals associated with abundance, like Citrine, can amplify the positive energies of Jupiter, attracting opportunities and supporting personal growth. Saturn, the planet of discipline and structure, reveals areas where lessons in responsibility and perseverance are required. Crystals like Amethyst, known for its calming and grounding properties, can help navigate the challenges associated with Saturn, promoting patience and resilience.

The outer planets—*Uranus, Neptune, and Pluto*—represent transformative energies that introduce profound shifts and awakenings. Understanding their transits can help you anticipate periods of intense change and utilize crystals to support the integration of these transformative energies. For example, during a Pluto transit, Black Tourmaline can be invaluable in shielding against negativity and supporting emotional processing.

Beyond individual planetary placements, the aspects formed between planets reveal the dynamic interplay of energies. Harmonious aspects, like trines and sextiles, indicate supportive energies, while challenging aspects, like squares and oppositions, represent areas requiring greater self-awareness and potential conflict resolution. In energy healing, challenging aspects can point towards specific chakras that may require attention and balancing. For instance, a challenging aspect between Mars and Saturn might indicate a need to address blockages in the root chakra (stability) and solar plexus chakra (self-esteem). Timing is crucial in energy healing, and astrology provides a powerful framework for optimizing the effectiveness of your sessions. By aligning healing sessions with favorable planetary transits or lunar cycles, you can amplify the positive energies and create a more conducive environment for healing. For example, a waxing moon is a potent time for healing practices focused on growth and manifestation, while a waning moon is ideal for releasing negative energies and blockages.

Furthermore, the astrological houses can also inform energy healing practices. Each house represents a different area of life, and understanding their energetic qualities can illuminate areas needing attention. For instance, the first house, representing self-identity, might suggest focusing on healing practices related to self-esteem and personal expression. The fourth house, representing home and family, might indicate a need for healing work related to emotional security and family dynamics.

Integrating astrology and energy healing is not a rigid system; it's a *fluid and dynamic process*. It's about understanding the energetic interplay between the cosmos and your inner world, using astrological insights to guide your healing practices, and empowering yourself to create a life of balance, harmony, and well-being. It's about listening to the whispers of the stars and the wisdom of your body, creating a harmonious symphony between your inner and outer worlds.

Consider this example: An individual with a strong emphasis on water signs in their birth chart, perhaps a Cancer Sun and Pisces Moon, might experience heightened emotional sensitivity. Astrologically, this suggests a need to focus on emotional regulation and self-care. In an energy healing session, the practitioner might incorporate techniques to balance the sacral chakra (emotions), utilizing calming crystals like Aquamarine and practicing gentle energy work to promote emotional flow and stability.

Another scenario might involve someone with a prominent Mars in their chart, perhaps a fiery Aries Mars, who experiences a challenging Mars transit. Astrologically, this indicates a potential increase in aggression or frustration. In this case, energy healing practices might focus on grounding and calming techniques, such as Reiki or crystal healing with grounding stones like Hematite, to help channel the excess Mars energy constructively.

Remember, this integration isn't about passively accepting astrological predictions but actively utilizing them as a tool for self-awareness and empowerment. It's about understanding the energetic currents within and around you, allowing the celestial wisdom to inform and enhance your healing journey. It's about harnessing the power of the cosmos to create a life of vibrant health, joy, and inner peace. This synergy unlocks a deeper level of self-understanding, fostering a more personalized and effective approach to holistic well-being. The celestial and earthly realms are not separate; they are interwoven, a dance of energy and consciousness that we can learn to navigate with grace and intention. The journey of self-discovery is a lifelong pursuit, and by combining the ancient wisdom of astrology with the transformative power of energy healing, we embark on a profound exploration of our own energetic landscape, aligning ourselves with the universal flow and creating a life of vibrant well-being.

Chapter 4: Unlocking the Secrets of Numerology

Numerology, a fascinating branch of ancient wisdom, offers a unique lens through which we can understand the energetic blueprint of our lives. Unlike astrology, which focuses on the celestial dance of planets at the time of our birth, numerology delves into the vibrational essence encoded within our birthdate. This vibrational signature, expressed through numbers, reveals profound insights into our personality, strengths, weaknesses, life purpose, and the karmic lessons we're here to learn. Central to numerological understanding is the *Life Path Number*, a powerful indicator of our core essence and the journey we're destined to undertake.

Calculating your Life Path Number is surprisingly simple. It involves reducing your full birthdate (month, day, and year) to a single digit. Let's say your birthday is October 26, 1985. First, convert the month to its numerical equivalent: October becomes 10. Then, add all the numbers together: 1 + 0 + 2 + 6 + 1 + 9 + 8 + 5 = 32. Since 32 is a two-digit number, we continue reducing until we reach a single digit: 3 + 2 = 5. Therefore, your Life Path Number is 5. This simple calculation reveals a powerful essence that permeates your life's trajectory. Your Life Path Number isn't merely a label; it's a vibrational key unlocking the deepest aspects of your personality and potential. It reflects the dominant energies shaping your character, your inherent talents, your life challenges, and your overall life purpose. It's a roadmap, guiding you through your unique journey, highlighting potential pitfalls, and revealing the lessons you're destined to learn.

Let's explore some examples of Life Path Numbers and their interpretations. These interpretations are not rigid definitions, but rather guiding principles, offering a framework for deeper self-understanding. Each individual embodies their Life Path Number in a unique and nuanced way.

Life Path Number 1: *The Pioneer*. Individuals with a Life Path Number 1 are natural leaders, independent, innovative, and self-reliant. They possess a strong will and an unwavering drive to achieve their goals. Their life lessons often involve learning to collaborate effectively, tempering their independent spirit with empathy and understanding. Challenges may arise from a tendency towards self-centeredness or an inability to delegate effectively. Crystals that resonate strongly with this number include clear quartz for clarity and amplification, and carnelian for courage and motivation. They are encouraged to embrace their leadership potential while also cultivating humility and cooperation.

Life Path Number 2: *The Diplomat*. Life Path Number 2 individuals are often highly sensitive, intuitive, and diplomatic. They excel at cooperation and thrive in harmonious environments. Their life lessons involve learning to assert themselves without compromising their compassionate nature. They often face challenges related to indecisiveness or a tendency to put others' needs before their own. Crystals such as moonstone for emotional balance and rose quartz for self-love are beneficial companions. They need to find balance between nurturing others and nurturing themselves.

Life Path Number 3: *The Creative Communicator*. These individuals are expressive, enthusiastic, and highly creative. They are gifted communicators and often find fulfillment in artistic endeavors. Their life lessons involve learning to manage their boundless energy and channel their creativity constructively. Challenges can stem from a tendency towards scattered energy or difficulty focusing on a single task. Crystals such as citrine for creativity and amber for optimism enhance their journey. Their journey is about finding structure and discipline within their vibrant energy.

Life Path Number 4: *The Builder*. Life Path Number 4 individuals are practical, reliable, and hardworking. They are excellent organizers and appreciate stability and security. Their life lessons involve learning to embrace change and flexibility while maintaining their grounded nature. They may face challenges relating to rigidity or an inability to adapt to unforeseen circumstances. Crystals like brown tourmaline for grounding and grounding them in their practical nature. They must find ways to release control and allow the flow of life to occur.

Life Path Number 5: *The Free Spirit*. These individuals are adventurous, versatile, and adaptable. They thrive on change and enjoy exploring new experiences. Their life lessons involve learning to balance their freedom-loving nature with responsibility and commitment. They might face challenges related to inconsistency or a lack of focus. Crystals that promote adaptability, such as lapis lazuli and amazonite, can support this vibrant life path. They are encouraged to find focus in their exploration.

Life Path Number 6: *The Nurturer*. Individuals with a Life Path Number 6 are loving, compassionate, and responsible. They value family and harmony and find fulfillment in nurturing others. Their life lessons often involve learning to set healthy boundaries and prioritize their own needs. They may face challenges related to over-giving or neglecting their own well-being. Crystals such as rose quartz for love and emerald for compassion guide their journey. They must cultivate self-care and set boundaries while maintaining their loving nature.

Life Path Number 7: *The Seeker*. Life Path Number 7 individuals are introspective, spiritual, and analytical. They possess a deep thirst for knowledge and understanding. Their life lessons involve learning to trust their intuition and embrace their unique spiritual path. They may face challenges related to isolation or a tendency towards overthinking. Crystals such as amethyst for intuition and selenite for clarity can aid their spiritual growth. They must learn to balance their deep inner life with meaningful connections.

Life Path Number 8: *The Achiever*. These individuals are ambitious, driven, and powerful. They possess a strong will and a capacity for leadership. Their life lessons involve learning to use their power responsibly and ethically. They may face challenges related to materialism or a lack of compassion. Crystals such as obsidian for grounding and black tourmaline for protection are helpful tools. Their task is to leverage their drive and ambition for good.

Life Path Number 9: *The Humanitarian*. Life Path Number 9 individuals are selfless, compassionate, and humanitarian. They are deeply connected to humanity and strive to make a positive impact on the world. Their life lessons involve learning to balance their compassion with self-care and setting healthy boundaries. They might face challenges related to burnout or a tendency to spread themselves too thin. Crystals such as clear quartz for amplification and amethyst for calming help them on their path. They must nurture their own spirit while extending their compassion to others.

Life Path Number 11: *The Master Teacher*. This is a Master Number, representing heightened intuition and spiritual awareness. These individuals are inspiring leaders and gifted communicators. Their life lessons involve learning to manage their intense energy and utilize their gifts for the betterment of others. Challenges may arise from a tendency towards perfectionism or an overwhelming sense of responsibility. Crystals such as amethyst and clear quartz work synergistically for amplification. They must harness their heightened sensitivity and insight for the greatest good.

Life Path Number 22: *The Master Builder*. Another Master Number, individuals with Life Path 22 are visionary leaders with the power to manifest their dreams on a grand scale. Their life lessons involve learning to balance their ambitious goals with practical action and sustainable growth. Challenges may include feeling overwhelmed by the scale of their ambitions or becoming disillusioned. Crystals that promote perseverance, such as garnet and tiger's eye, are valuable allies. They must maintain perspective and take consistent action. Understanding your Life Path Number is a powerful step towards self-discovery. It's not a rigid prediction, but rather a guide, a map of your energetic terrain, highlighting your strengths, potential challenges, and the lessons you're here to learn.

By consciously embracing the insights revealed by your Life Path Number, you can navigate your journey with greater clarity, intention, and empowerment, aligning your actions with your truest purpose and creating a life of authenticity, fulfillment, and joy. Remember to combine this numerological understanding with other modalities, such as chakra balancing, crystal healing, and astrological insights, for a truly holistic approach to self-discovery and personal growth. The journey is unique to each individual and a lifelong adventure of learning and self-improvement.Beyond the Life Path Number, a rich tapestry of numerological insights awaits, revealing further layers of your unique energetic blueprint. The Destiny Number, Soul Urge Number, and Personality Number, each offer a distinct perspective on your inherent traits, desires, and the way you present yourself to the world. Understanding these numbers, and the interplay between them, provides a more comprehensive understanding of your multifaceted self.

The Destiny Number, often referred to as the **Expression Number**, *represents your overall potential and the impact you are destined to have on the world*. Unlike the Life Path Number, which is derived solely from your birthdate, the Destiny Number incorporates the numerical values of all the letters in your full name. This calculation reveals the sum total of your inherent talents and the vibrational energies you bring to the world. To calculate your Destiny Number, assign numerical values to each letter of your name (A=1, B=2, C=3, and so on, until Z=8. Some systems use a different alphabetic numerology chart. This difference in assigning numbers to alphabets is not going to affect the basic meaning. You just might need to adjust the interpretation slightly). Sum the values for all letters in your full name, and then reduce the resulting number to a single digit.

For instance, let's consider the name "Amelia Grace." A=1, M=4, E=5, L=3, I=9, A=1, G=7, R=9, A=1, C=3, E=5. Adding these values together: 1+4+5+3+9+1+7+9+1+3+5 = 48. Reducing this to a single digit: 4+8=12; 1+2=3. Amelia Grace's Destiny Number is 3, suggesting a natural inclination towards creativity, communication, and self-expression. Interpreting the Destiny Number is similar to interpreting the Life Path Number, yet it unveils a different facet of your being. It shows what your natural skills are, and what you are best suited to achieve with minimal effort. It's the potential that's inherent within you, waiting to be realized. It speaks to your public image. It's the role you play on the world's stage. For example, a Destiny Number 1 might indicate a natural aptitude for leadership, while a Destiny Number 7 might suggest a profound interest in spiritual exploration or intellectual pursuits. However, the Destiny number is not always in sync with the life path. This is where the Soul Urge number and the Personality number come into play.

The **Soul Urge Number**, also known as the **Heart's Desire Number**, *delves deeper into your subconscious motivations, desires, and the inner yearnings that drive your actions.* This number is calculated by adding up the numerical values of the vowels in your full name. It unveils your deepest, most authentic self, the part of you that yearns for fulfillment and true happiness. It reveals the things that will make you feel truly satisfied and content. It's the driving force of your passions, which are not necessarily expressed publicly or fully realized. It's the silent whisper of your soul.

Continuing with "Amelia Grace," the vowels are A, E, A, and E. A=1, E=5, A=1, E=5. Adding these together: 1+5+1+5 = 12, reduced to 3. Amelia Grace's Soul Urge Number is 3, indicating a strong desire for creative expression, communication, and a life filled with joy and enthusiasm.

The interplay between the Destiny Number and the Soul Urge Number is fascinating. If these numbers are the same, it suggests a strong alignment between your outward expression and your inner desires. If they differ, it highlights the potential for inner conflict or the need to bridge the gap between what you outwardly project and what truly motivates you. This might reveal why someone is successful in a particular field but feels unfulfilled. This gap needs to be bridged through self-awareness and taking steps to align inner desires with outer actions. This will manifest a more fulfilled life.

Finally, the **Personality Number** reveals *how you present yourself to the world*. It's the mask you wear, the persona you project, the first impression you make. This number is calculated by adding up the numerical values of the consonants in your full name. It illuminates your outer personality, the way you interact with others, and the image you cultivate. This might not necessarily reflect your true nature; instead, it is the role you choose to play in social settings.

For "Amelia Grace," the consonants are M, L, M, G, R, C. M=4, L=3, M=4, G=7, R=9, C=3. Adding these together: 4+3+4+7+9+3 = 30, reduced to 3. Amelia Grace's Personality Number is 3, suggesting an outgoing, expressive, and engaging personality.

The combination of the Life Path, Destiny, Soul Urge, and Personality Numbers paints a *vibrant portrait of your unique energetic profile*. It highlights the potential for synergy or conflict between your inner world and outer presentation, your aspirations and your capabilities. A detailed understanding of these numbers fosters self-awareness, providing valuable insights into your strengths, weaknesses, motivations, and the path toward fulfilling your life's purpose. This intricate numerological tapestry unfolds not as a rigid prediction, but as a dynamic map of your energetic landscape, guiding you towards a deeper understanding of yourself and your place in the universe.

For instance, if someone has a Life Path Number 1 (the pioneer), a Destiny Number 7 (the seeker), a Soul Urge Number 2 (the diplomat), and a Personality Number 8 (the achiever), we can begin to see a fascinating interplay of energies. The Life Path suggests a natural leadership potential, but the Destiny Number hints towards a more introspective and spiritual journey. The Soul Urge points to a deep-seated need for harmony and collaboration, while the Personality Number indicates an outward ambition and drive for success. This individual might experience internal conflict between their desire for independence (Life Path 1) and their need for connection (Soul Urge 2), or between their ambitious nature (Personality 8) and their spiritual inclinations (Destiny 7). By understanding these nuances, the individual can consciously work to integrate these different aspects of their personality, creating a more balanced and harmonious life.

Moreover, understanding these numbers *facilitates effective self-management*. If you know your Soul Urge is to nurture others but your Personality Number shows a tendency to be driven and independent, you can consciously strive for balance, ensuring you satisfy your inner needs while still acting as a successful and driven individual.

Furthermore, the relationship between these numbers can *provide insights into potential life challenges*. For example, a significant discrepancy between the Destiny and Soul Urge Numbers might indicate a struggle to reconcile your public persona with your true inner desires. Recognizing this conflict enables you to address it consciously, making choices that foster greater alignment between your inner self and your outer expression. This process of self-discovery is not about changing who you are, but rather about becoming more aware of the various facets of your being and learning to integrate them harmoniously.

In essence, numerology acts as a powerful tool for *self-reflection and personal growth*. By delving deeper into the multifaceted nature of these key numerological numbers, you gain a richer understanding of your unique energetic landscape, paving the way for greater self-acceptance, alignment, and ultimately, a more fulfilling and authentic life. Remember to use these insights as a guide, not as a rigid prediction, allowing for the organic unfolding of your individual journey. The integration of numerological insights with other holistic practices such as chakra balancing, crystal healing, and astrological interpretations provides a truly holistic and enriching pathway to self-discovery and personal growth.Beyond the individual journey of self-discovery through numerology, lies a fascinating application of this ancient wisdom: understanding the dynamics of relationships and assessing compatibility between individuals. While numerology cannot predict the future of a relationship with absolute certainty, it can offer valuable insights into the inherent energies and potential challenges or harmonies between two people. This understanding empowers individuals to navigate their relationships with greater awareness and intention, fostering healthier and more fulfilling connections.

The core principle lies in comparing the various numerological numbers of each individual. We can compare Life Path Numbers, Destiny Numbers, Soul Urge Numbers, and Personality Numbers to gain a multi-faceted perspective on the potential dynamics between two people. For example, consider two individuals: one with a Life Path Number 1 (the independent leader) and the other with a Life Path Number 2 (the harmonious collaborator). The inherent energies of these numbers suggest a potential for both friction and synergy. The number 1's independent drive might clash with the number 2's need for partnership and collaboration, creating potential for conflict if not managed consciously. However, this difference in energies can also be a source of strength, with the number 1 providing direction and the number 2 offering balance and support. Understanding this inherent dynamic enables the couple to anticipate potential challenges and develop strategies for effective communication and conflict resolution.

The Destiny Numbers reveal how each individual is likely to express themselves in the world and the impact they are destined to have. A comparison of these numbers can highlight areas of potential alignment or divergence in goals and values. For instance, if one partner has a Destiny Number 7 (the spiritual seeker) and the other has a Destiny Number 5 (the free spirit), their shared desire for exploration and experience might create a strong bond. However, the vastly different approaches – the 7's introspective spiritual quest and the 5's love of adventure – might necessitate conscious effort to understand each other's needs and find common ground.

The Soul Urge Numbers, representing the deepest inner desires, can unveil areas of potential emotional resonance or conflict. If both partners share similar Soul Urge Numbers, it suggests a strong emotional connection and shared values. However, discrepancies between these numbers can highlight potential areas of misunderstanding or unmet needs. Consider a couple where one partner has a Soul Urge Number 4 (the builder, seeking stability) and the other has a Soul Urge Number 9 (the humanitarian, seeking to make a difference in the world). The 4's need for security might clash with the 9's desire for expansive humanitarian work, potentially leading to conflict if not addressed with empathy and understanding.

The Personality Numbers reveal how each individual presents themselves to the world, influencing the initial interactions and the ongoing dynamics of the relationship. Comparing Personality Numbers provides insight into how each partner interacts with the other and how they navigate social situations together. For example, a couple where one partner has a Personality Number 3 (the expressive communicator) and the other has a Personality Number 6 (the nurturing caregiver) might experience a harmonious blend of energy, with the 3 providing enthusiasm and the 6 offering support and stability. However, the 3's need for constant stimulation might occasionally clash with the 6's preference for calm and quiet time.

Beyond these core numbers, further explorations can be undertaken by calculating the numerological value of the couple's combined names, creating a "relationship number" which offers an overview of the unique energetic signature of their partnership. This process goes beyond simply adding the individual numbers. It involves a deeper symbolic interpretation based on the combined qualities and potential challenges implied by the number. This number might reveal the underlying energies governing their interaction, highlighting potential strengths and areas for growth. For instance, a relationship number 7 might indicate a deep spiritual connection and a shared desire for personal growth, whereas a relationship number 3 might suggest a vibrant, creative partnership full of joy and communication.

It's crucial to remember that numerology is a *tool for insight,* not a definitive predictor of relationship success or failure. A lack of compatibility indicated by the numerology does not necessarily doom a relationship. Rather, it offers a map of potential challenges and areas where conscious effort and mutual understanding are needed. Couples can use this information to proactively address potential conflicts, strengthen communication, and nurture a more harmonious and fulfilling partnership. The aim is not to find a perfect match based on numbers, but rather to foster self-awareness, understanding, and conscious creation of a supportive relationship.

A strong, healthy relationship thrives on open communication, mutual respect, and a shared vision. Numerology can contribute by highlighting the inherent energies and potential dynamics within the partnership, enabling couples to navigate challenges with greater awareness and intention. By understanding their individual numerological profiles and the interaction between them, couples can gain deeper insight into their strengths, weaknesses, and potential areas of growth. This awareness empowers them to cultivate a more balanced and fulfilling relationship, fostering harmony and mutual understanding.

Moreover, the principles of numerology, when combined with other holistic practices such as chakra balancing and energy work, can enhance the effectiveness of relationship building and conflict resolution. For instance, understanding the relationship between the partners' dominant chakras (e.g., heart chakra for love and connection, root chakra for stability and security) can provide further insight into their emotional needs and communication styles. Using crystal healing, guided meditation or energy balancing techniques can facilitate emotional healing and strengthen the bond between partners, addressing energetic imbalances that might otherwise create friction.

Ultimately, numerology offers a unique lens through which to view relationships. It can offer a deeper understanding of the energetic interplay between partners, revealing potential areas of harmony and conflict. But the success of any relationship rests not solely on numbers, but on conscious effort, communication, and a willingness to grow and adapt together. Using numerology as a tool for self-awareness and understanding can enhance any relationship by helping couples navigate challenges with greater understanding and cultivate a more harmonious and fulfilling connection. It's a map, not a destination. The journey of love and partnership remains a dynamic and evolving process, guided by intention, empathy, and mutual growth. The insights gained through numerology provide a valuable framework, enriching the process of self-discovery and strengthening the bonds of connection.

Understanding this framework allows for a more conscious and intentional approach to building and maintaining a healthy relationship. And in the end, that is the true magic.

Beyond understanding relationships, numerology offers a powerful tool for navigating the ebb and flow of time itself. It allows us to identify optimal moments for action, aligning our intentions with the energetic currents of the universe to maximize our chances of success and fulfillment. This is not about predicting the future with absolute certainty, but rather about working *with* the energies at play, increasing the likelihood of positive outcomes.
The core principle rests on understanding the vibrational essence of numbers. Each number carries a unique energetic signature, influencing the overall energetic landscape of a specific period. By understanding these vibrations and their interplay, we can discern periods of heightened energy, conducive to specific endeavors, and periods that might be better suited for reflection and planning. This understanding empowers us to time our actions strategically, capitalizing on favorable energetic currents.

One of the most fundamental applications is examining the numerical value of dates. Converting dates into single-digit numbers (by adding the digits together until a single-digit remains) reveals the underlying energy of that particular day. For example, let's analyze October 26th, 2024. We add the digits of the month (1+0 = 1), the day (2+6 = 8), and the year (2+0+2+4 = 8). Adding these together (1+8+8 = 17, then 1+7=8), we arrive at the number 8. The number 8 resonates with ambition, power, and material success, suggesting this day might be particularly auspicious for initiating ambitious projects or making significant business decisions. However, it's crucial to consider the overall context and personal numerological profile, as this is simply one piece of the puzzle.

Similarly, we can apply this principle to months and years. Analyzing the numerical vibrations of each month and year can reveal overarching energetic themes and identify periods ideal for specific goals. For instance, a year reducing to a 1 might be highly productive for starting new ventures, while a year reducing to a 7 could be more conducive to introspection and spiritual growth. This broader perspective allows for long-term planning, ensuring that important decisions are aligned with the overarching energetic trends.

However, relying solely on numerical calculations can be limiting. *Intuition* plays a crucial role in harnessing the power of numerology for timing. While the numbers provide a framework, it's our inner guidance that ultimately determines the most opportune moment for action. We must listen to our inner voice, paying attention to subtle cues and feelings. A favorable numerological alignment might indicate a period of opportunity, but our intuition will help us to recognize the specific signs that point towards optimal timing within that window.

Consider, for example, an individual planning to launch a new business. Numerology might indicate that a particular month has a highly favorable energetic signature, say, a number 5 representing freedom and adaptability. However, this individual might experience a period of uncertainty or fear during this time, prompting them to postpone the launch. This inner hesitation might be a crucial piece of information, indicating that despite the auspicious numerological alignment, the timing is not yet right for *this individual*. Ignoring such intuitive cues could lead to a less successful outcome, even if the numerical indicators are favorable.

The interplay between numerology and other holistic modalities further enhances our ability to identify optimal times for action. For instance, connecting numerological insights with astrological transits can provide a more nuanced perspective. A powerful numerological alignment coupled with supportive astrological aspects might point to an exceptionally potent period for manifesting desires. Similarly, understanding the influence of different chakra energies can help determine when specific endeavors are energetically supported. For instance, a project requiring immense creativity might thrive during periods when the solar plexus chakra, the seat of personal power, is actively stimulated.

Crystal healing can further augment this process. Specific crystals are associated with different energies and can amplify our intentions, enhancing the effectiveness of action taken during favorable numerological periods. For instance, *Citrine*, associated with abundance and prosperity, might be used to enhance the success of financial endeavors during a numerically auspicious period. This combined approach allows for a more holistic and effective approach to timing, weaving together ancient wisdom and modern techniques to create a synergistic effect.

It's crucial to remember that numerology is a tool, not a rigid set of rules. *It's a guide to assist us in aligning our actions with the universal flow, not a crystal ball predicting the future.* Flexibility and intuition are paramount. Even during periods marked by favorable numerical alignments, unexpected obstacles might arise. The key is to remain adaptable and respond to these challenges with awareness and intention. The numerological insights provide a framework, but true success lies in our ability to navigate the complexities of life with grace and wisdom.

Furthermore, the personal numerological profile should always be considered. For example, an individual with a Life Path Number 1, often independent and proactive, might find more success in launching new ventures during periods favored by numbers associated with independence and leadership. Conversely, an individual with a Life Path Number 2, usually more collaborative and harmonious, might find more success during periods aligned with partnerships and cooperation.

Therefore, identifying optimal times for action is a deeply personal process. It requires a harmonious blend of numerological knowledge, intuitive guidance, and mindful consideration of our individual strengths and weaknesses. Numerology provides a roadmap, guiding us toward moments of heightened potential. However, it is the synergy between our understanding of the numbers and our own inner compass that truly unlocks the power of optimal timing.

Ultimately, the art of harnessing numerology for timing is a *journey of self-discovery*. It's about cultivating a deeper connection with our intuition and learning to trust our inner voice. As we become more attuned to the subtle energies around us, and as our understanding of numerology deepens, we can effectively time our actions, maximizing our chances of success and creating a more fulfilling life. It's about aligning our actions with the cosmic rhythm, creating harmony between our intentions and the universe's energetic flow. The more we practice and refine this skill, the more intuitive and accurate we become in recognizing the perfect moment to act, leading to a more empowered and aligned existence. The true mastery lies not just in understanding the numbers, but in understanding ourselves and our connection to the universe's inherent timing.Integrating numerology with energy healing opens a powerful avenue for amplifying the effectiveness of healing modalities. Just as numbers vibrate with specific energies, so too do our bodies, our chakras, and the crystals we use for healing. Understanding this interconnectedness allows us to harness the synergistic power of both systems, creating a more potent and targeted healing experience.

One of the most immediate applications is in choosing the right crystals for a healing session. *Each crystal resonates with specific vibrational frequencies, corresponding to particular numbers and chakra energies.* By understanding the numerological profile of an individual and their current life challenges, we can select crystals that amplify the healing process. For instance, someone struggling with emotional imbalance, whose numerological profile suggests a need for emotional grounding (perhaps a Life Path Number 4 associated with stability and structure), might benefit from grounding crystals like Hematite or Black Tourmaline, which vibrate at frequencies conducive to stability and emotional regulation. Conversely, someone needing to boost their creativity, represented perhaps by a Life Path Number 3 associated with expression and joy, could benefit from crystals like Citrine or Carnelian, which carry the energetic frequency to unlock creative potential and joyful expression.

Furthermore, numerology can *inform the timing of healing sessions*. Just as specific days might be more energetically conducive to certain endeavors, the same holds true for healing. By calculating the numerical value of a particular date – similar to the date analysis explained in the previous section – we can determine if that day aligns favorably with the desired healing outcome. A date reducing to a number 6, associated with harmony and balance, might be ideal for a session focusing on emotional healing or restoring energetic equilibrium. Similarly, a date reducing to a number 2, associated with cooperation and partnerships, may be more suitable for collaborative healing sessions or working with a healing partner. The individual's personal numerology should, of course, be taken into account – a Life Path 8, often associated with ambition and drive, might find more benefit from scheduling healing sessions during days associated with higher achievement-oriented numbers, such as 8 itself or a 1, signifying new beginnings and leadership.

This approach extends beyond simply choosing the right date. Even the time of day can be considered. The energetic landscape changes throughout the day, mirroring the natural rhythms of the earth. Sunrise and sunset, for example, mark significant energetic shifts. A morning session might be ideal for invigorating energy and clearing blockages, while an evening session may be more suitable for relaxation and deep healing. Understanding these daily energy cycles and relating them to the numerological significance of the date can help pinpoint the most potent time for a healing session. Intuitive guidance should always complement these calculations; if a specific time or date, despite favorable numerological alignments, feels off to the individual or healer, it's crucial to trust that intuition and reschedule accordingly.

Numerology can also *illuminate personal energy patterns over time.* By analyzing the numerological significance of a person's birth date, their Life Path Number, and other relevant numbers in their numerological chart, we can gain insight into their inherent energetic strengths and weaknesses. This understanding can inform the ongoing energy healing journey. For example, someone with a Life Path Number 7, often associated with introspection and spiritual growth, may be prone to periods of heightened sensitivity or withdrawal. Understanding this inherent energetic pattern allows the healer to tailor sessions to support the individual's specific needs during those times, providing grounding techniques or focusing on specific chakras that may require extra attention.

The integration of numerology also extends to working with the chakra system. Each chakra resonates with specific colors, numbers, and crystals. Understanding the numerological value of a specific period can help determine which chakras are most active or in need of attention. For example, a period reducing to a number 1 might highlight the root chakra (associated with security and grounding), while a period reducing to a 7 might emphasize the crown chakra (connected to spiritual awareness and higher consciousness). This numerological understanding allows for a targeted approach to chakra balancing and healing, maximizing the effectiveness of energy work.

Consider, for example, an individual experiencing recurring issues with their sacral chakra (associated with creativity, pleasure, and abundance). Their numerological profile, perhaps revealed through a challenging year number or a personal year associated with blockages, suggests a need to focus on this area. The healer could then incorporate crystals associated with the sacral chakra, such as orange carnelian or sunstone, during healing sessions. They could also choose dates that resonate with the sacral chakra's energy, taking into account the numerological significance of those days. This multi-faceted approach—combining numerology, chakra balancing, and crystal healing—creates a more holistic and impactful healing experience, aligning the individual's energy with their inherent numerological predispositions and the beneficial vibrational energies.

Moreover, the use of numerology in energy healing extends beyond individual sessions. It can be incorporated into longer-term healing plans. By analyzing the numerological significance of entire years or months, we can anticipate periods of heightened energetic challenges or opportunities. This foresight allows the healer and client to collaboratively plan and adjust the healing process accordingly. If a particular year is numerologically challenging, the healing plan might incorporate stronger preventative measures, while a numerologically favorable year might offer an opportunity to work on more ambitious healing goals.

Beyond individual healing, the combined power of numerology and energy healing can be applied to group settings. Workshops or retreats focused on specific healing themes could be scheduled to coincide with periods numerologically conducive to that theme. A retreat focused on emotional release might be scheduled during a month reducing to a number 2, emphasizing collaboration and harmony, while a retreat aimed at boosting self-confidence might be scheduled during a period reducing to a number 1, highlighting the energy of new beginnings and independence. This strategic approach maximizes the effectiveness of the group healing experience.

It's vital to remember that the integration of numerology into energy healing is not about rigid adherence to rules, but rather about *using numerical insights as a guide to enhance intuition and personalize the healing process.* It's a tool to complement, not replace, the healer's intuition and the individual's self-awareness. Numerology provides a framework for understanding underlying energy patterns, but the true power lies in the synergistic combination of these insights with the healer's intuitive guidance and the individual's personal journey.

The beauty of this combined approach lies in its customization. The synergy between numerology and energy healing allows for tailored healing plans that resonate deeply with each individual's unique energetic makeup. It's a journey of self-discovery, where the numbers act as a roadmap, guiding the individual and the healer toward a more harmonious and balanced state of being. This holistic approach allows individuals to access their inner wisdom and harness the universe's inherent healing power. Ultimately, it's about creating a more conscious and effective path toward self-healing and well-being. **The practice is a continuous learning process, a deepening relationship with numbers, energy, and the intuitive self, leading to a more fulfilling and aligned life.**

Chapter 5: The Art of Reiki Healing

Reiki, pronounced "ray-key," is a *Japanese energy healing technique that channels universal life force energy, often referred to as Ki, Qi, or Prana, to promote physical, emotional, and spiritual well-being.* It's a gentle yet powerful method that works on multiple levels, addressing not just the symptoms of imbalance but also the root causes. Unlike other healing modalities that rely heavily on the practitioner's own energy, Reiki acts as a conduit, allowing the universal life force energy to flow through the practitioner and into the recipient. This energy is intelligent and self-regulating, intuitively finding the areas that require healing and support.

The history of Reiki is rich and fascinating, tracing back to Mikao Usui, a Japanese Buddhist monk, in the early 20th century. Usui, seeking to understand the healing methods mentioned in ancient Buddhist scriptures, embarked on a rigorous spiritual journey. Legend tells of a 21-day retreat atop Mount Kurama, during which he achieved enlightenment and rediscovered the lost art of Reiki. Through this experience, he reportedly received the ability to channel universal life energy for healing. He subsequently established the Usui Reiki Ryoho Gakkai, disseminating his teachings and establishing a lineage of Reiki practitioners.

Usui's original Reiki system, often called Usui Shiki Ryoho, focused on self-healing and the treatment of others. It incorporated meditative practices, moral principles, and specific hand positions to direct the flow of Reiki energy. Over time, different lineages and styles of Reiki have emerged, each with its own variations and interpretations. However, the core principles and the fundamental concept of channeling universal life energy remain consistent across all lineages. The evolution of Reiki demonstrates its adaptability and its capacity to integrate with diverse spiritual and philosophical perspectives. Many modern Reiki practitioners blend aspects of other energy healing techniques, such as crystal healing or chakra balancing, to enhance the effectiveness of their treatments. This integration further underscores Reiki's versatility and its capacity to be tailored to individual needs and preferences.

Central to the practice of Reiki are its five guiding principles, often referred to as the Reiki precepts. These principles, originally written in Japanese by Usui, provide a framework for ethical living and personal development, promoting inner harmony and contributing to a more fulfilling healing experience.

They are:

Just for today, do not anger: This principle encourages cultivating patience, compassion, and understanding, releasing resentment and negativity that can hinder healing on all levels. It emphasizes the importance of emotional self-regulation, recognizing that unresolved anger can manifest as physical tension and energetic blockages.

Just for today, do not worry: This principle promotes letting go of anxieties and fears that often drain energy and impede the healing process. It emphasizes the importance of living in the present moment, focusing on what is within one's control, and trusting in the unfolding of life's events. Letting go of excessive worry creates space for positive energy to flow freely.

Just for today, be grateful for your blessings: This principle encourages fostering an attitude of gratitude, appreciating the good in one's life, and acknowledging the support received from others and the universe itself. Gratitude promotes positive energy and creates a receptive environment for healing.

Just for today, do your work honestly: This principle encourages integrity, ethical conduct, and responsible actions. It emphasizes the importance of aligning one's actions with one's values, fostering a sense of purpose and contributing to personal growth. Honest work strengthens one's character and creates a foundation for positive energy flow.

Just for today, be kind to yourself and others: This principle emphasizes compassion, self-love, and extending kindness to all beings. It encourages empathy, forgiveness, and non-judgment, creating a harmonious environment conducive to healing. Kindness nourishes the soul and enhances the overall healing process.

These principles are not simply rules to follow but rather *guidelines for cultivating a mindful and compassionate approach to life.* They are integral to the Reiki practice because they create an inner state of balance and harmony, enabling the practitioner to become a more effective conduit for universal life force energy. Integrating these principles into daily life fosters a holistic approach to well-being, impacting all aspects of life and enhancing the effectiveness of Reiki healing.

Reiki is often described as operating through different levels, or degrees, of initiation. Each level introduces new techniques and deeper understandings of the energy flow.

The first level, **Reiki I**, usually involves a one-day or weekend workshop, which focuses on self-healing and treating others. Practitioners learn basic hand positions and the fundamental principles of Reiki. This level provides a solid foundation for understanding and practicing Reiki, and lays the groundwork for further advancement.

Reiki II introduces a range of symbols that enhance the energy flow and expand the practitioner's capabilities. These symbols act as energetic amplifiers, enhancing the intention and focus of the healing session. They also allow for distance healing, meaning that Reiki can be sent across distances, to individuals who are not physically present. This level expands the practitioner's range and allows for a more comprehensive approach to healing.

Reiki III, also known as Reiki Master level, involves a deeper level of spiritual training and empowerment. At this level, individuals are typically initiated into a higher level of mastery, empowering them to teach and initiate others into the Reiki practice. This level involves a deeper dive into the energetic principles, allowing the practitioner to develop a more intuitive and profound understanding of the energy flow. It builds upon the self-healing techniques learned in previous levels and establishes the foundation for lifelong spiritual practice. This often includes intensive self-reflection and work on personal development.

The practice of Reiki is deeply intertwined with *ethical considerations*. Reiki practitioners should uphold the highest ethical standards in their practice. This includes maintaining confidentiality, respecting the autonomy of the recipient, avoiding making unrealistic promises, and always recommending conventional medical care when appropriate. Reiki is a complementary therapy, and practitioners should never represent it as a replacement for conventional medical treatment. It's also essential for practitioners to adhere to a code of ethics that prioritizes client well-being and maintains the integrity of the Reiki practice. Integrity and trustworthiness are paramount in any therapeutic relationship and are especially crucial within this context.

The practice of Reiki emphasizes the inherent *self-healing ability of the body and its innate capacity to restore balance and harmony*. It is not about imposing the practitioner's will or energy onto the recipient but rather about creating a space for the recipient's own healing process to unfold naturally. The practitioner acts as a facilitator, channeling universal life force energy and guiding the recipient toward a state of greater well-being. The effectiveness of Reiki is often attributed to its ability to reduce stress, promote relaxation, and enhance the body's natural healing capabilities. It works subtly, allowing the body to heal itself at its own pace, guided by the universal intelligence of Reiki energy.

Beyond its physical effects, Reiki has the potential to facilitate profound emotional and spiritual transformations. By releasing blockages and promoting energy flow, Reiki can address underlying emotional wounds and trauma, enabling individuals to achieve greater emotional balance and resilience. It can also foster a deeper connection to one's inner self, facilitating spiritual growth and expanding awareness.

Ultimately, Reiki is a holistic healing modality that addresses the interconnectedness of mind, body, and spirit. Its profound effects extend far beyond the physical, nurturing emotional resilience and spiritual growth. By combining its use with other holistic practices such as those discussed earlier in the context of numerology and chakra work, Reiki offers a comprehensive approach to self-care and personal development. As a path of self-discovery, Reiki opens up doors to self-healing and a journey towards a more balanced and fulfilling life, in harmony with the universe. Preparing for a Reiki self-treatment session is as much about cultivating the right atmosphere as it is about the physical act of placing your hands. Think of it as preparing a sacred space, a sanctuary where your body and spirit can surrender to the healing energy. The environment you create significantly impacts the effectiveness of the session, allowing you to fully immerse yourself in the experience and receive the benefits Reiki offers. Begin by selecting a quiet space where you won't be disturbed for at least 30 to 45 minutes. This could be your bedroom, a meditation corner, or even a quiet spot in nature. The key is to find a place where you feel safe, comfortable, and protected from external interruptions.

Once you've found your space, begin **decluttering it, both physically and energetically**. Remove anything that might distract you—electronics, clutter, or anything that visually or mentally disrupts the peace you're aiming for. Consider the energy of the space; if it feels cluttered or heavy, take a few moments to cleanse it. You could do this through simple methods like opening a window to let fresh air circulate, burning incense or sage to purify the air, or even visualizing white light filling the space, washing away any stagnant or negative energy. This cleansing ritual helps to set a positive intention for your session, ensuring that you're working within a calm and receptive atmosphere.

Next, focus on creating a **calming ambiance**. Soft lighting is crucial; dim the lights or use candles—real candles are particularly effective for their flickering, meditative quality, although always prioritize safety. If candles aren't suitable, opt for a soft lamp, or even natural light if possible. Consider the soundscape; gentle, ambient music, nature sounds, or even silence can all be beneficial. Experiment with different sounds to determine what best promotes relaxation and helps you achieve a meditative state of being. The goal is to create a sensory experience that fosters a sense of tranquility and promotes deep relaxation. This prepares your mind and body to receive the healing energy more effectively.

Now, turn your attention to yourself. Choose comfortable clothing that allows for free movement and doesn't restrict your circulation. Loose, natural fabrics are ideal, allowing your body to breathe freely. Remove any jewelry that might impede the flow of energy, especially metal jewelry which can sometimes disrupt the energy flow during a Reiki session. This is particularly important if you choose to lie down, as you want to ensure there's nothing that will cause discomfort or impede your comfort during your self-healing session.

Before beginning your Reiki self-treatment, *engage in a few grounding and centering techniques.* A simple grounding exercise involves feeling your feet firmly planted on the floor, connecting with the earth's energy, stabilizing your energy field. This provides a sense of stability and helps to anchor your energy before beginning the Reiki session. Consider practicing some deep, conscious breathing exercises. Inhale slowly and deeply through your nose, feeling the air fill your lungs, expanding your chest and belly. Hold for a few seconds, and then exhale slowly and completely through your mouth, releasing any tension or stress. Repeat this several times, focusing on the rhythm of your breath and the sensation of your body relaxing with each exhale. This mindful breathing helps to calm your nervous system and prepare you for the meditative state required for effective Reiki self-treatment.

Once you feel grounded and centered, *set your intention* for the session. What areas of your being need healing? What imbalances do you hope to address? Setting a clear intention before beginning allows you to direct the Reiki energy to the specific areas that need attention. This could be physical pain, emotional distress, or simply a general feeling of imbalance. Your intention doesn't need to be complex; it could be something simple like, "I intend to invite Reiki energy to flow through me, promoting healing and balance." This focused intention guides the energy to the areas that need attention most during your Reiki self-treatment.

The use of crystals and essential oils can enhance your Reiki self-treatment. Crystals amplify and direct energy, so placing specific crystals around your body or on your chakras can enhance the healing process. Amethyst is excellent for spiritual growth and promotes deep relaxation; clear quartz amplifies energy and promotes clarity, rose quartz opens the heart chakra, while selenite cleanses and protects your energy field. Research different crystals and their properties to select those that resonate with your needs and intentions. Similarly, certain essential oils can enhance the meditative state and promote relaxation, assisting in the overall effectiveness of your Reiki self-treatment session. Lavender, chamomile, and sandalwood are popular choices due to their calming and soothing properties. Always ensure the essential oils you select are pure and undiluted, using an appropriate diffuser or applying them topically with a carrier oil.

Before you begin the hand placements, spend a few minutes silently reflecting on your intention and focusing on your breath. Let go of any thoughts or distractions that might arise, allowing yourself to be present in the moment. Visualize yourself bathed in white light, feeling the energy flowing through you, filling you with peace and serenity. This preparatory period is crucial for establishing a connection with your inner self and the universal life force energy you're about to channel. It creates a bridge between your conscious intentions and the subconscious healing process.

Choosing your body position for your Reiki self-treatment is important. You can perform Reiki either lying down or sitting comfortably. If lying down, choose a comfortable surface such as a bed or yoga mat. Ensure your spine is straight, your limbs are relaxed, and you're in a comfortable and supportive posture. If sitting, maintain a good posture with your back straight and your hands resting gently on your lap or knees. The key is to find a position that promotes relaxation and allows the energy to flow freely. Your body should feel supported and comfortable, enabling you to relax fully and be receptive to the Reiki energy.

Remember, the key to a successful Reiki self-treatment lies in the intention and the creation of a safe, relaxing atmosphere. Your preparation should foster a state of deep relaxation, allowing you to fully receive the healing benefits of the Reiki energy. Embrace this time for self-care and nurturing, allowing yourself to be present and receptive to the healing that is unfolding within. This preparation, as much a ritual as a practical process, sets the stage for a profoundly beneficial self-healing experience. It's a journey inward, a connection with your inner self, and a gentle embrace of the healing power that resides within you. With consistent practice, you'll become more attuned to the subtle energies within and develop a deeper understanding of the transformative potential of Reiki. This self-treatment is not just a healing practice but also a meditative practice—a time for self-reflection, introspection, and connection with your inner self.Now that you've prepared your sacred space and centered yourself, we can begin the actual Reiki self-treatment. Remember, this is a journey inward, a gentle dance with your own energy. There's no right or wrong way to do this; trust your intuition and allow the energy to guide you.

The core of Reiki self-treatment lies in the *hand positions*. These positions are not rigid rules but rather suggestions, guiding the energy flow to specific areas of your body. Begin by sitting or lying down in your chosen comfortable position. Close your eyes gently, and allow your breath to settle into a slow, deep rhythm. Visualize a soft, white light surrounding you, enveloping you in its warmth and protection. This light represents the universal life force energy, the very essence of Reiki.

We'll start with the basic hand positions, focusing on the major energy centers or chakras. However, if you feel drawn to place your hands elsewhere, trust your intuition. The energy will guide you to where it's most needed. Remember, this is your personal journey, and your intuition is your most valuable guide.

The first position is on the *crown chakra*, located at the top of your head. Gently place your hands on your head, palms down, feeling the warmth and energy flowing into you. Hold this position for 3-5 minutes, breathing deeply and consciously, allowing the energy to gently cleanse and balance the crown chakra, connecting you to your higher self and spiritual awareness. Pay attention to any sensations you may feel—a tingling sensation, warmth, or coolness. These are all signs of the energy working its magic. Don't judge or analyze; simply observe and acknowledge these subtle changes.

Next, move your hands to your forehead, specifically between your eyebrows, the area of your *third eye chakra*. This chakra governs intuition, insight, and psychic abilities. Hold this position for another 3-5 minutes, visualizing the energy dissolving any blockages and enhancing your clarity and intuition. Allow any thoughts or emotions to surface without judgment; simply observe them and let them go with each exhale. Feel the energy calming your mind, easing any mental tension or stress. You might experience a sense of lightness, increased mental focus, or even a sudden burst of insight or inspiration.

Now, bring your hands to your *throat chakra*, located at the base of your throat. This energy center governs communication, self-expression, and creativity. Place your palms gently on your throat, feeling the energy flowing through this area. Hold for 3-5 minutes, focusing on any emotional blockages that might be hindering your ability to express yourself authentically. Visualize the energy clearing away any tension or constriction in your throat, allowing for free and honest self-expression. You might feel a release of tension in your neck and shoulders, a sense of ease in your throat, or a renewed sense of confidence in your ability to communicate.

The next position is on your *heart chakra*, located in the center of your chest. This is the seat of love, compassion, and emotional balance. Place your hands gently over your heart, palms down, feeling the warmth and energy flowing into you. Hold this position for 5-7 minutes, allowing the energy to nurture and heal any emotional wounds or imbalances. Visualize a radiant green light filling your heart chakra, expanding your capacity for love, forgiveness, and self-acceptance. You may feel a deep sense of peace, compassion, and connection with yourself and others. You may also experience a release of emotions, such as sadness, grief, or anger. Allow these emotions to flow through you without resistance, knowing that they are being healed and transformed.

Move your hands down to your *solar plexus chakra*, located just above your navel. This chakra governs your personal power, self-esteem, and willpower. Place your hands over this area, palms down, and hold for 3-5 minutes. Visualize a vibrant yellow light filling this chakra, empowering you with confidence and self-assurance. You might feel a surge of energy, a renewed sense of vitality, or a greater sense of control over your life.

Now, place your hands on your *sacral chakra*, located below your navel. This chakra is associated with creativity, sensuality, and emotional well-being. Hold for 3-5 minutes, visualizing an orange light flowing into this area, balancing your emotions and enhancing your creativity. You might experience a sense of warmth, increased creativity, or a feeling of groundedness and stability.

Finally, place your hands on your *root chakra*, located at the base of your spine. This chakra is your connection to the earth, providing a sense of grounding, security, and stability. Hold for 3-5 minutes, visualizing a deep red light filling this chakra, grounding you in the present moment and anchoring your energy. You may feel a sense of stability, security, and connection to the earth.

After working with each chakra, you can choose to linger on any area that feels particularly stagnant or requires more attention. *Trust your intuition*; it will guide you to where the energy is most needed. You may also choose to spend more time on certain chakras depending on your current needs and intentions. For example, if you've been feeling stressed and overwhelmed, you may want to spend more time on the crown and third-eye chakras to calm your mind and improve clarity. Or, if you've been experiencing emotional difficulties, you might focus more time on your heart chakra to nurture and heal emotional wounds.

Throughout the entire process, maintain a gentle and mindful awareness of your breath, allowing it to anchor you to the present moment. Observe any sensations that arise, without judgment or expectation. Simply allow the energy to flow, trusting in its inherent wisdom and healing power. The sensations you experience can vary widely. Some people feel intense heat or cold, tingling, or a pulsing sensation. Others may experience a deep sense of relaxation, peace, or even emotional release. There may be moments of stillness and clarity, or a flood of emotions and thoughts. Whatever you experience, embrace it as part of the healing process.

Once you've completed the hand positions, take a few moments to simply rest and integrate the energy. You may want to lie quietly, allowing the energy to settle and permeate your being. You may also choose to sit and reflect on your experience, noticing any shifts in your energy or emotional state. Remember, the effects of Reiki often unfold gradually, so be patient and kind to yourself. Self-compassion is key to the healing process.

After your self-treatment session, gently bring your awareness back to your surroundings. Take a few deep breaths, and slowly open your eyes. Drink some water to help hydrate your body and aid in the energy integration. Notice how you feel, both physically and emotionally. You may feel more relaxed, energized, or centered. You may also notice shifts in your mood, emotions, or thought patterns. Keep a journal to track your experience and notice any recurring patterns or insights. Remember, consistency is key to experiencing the full benefits of Reiki. Regular self-treatment sessions can significantly enhance your overall well-being, fostering emotional balance, spiritual growth, and a deeper connection with your inner self.

This basic Reiki self-treatment is just a starting point. As you become more comfortable with the process, you can experiment with different hand positions, visualizations, and affirmations to enhance your healing journey. You can also incorporate other modalities, such as crystals or essential oils, to further support the healing process. Always trust your intuition, and allow the energy to guide you. Reiki is a powerful tool for self-healing and personal growth, empowering you to take charge of your well-being and live a more fulfilling and meaningful life. Remember, this is not just a technique; it's a journey of self-discovery and connection with your inner wisdom and the universal life force energy. Embrace the process, nurture yourself, and allow the healing to unfold naturally. The more you practice, the more attuned you'll become to the subtle energies within, deepening your understanding of the transformative power of Reiki. Each session is a step toward deeper self-awareness and a more harmonious connection with yourself and the universe. Enjoy the journey. Expanding your Reiki practice beyond self-healing opens up a world of possibilities, a realm where you can extend the healing touch to others, regardless of distance. This is the essence of distant healing, a powerful technique that leverages the boundless nature of Reiki energy. Imagine sending healing energy across continents, offering solace and support to someone in need, simply through focused intention and the guidance of your Reiki attunement. It's a testament to the universal energy field that connects us all, a field that Reiki taps into with remarkable grace and effectiveness.

Before embarking on distant healing, a clear understanding of ethical considerations is paramount. Respect for the recipient's free will is non-negotiable. Distant healing should never be imposed; it's a gift offered, not a forceful intervention. Always seek the recipient's consent, ensuring they are aware of the process and comfortable receiving your energy. This respect extends to respecting their boundaries and their journey; your role is to offer support, not dictate their healing path. Remember, you're facilitating their connection to their own innate healing capacity, not replacing it.

The process of distant healing mirrors the principles of self-healing, yet with a subtle shift in focus. Instead of directing energy directly to your physical body, you focus your intention on the recipient. Begin by creating your sacred space, just as you would for a self-healing session. This sets the tone for a focused and effective transmission of energy. Clear your mind of distractions, allowing yourself to become a conduit for the universal life force. You can visualize a cord of light connecting you to the recipient, a vibrant stream of energy flowing between you, carrying healing and support.

Consider using the recipient's photograph or a personal item that holds their energy. This acts as a focal point for your intention, helping to direct the healing energy effectively. The photograph or item allows you to connect with the person on a deeper level, enhancing the strength and focus of your transmission. However, if this isn't possible, don't be discouraged. The power of Reiki lies in the intention itself; focusing on the recipient's name and their well-being is sufficient for the energy to reach its destination.

Now, visualize the recipient surrounded by a soft, white light, representing the universal life force energy. See this light gently cleansing and balancing their energy field, healing any imbalances or blockages. Focus on the areas where they need healing, be it physical pain, emotional distress, or spiritual stagnation. Visualize the Reiki energy dissolving the negativity, replacing it with a sense of peace, well-being, and vitality. You can use affirmations, silently repeating phrases such as "I send healing energy to [recipient's name], promoting their well-being and wholeness," or similar positive affirmations that resonate with you.

The length of a distant healing session can vary. A shorter session of 15-20 minutes can be remarkably effective, but feel free to extend it based on your intuition and the recipient's needs. Trust your inner guidance; the energy will flow as needed. After the session, ground yourself and disconnect from the energy flow. Take a moment to reflect on the experience, noticing any sensations or insights that arose during the transmission.

Just as with self-healing, you might experience various physical sensations during distant healing. These could range from tingling in your hands to a sense of warmth or coolness. Some practitioners experience a sense of connection with the recipient, intuitively understanding their energy state. It is crucial to acknowledge these sensations without judgment; they are indicators of the energy exchange, and your capacity to channel it. If you feel overwhelmed at any point, it's essential to ground yourself immediately, gently disconnecting from the energy flow and returning your attention to your physical body and surroundings. Your well-being is also a priority in this process.

Distant healing, like all Reiki practices, is enhanced by consistent practice. Regular practice strengthens your ability to focus your intention and channel the Reiki energy effectively. Don't be disheartened if you don't experience dramatic changes immediately. The healing process is gradual and unique to each individual. The effects of distant healing may not be immediately apparent to the recipient, but the energy is working subtly, promoting balance and healing on all levels. You are acting as a facilitator, supporting their own inherent healing journey.

The application of Reiki symbols enhances the power and effectiveness of distant healing. Each symbol holds a unique vibrational frequency that amplifies the healing energy and enhances specific aspects of the healing process. The use of symbols requires a proper attunement from a qualified Reiki teacher. It's not advisable to use symbols without receiving the proper attunements and guidance, as incorrect use can be counterproductive.

The Cho Ku Rei symbol, often described as the power symbol, is frequently used to *amplify the intention and energy flow*. Visualize this symbol brightly, infusing your healing energy with focused power. It strengthens the connection with the recipient, ensuring the energy reaches its destination with precision.

The Sei He Ki symbol, often associated with emotional and mental healing, *works on a deeper level, addressing the emotional and mental aspects underlying the physical ailment*. It can help to release emotional blockages, promoting mental clarity and emotional balance. Visualize the Sei He Ki symbol gently cleansing and harmonizing the recipient's emotional and mental field.

The Hon Sha Ze Sho Nen symbol is specifically designed for distant healing. It acts as a bridge, *connecting you to the recipient regardless of distance*. Visualize this symbol as a radiant beam of light, connecting you to the recipient, carrying the healing energy directly to them. It's essential to use this symbol correctly in order to successfully perform distant healing. Ensure you are properly attuned to this symbol before attempting distant healing with it.

The Dai Ko Myo symbol, often regarded as the master symbol, *enhances all other symbols and amplifies the overall healing effect.* This symbol increases the potential and effectiveness of the entire distant healing process, creating a powerful wave of positive energy. However, this symbol, being the most potent of the core Reiki symbols, requires advanced mastery and understanding. Its use is generally reserved for practitioners with advanced Reiki training and experience.

Integrating these symbols into your distant healing practice requires mindful intention and a clear understanding of their respective properties. Visualize the symbols clearly and feel their vibrational essence as you direct the Reiki energy to the recipient. Remember that these symbols are tools to amplify your intention and enhance the healing process; they are not the source of the healing itself. The healing comes from the universal life force energy and the practitioner's intention and focus.

Incorporating other holistic techniques, such as crystal healing or aromatherapy, can further complement the distant healing process. For example, you could place a crystal such as amethyst or clear quartz near the recipient's photograph or personal item to enhance the healing energy. Alternatively, you could use specific essential oils, such as lavender or chamomile, to create a calming and healing atmosphere. This holistic approach enhances the overall healing experience, creating a synergistic effect that supports the recipient's journey to wholeness.

Remember, the journey of Reiki is a personal one, filled with constant learning and refinement. As you gain more experience, your understanding of distant healing will deepen.

The more you practice, the more attuned you will become to the subtle energies involved, fostering a profound connection with both the recipient and the universal life force energy. This continuous evolution and deepening of understanding is an integral part of the Reiki journey, transforming you into a conduit of healing and empowering others to embark on their own transformative journeys. Continue to nurture your practice, seek guidance when needed, and always approach distant healing with respect, compassion, and a deep commitment to ethical conduct.The power of Reiki extends far beyond its solitary application. Its gentle yet potent energy acts as a beautiful foundation, seamlessly integrating with other energy healing modalities to create a holistic and profoundly transformative healing experience. Think of Reiki as the conductor of an orchestra, harmonizing various instruments – chakra balancing, crystal healing, aromatherapy, numerology, and even astrology – to create a symphony of healing. This synergistic approach elevates the healing process, addressing imbalances on multiple levels: physical, emotional, mental, and spiritual.

One of the most natural integrations is with chakra balancing. Reiki's ability to cleanse and revitalize the energy system aligns perfectly with the practice of harmonizing the seven main chakras. Before beginning a Reiki session focused on chakra balancing, it's beneficial to assess the client's energy field. This might involve intuitive sensing, pendulum dowsing, or even simply observing their posture and demeanor. Notice any areas of tension or imbalance; these often correlate with specific chakras. For instance, a feeling of rootlessness or insecurity might indicate an imbalance in the root chakra, while a constricted throat chakra might manifest as difficulty expressing oneself.

Once you've identified potential imbalances, you can incorporate Reiki treatments to address these energy centers. Start by performing a standard Reiki session, allowing the energy to flow naturally through the body. As you feel the energy flowing, consciously direct it towards the imbalanced chakras. Visualize each chakra spinning freely and vibrantly, its natural color radiating with health and vitality. You might use specific Reiki symbols, such as Sei He Ki, which is particularly effective in emotional healing, to further support the chakra's balancing. For the root chakra, you might visualize a deep grounding energy connecting the person to the earth, fostering a sense of stability and security. For the crown chakra, you might envision a connection to the divine, opening the flow of spiritual energy.

The integration of crystal healing with Reiki amplifies the healing process significantly. Crystals, with their inherent vibrational frequencies, act as potent energy amplifiers and conduits. Each crystal carries unique properties and resonates with different chakras and energies. For instance, amethyst is often used for spiritual growth and emotional healing, while rose quartz promotes love and compassion. Clear quartz is a versatile amplifier that can enhance the effects of other crystals and Reiki energy.

During a combined Reiki and crystal healing session, strategically place crystals on or around the client's body while performing the Reiki treatment. The crystals' energy will work in concert with the Reiki energy, amplifying its effects and directing it to specific areas. For instance, placing amethyst on the third eye chakra can enhance intuition and spiritual awareness while a rose quartz on the heart chakra can facilitate emotional healing and self-love. The placement of crystals can be guided by your intuition, the client's needs, and the specific properties of the crystals used. Remember to cleanse and program the crystals before each session to ensure their energy is clear and focused.

Aromatherapy, with its diverse range of essential oils, adds another layer of depth to the Reiki healing experience. Essential oils, extracted from plants, possess unique aromatic and therapeutic properties that can impact our emotional and physical well-being. The inhalation of these oils stimulates the limbic system, the emotional center of the brain, influencing our mood, thoughts, and emotions. Certain oils, like lavender, promote relaxation and reduce stress, while others, like peppermint, enhance focus and mental clarity.

Integrating aromatherapy into a Reiki session is as simple as diffusing essential oils in the treatment area or applying them topically during the session. However, it is crucial to always use pure, high-quality essential oils and perform a patch test before applying them directly to the skin. Remember to use a carrier oil, such as jojoba or sweet almond oil, when applying essential oils topically. The scent itself can enhance the overall atmosphere of the healing space, creating a calming and supportive environment for the client.

Numerological insights can enhance the understanding and interpretation of a Reiki session. By analyzing the client's birth date and name, you can gain insights into their life path, personality traits, and karmic patterns. This information can be incredibly helpful in tailoring the Reiki treatment to address specific challenges and support their overall well-being. For example, a numerology reading might reveal a pattern of self-sabotage or a tendency to avoid emotional vulnerability. Knowing this, you can focus the Reiki energy on releasing those patterns and empowering the client to embrace self-compassion and healthy boundaries.

Similarly, **astrology** can offer valuable insights into the client's energetic state. By understanding the current planetary transits and the client's astrological chart, you can gain a deeper understanding of their emotional and spiritual state. This information can help you tailor the Reiki treatment to address specific energetic challenges and support their overall well-being during a particular time. For example, if a client is experiencing emotional turmoil during a challenging planetary transit, Reiki can help them navigate those difficult periods with grace and resilience.

The *combination of these modalities*, guided by intuition and intention, provides a powerful and customized healing approach. Consider the client's specific needs, energy imbalances, and personal preferences when selecting and integrating these tools. There is no one-size-fits-all approach; rather, the art lies in intuitively selecting the modalities and techniques that best support the individual's healing journey.

This holistic approach doesn't end with the session itself. It extends into empowering the client to continue their healing journey through self-care practices and conscious living. This could include guided meditation, mindful movement, healthy diet, and regular engagement in practices that resonate with their spiritual growth. The Reiki session becomes a starting point, providing the tools and guidance for the client to cultivate a sustainable path of well-being and self-discovery. Remember, your role as a healer extends beyond the treatment itself; it is to empower and inspire your clients to cultivate a life of balance and harmony. The combined power of Reiki and these other modalities provides a transformative experience, enriching both the client's life and the practitioner's journey of service. The journey of holistic healing is a dance of energy, intuition, and compassion, a journey of constant learning and deepening understanding. The more you practice, the more intuitive and effective your integration of these modalities will become. Embrace the art of synergy, allowing your knowledge and intuition to guide you, and watch as the healing unfolds in unexpected and profound ways.

Chapter 6: The Power of Crystal Healing

Crystals, with their captivating beauty and inherent energy, have been revered for centuries for their healing properties. Far from mere decorative objects, these geological wonders hold a potent vibrational energy that can interact with and influence our own energy fields, contributing to our physical, emotional, and spiritual well-being. Crystal healing, therefore, is not about the crystals themselves possessing inherent curative powers, but rather about *harnessing their unique vibrational frequencies to facilitate healing and balance within the individual. It's about working with the crystal's energy, not through it as a magical cure-all.* The fundamental principle of crystal healing lies in the concept of *energy transference*. Every living thing, including ourselves, emits and absorbs energy. This energy, often referred to as bio-energy or life force, flows through our bodies along pathways known as meridians or nadis, influencing our physical and emotional states. When these energy pathways become blocked or disrupted – due to stress, illness, or emotional trauma – it can lead to physical ailments, emotional imbalances, and spiritual disharmony. Crystals, with their stable and consistent vibrational frequencies, can act as conduits, helping to clear blockages, balance energy flow, and restore harmony within the body's energetic system. They essentially act as tuning forks, gently nudging our energy fields back into resonance.

The history of crystal healing is rich and spans various cultures and time periods. Ancient civilizations, including the Egyptians, Greeks, and Romans, utilized crystals for their perceived medicinal properties. Shamans and healers in many indigenous traditions have long incorporated crystals into their healing practices, attributing to them spiritual significance and potent healing capabilities. The use of crystals for healing experienced a resurgence in the latter half of the 20th century, gaining popularity alongside the rise of holistic and alternative medicine.

However, it's crucial to approach crystal healing with a balanced perspective. While crystals can be a valuable tool in a holistic approach to well-being, they should never be considered a substitute for conventional medical treatment. If you are experiencing a medical condition, it's vital to seek professional medical advice from a qualified healthcare practitioner. Crystals can be a supportive adjunct to traditional medicine, but they should not replace necessary medical care.

The diverse range of crystals available, each with its own unique properties and energetic signature, contributes to the richness and versatility of crystal healing. This isn't simply a matter of aesthetic preference; the different chemical compositions and crystalline structures of various minerals translate into distinct vibrational frequencies, each resonating with specific chakras and addressing various imbalances.

Amethyst, for example, with its calming violet hues, is widely recognized for its ability to *soothe the mind, promote relaxation, and enhance spiritual awareness.* Its gentle energy often helps to alleviate stress, anxiety, and insomnia, making it a valuable tool for those seeking emotional and mental tranquility. Often placed near the third eye chakra (Ajna chakra) or crown chakra (Sahasrara chakra) during meditation, it can amplify the experience and deepen the connection to inner wisdom. Amethyst's vibrational frequency is also particularly effective in clearing the aura of negative energy and promoting a sense of peace.

Rose quartz, a stone of *unconditional love, fosters compassion, self-acceptance, and emotional healing.* Its soft pink energy gently opens the heart chakra (Anahata chakra), *promoting forgiveness, healing past wounds, and cultivating self-love and healthy relationships.* Its soothing energy can be immensely comforting during times of heartbreak or emotional turmoil, helping to mend emotional wounds and foster inner peace. Holding a piece of rose quartz can be a potent way to connect with the energy of compassion and self-acceptance.

Clear quartz, often referred to as the "master healer," is a remarkably versatile crystal known for its amplification properties. It doesn't hold a specific energy of its own but rather *amplifies the energy of other crystals and even amplifies the intention of the healer.* This makes it a powerful tool for enhancing the effectiveness of other crystals and energy healing modalities. It can be used to amplify the energy flow during Reiki sessions or placed alongside other crystals to boost their healing properties. Clear quartz can also be programmed with specific intentions, making it a powerful tool for manifestation and positive affirmation.

Citrine, with its radiant yellow color, is associated with *abundance, prosperity, and creativity.* Its vibrant energy is often used to stimulate the solar plexus chakra (Manipura chakra), fostering self-confidence, self-esteem, and personal empowerment. It can help to boost energy levels, enhance motivation, and attract positive opportunities. Keeping a citrine near your workspace or carrying it with you can help to boost creativity and attract abundance into your life.

Selenite, a luminous white crystal, is known for its purifying and cleansing properties. Its energy is exceptionally powerful at clearing negative energy from spaces and individuals. It's frequently used to cleanse other crystals and to purify the energy field of a person or a room. Selenite's high vibrational frequency can help to dissolve stagnant energy, promote clarity, and enhance spiritual connection. It is also often associated with tranquility, peace, and clarity of thought.

Turquoise, with its distinctive blue-green hue, is connected to *communication, self-expression, and emotional balance.* It is frequently associated with the throat chakra (Vishuddha chakra), helping to facilitate clear and confident communication. It assists in expressing one's truth authentically while overcoming communication barriers. Turquoise can also aid in emotional healing, helping to release repressed emotions and promote emotional balance.

These are just a few examples of the many crystals used in healing practices. Each crystal carries its unique energetic signature, resonating with specific chakras and addressing various aspects of our well-being. The selection of crystals for a particular purpose depends on the individual's needs, the desired outcome, and the intuition of the practitioner.

Selecting the right crystals is often guided by intuition. Often, you might find yourself drawn to a particular crystal without knowing why. This is often a sign that the crystal's energy resonates with your current energetic needs. You can also use charts or guides that link crystals to specific chakras or ailments, but trust your intuition above all. It's important to handle crystals with respect and care, appreciating their inherent beauty and power. Regular cleansing and charging of crystals is crucial to maintain their energetic integrity. This can be done through various methods, including smudging with sage, placing them under moonlight, or using selenite to cleanse them energetically.

The integration of crystal healing within a broader holistic healing framework, such as the one explored earlier with Reiki, chakra balancing, and aromatherapy, significantly amplifies its effectiveness. Imagine a Reiki session where amethyst is placed on the third eye chakra to enhance intuition, rose quartz on the heart chakra to foster self-love, and clear quartz strategically placed to amplify the overall energy flow. The synergistic effect of these modalities creates a powerful, holistic healing experience, addressing imbalances on multiple levels.

The journey into crystal healing is a journey of self-discovery. It's about learning to listen to your intuition, understanding the subtle energies that surround us, and appreciating the power of natural elements to support our well-being. Remember always to approach crystal healing with an open mind, respect for the stones, and a realistic understanding of its potential within a broader healing framework. It's a beautiful complement to other modalities, enriching the overall healing experience and fostering a deeper connection with oneself and the universe. The power lies not only in the crystal itself but in the intention, the connection, and the belief in the healing process.Choosing the right crystals is a deeply personal journey, one that often transcends logic and speaks directly to the intuitive heart. It's not simply about picking a pretty stone; it's about selecting a vibrational partner, a mineral ally that resonates with your current energy needs and intentions. While guides and charts linking crystals to specific chakras or ailments can be helpful, the most powerful selection comes from listening to your inner wisdom. Pay attention to the subtle pull, the inexplicable magnetism that draws you toward a particular crystal. That visceral connection is your intuition whispering, guiding you towards the perfect energetic match.

This intuitive connection goes beyond visual appeal. You might find yourself drawn to a crystal's texture, its weight in your hand, or even a particular imperfection within its structure. Each of these details plays a role in the overall energetic resonance. Don't dismiss these subtle cues; they're often the most reliable indicators of a crystal's suitability for you at that moment. Hold different crystals, feel their energy, and trust the subtle guidance of your intuition. It's a conversation between you and the crystal, a silent exchange of energy that precedes any conscious understanding.

Let's say, for example, you're feeling overwhelmed by stress and anxiety. You might find yourself instinctively drawn to the soothing violet hues of amethyst, its calming energy a natural balm for your frayed nerves. Or perhaps you're struggling with self-love and acceptance. In that case, the soft pink glow of rose quartz might gently call to you, its gentle embrace promising comfort and healing. The process is unique to each individual and each crystal; there's no right or wrong way to choose. Trust the process, trust your intuition, and allow yourself to be guided by the subtle whispers of the stones.

Remember, the relationship you cultivate with your crystals is paramount. It's a relationship built on respect, understanding, and intention. Approach each crystal with reverence, acknowledging its inherent power and the energetic exchange that occurs between you. Handle your crystals with care, appreciating their unique beauty and the wisdom they hold. Consider them not just as objects but as living entities, each with its own distinct personality and energetic signature. This mindful approach deepens the connection and amplifies the healing potential.

Once you've chosen your crystals, the next crucial step is *cleansing*. Just as we cleanse our bodies through showering or bathing, crystals require cleansing to maintain their energetic integrity. Crystals absorb energy from their surroundings – both positive and negative – and over time, this can dull their vibrational frequency and diminish their healing power. Regular cleansing removes any accumulated negative energy, resetting the crystal and restoring its vibrancy. It's akin to clearing the channel, ensuring that the crystal's energy flows freely and powerfully.

One of the most common and effective methods is *smudging*. This ancient practice involves using the smoke of sacred herbs, such as white sage, to cleanse and purify objects and spaces. Simply light a smudge stick, gently fanning the smoke around your crystal, visualizing the negative energy being released and replaced with pure, positive energy. Intention is key here; visualize the smoke washing over the crystal, dissolving any stagnant or negative energy. The intention behind the act powerfully enhances the effectiveness of the cleansing process. Water cleansing is another effective method, particularly suitable for crystals that are relatively hard and non-porous. This involves gently rinsing your crystals under running water, preferably from a natural source like a stream or river. As you rinse the crystal, visualize the water washing away any negative energy, leaving the crystal cleansed and refreshed. You can also use a bowl of purified water for crystals that are more delicate, ensuring they are not submerged for extended periods. The power of running water, with its inherent cleansing properties, is beautifully synergistic in this process.

Sunlight is another powerful tool for cleansing crystals. The sun's radiant energy has a naturally purifying effect, charging and revitalizing crystals. However, be mindful that prolonged exposure to direct sunlight can fade the color of some crystals, so it's best to use this method judiciously. Place your crystals in direct sunlight for a few hours, focusing your intention on their cleansing and rejuvenation. Visualize the sunlight's energy infusing the crystal, clearing away any negativity and amplifying its positive vibrations.

Selenite, as previously mentioned, is a *powerful cleansing agent for other crystals*. Because of its exceptional ability to purify the energy field, placing other crystals on a selenite slab for a few hours is an excellent way to cleanse them energetically. This is particularly useful for crystals that are sensitive to water or sunlight. The high vibrational frequency of selenite effectively clears away any accumulated negativity, restoring the crystals' vibrancy and enhancing their energetic potential.

Beyond these traditional methods, you can infuse your own personal cleansing rituals. Perhaps you incorporate *sound healing*, such as playing a singing bowl or tuning forks near your crystals, allowing the vibrations to cleanse and energize them. Or maybe you prefer to connect with nature, burying your crystals in the earth for a period, allowing Mother Earth to restore their balance and vitality. Whatever method you choose, remember that the intention behind the act is paramount. Your focused intention acts as a catalyst, amplifying the effectiveness of the cleansing process and creating a stronger connection between you and your crystals.

The power of intention is paramount in crystal healing. It's not simply about mechanically following prescribed steps; it's about consciously participating in the energetic exchange. Your intentions, your beliefs, and your connection to the crystal profoundly influence the effectiveness of the healing process. Whether you're choosing your crystals, cleansing them, or using them in a healing session, infuse your actions with intention. Visualize the energy flowing, feel the connection, and trust the inherent power of both the crystal and your own intention to work together in harmony. This conscious engagement transforms the process from a mere procedure into a potent spiritual practice.

The cleansing process isn't just about removing negativity; it's also about preparing the crystal for its intended purpose. Before using a crystal in a healing session or for a specific intention, cleanse it thoroughly, setting your intentions for its use. This focuses the crystal's energy and strengthens its ability to serve your purpose. For instance, if you plan to use amethyst for meditation to enhance intuition, cleanse it beforehand, visualizing its energy becoming a conduit for heightened spiritual awareness. This conscious preparation strengthens the bond between you and the crystal, enhancing its effectiveness in the healing process.

Similarly, when cleansing a crystal, remember to set an intention for what you want the process to achieve. Are you clearing away accumulated negativity, infusing it with positive energy, or simply preparing it for a specific purpose? This mindful approach transforms the act of cleansing into a powerful energetic exchange, enhancing the crystal's vibrancy and its ability to serve its purpose. It is a powerful demonstration of the synergy between human intention and the inherent power of crystals.

The journey of choosing and cleansing your crystals is more than just a practical exercise; it's a spiritual practice. It's a path of self-discovery, a deepening of your connection with the subtle energies of the universe, and an acknowledgement of the powerful partnership you forge with these extraordinary natural elements. Embrace this journey with an open heart, a curious mind, and a reverence for the inherent power held within each crystal. Through this process, you not only cleanse and energize your crystals but also deepen your own inner connection to the healing potential of the universe.Now that we've explored the art of choosing and cleansing your crystals, let's delve into the fascinating world of chakra balancing using these potent tools. Each of our seven chakras, those swirling vortexes of energy along our spine, corresponds to specific aspects of our being – physical, emotional, and spiritual. When these chakras are balanced and flowing freely, we experience a sense of wholeness, harmony, and vitality. However, imbalances can manifest as physical ailments, emotional distress, or spiritual stagnation. Crystals, with their unique vibrational frequencies, can be powerful allies in restoring this equilibrium.

The *root chakra*, located at the base of the spine, is our foundation, grounding us in the physical world and providing a sense of security and stability. When this chakra is imbalanced, we may experience feelings of fear, insecurity, and lack of grounding. Red Jasper, Garnet, and Hematite are excellent crystals for balancing the root chakra. Their grounding energy helps to instill a sense of stability and security, anchoring us to the present moment and promoting feelings of safety and self-confidence. To use these crystals, you can place them on your sacral chakra, visualize their energy anchoring you to the earth, and feel a sense of stability permeating your being. You could also carry a tumbled Red Jasper in your pocket throughout the day, allowing its grounding energy to subtly support you.

Moving upwards, the *sacral chakra*, located in the lower abdomen, governs our creativity, sexuality, and emotional expression. Imbalances here can manifest as emotional instability, sexual dysfunction, or a lack of creativity. Carnelian, Orange Calcite, and Sunstone are potent crystals for harmonizing the sacral chakra. Their vibrant energy encourages self-expression, boosts creativity, and fosters emotional balance. Place a smooth Carnelian stone on your sacral chakra during meditation, visualizing its warm energy flowing through you, igniting your creativity and fostering emotional freedom. Alternatively, you can wear a Carnelian pendant, allowing its uplifting energy to support you throughout the day.

The *solar plexus chakra*, situated in the upper abdomen, is our center of personal power, self-esteem, and will. Imbalances can lead to feelings of low self-esteem, lack of confidence, or digestive issues. Yellow Calcite, Citrine, and Tiger's Eye are powerful allies in balancing this chakra. Their vibrant energy boosts self-confidence, strengthens willpower, and promotes a sense of personal power. Hold a piece of Citrine in your hand while affirming your self-worth, visualizing its golden energy filling you with confidence and strength. You could also place a Yellow Calcite on your solar plexus during meditation, allowing its energy to infuse you with self-assurance and empowerment.

The *heart chakra*, located in the center of the chest, governs love, compassion, and emotional healing. Imbalances can manifest as feelings of loneliness, heartbreak, or emotional coldness. Rose Quartz, Green Aventurine, and Emerald are beautiful crystals for nurturing the heart chakra. Their gentle energy promotes emotional healing, encourages forgiveness, and fosters self-love and compassion. Hold a Rose Quartz close to your heart while meditating on feelings of self-love and compassion, allowing its gentle energy to soothe emotional wounds. You could also wear a Green Aventurine necklace, allowing its nurturing energy to support you throughout the day, promoting feelings of harmony and connection.

The *throat chakra*, located in the throat area, governs communication, self-expression, and truth. Imbalances can lead to difficulty communicating, suppressed emotions, or throat problems. Blue Lace Agate, Turquoise, and Aquamarine are excellent crystals for opening and balancing the throat chakra. Their calming energy promotes clear communication, encourages self-expression, and facilitates the release of suppressed emotions. Place a Blue Lace Agate on your throat chakra during meditation, visualizing its soothing energy dissolving any blockages and facilitating clear, confident communication. You can also wear a Turquoise pendant, reminding yourself to express your truth with honesty and integrity.
The third eye chakra, located in the center of the forehead, governs intuition, insight, and spiritual awareness. Imbalances can lead to a lack of intuition, confusion, or headaches. Amethyst, Lapis Lazuli, and Sodalite are potent crystals for activating and balancing the third eye chakra. Their intuitive energy enhances psychic abilities, promotes clarity of thought, and fosters spiritual growth. Place an Amethyst on your third eye chakra during meditation, visualizing its violet energy expanding your intuition and deepening your spiritual awareness. You could also carry a Lapis Lazuli stone with you to enhance your intuitive insights throughout the day.

Finally, the *crown chakra*, located at the top of the head, connects us to higher consciousness, spiritual awareness, and universal energy. Imbalances can lead to feelings of disconnection, lack of purpose, or spiritual emptiness. Clear Quartz, Selenite, and Amethyst are powerful crystals for balancing the crown chakra. Their high vibrational energy enhances spiritual connection, promotes feelings of peace and enlightenment, and strengthens the link to universal consciousness. Place a Clear Quartz on your crown chakra during meditation, visualizing its energy connecting you to the divine, infusing you with a sense of peace, purpose, and spiritual wholeness. Regular meditation with Clear Quartz can significantly strengthen the flow of energy through your crown chakra.

Beyond placing crystals directly on your chakras, consider strategically placing them in your environment. For example, placing a large Amethyst geode in your meditation space can infuse the room with calming, intuitive energy, enhancing the effectiveness of your practice. Similarly, placing Rose Quartz in your bedroom can promote restful sleep and foster feelings of love and compassion. Experiment with different placements and observe how the energy of the crystals interacts with your environment and your own personal energy field. The effectiveness of crystal healing is also deeply intertwined with your intention. Approach your crystal healing practices with mindfulness and focused intention. Visualize the energy flowing from the crystal into your chakras, dissolving blockages and promoting balance. Affirm your intention for healing and well-being. The power of your intention significantly amplifies the crystal's healing potential.

Remember that crystal healing is a gentle, supportive process. It complements other healing modalities and does not replace medical or psychological treatment. If you are experiencing significant health challenges, consult with qualified healthcare professionals. Crystal healing is a journey of self-discovery, a path towards greater balance and harmony. Approach it with an open heart, a curious mind, and trust in the inherent wisdom of these natural wonders. Embrace the subtle energies, allowing them to guide you toward a state of wholeness and well-being. The journey unfolds uniquely for each person, and the crystals are simply guides along the way.

The beauty of crystal healing lies not only in its effectiveness but also in the profound connection it fosters with the natural world and the subtle energies that permeate our existence. As you work with crystals, take time to appreciate their beauty, their unique energy signatures, and the deep connection they offer to the earth's ancient wisdom. This connection goes beyond mere healing; it's a path of spiritual growth, a deepening of your intuitive abilities, and a strengthening of your connection to the universe.

The process is as much about the journey as it is about the destination. Each crystal, each chakra, each session holds a unique lesson, a unique opportunity for growth and understanding. Be patient with yourself, be open to the subtle shifts in energy, and trust in the unfolding process. The transformative power of crystal healing is subtle yet profound, guiding you towards a state of greater balance, harmony, and vibrant well-being.

As you continue your journey with crystals, you will discover a deeper understanding of yourself, your energetic body, and the interconnectedness of all things. The path of crystal healing is a continuous exploration, a dynamic interplay between the stones and your own innate healing capacity. Embrace this path with curiosity, respect, and a deep appreciation for the transformative power of nature's gifts. And remember, the journey itself is a profound act of self-care, a testament to your commitment to your holistic well-being. The more you work with your crystals, the more attuned you will become to their subtle energies, and the more effectively you will be able to use them to support your physical, emotional, and spiritual growth. It's a journey of continuous discovery and deepening connection, both with the crystals themselves and with the powerful, innate healing potential that resides within you.Having explored the individual power of crystals and their application in chakra balancing, we now move to a more advanced technique: crystal grids. Think of a crystal grid as a powerful amplifier, a focused intention manifested in a geometric arrangement of crystals. Each crystal, carefully selected and placed, contributes its unique energy to the overall intention of the grid, creating a synergistic effect far exceeding the sum of its parts. This sophisticated method allows for targeted energy work, magnifying your intentions and manifesting desired outcomes with remarkable efficacy.

The *construction* of a crystal grid is both a creative and spiritual process. It's not simply about placing crystals in a pattern; it's about infusing the grid with your intention, setting a clear and focused purpose that will guide the energy flow. Begin by defining your intention. What do you wish to manifest? Clarity is paramount; the more precise your intention, the more effective the grid will be. Are you aiming for healing, abundance, love, or clarity? Perhaps you seek protection, enhanced creativity, or deeper spiritual connection. Writing your intention down is a crucial first step, allowing you to focus your energy and solidify your purpose. Once your intention is clear, you need to choose the appropriate crystals. Each crystal vibrates at a specific frequency, resonating with different energies and intentions. For example, Rose Quartz is ideal for fostering love and compassion, Citrine attracts abundance and prosperity, Amethyst promotes intuition and spiritual growth, and Clear Quartz amplifies the energy of other crystals. Your choice of crystals should align with your intention, carefully considering the properties and vibrational frequencies of each stone. Consider the specific energies needed to achieve your goal. Do you need grounding energy? Are you aiming to open your heart? Or perhaps you require enhanced mental clarity? Select crystals that complement each other and enhance the overall energy of the grid.

The *shape and size* of your grid also matter. Various geometric shapes hold symbolic meaning and influence the energy flow. Circles represent wholeness and completion; squares symbolize stability and grounding; triangles represent manifestation and growth; and hexagons are associated with balance and harmony. The size of your grid depends on your intention and the space available. A small grid may suffice for personal healing, while a larger grid could be used for more expansive intentions, such as enhancing the energy of an entire room.

The *placement* of the crystals within the grid is equally important. Consider the symbolism of each crystal's position and its relationship to other stones. You can create your own unique design or follow established grid patterns. There are many resources available online and in books that offer guidance on designing effective crystal grids. Intuition also plays a vital role; allow yourself to be guided by your inner wisdom, trusting your instincts in placing each crystal.

Once you've chosen your crystals and decided on your grid's design, it's time to cleanse and activate them. Cleansing removes any stagnant or negative energy the crystals may have absorbed. You can cleanse your crystals using several methods, such as smudging with sage, burying them in the earth, or placing them under running water. Activation aligns the crystals with your intention, infusing them with your focused energy. Hold each crystal in your hand, visualize your intention, and mentally program the stone to assist you in manifesting your goal.

After cleansing and activating your crystals, carefully arrange them according to your chosen design. As you place each crystal, visualize the energy flowing from the stone into the grid, amplifying your intention. You can create a physical grid by placing crystals on a flat surface, such as a table or a piece of fabric. Alternatively, you can create a grid using visualization techniques, mentally placing crystals in a designated space.

Once your grid is complete, it's essential to maintain its energy. Spend some time with your grid each day, focusing on your intention and visualizing its manifestation. Regularly cleanse your crystals to maintain their energetic integrity, using the same techniques you employed during the initial preparation. After your intention has manifested or the necessary time has passed, it's crucial to dismantle the grid. This prevents the energy from becoming stagnant. Gratefully thank each crystal for its contribution, and then cleanse them before storing them for future use.

Let's explore some specific examples of crystal grids and their applications:

Grid for Abundance and Prosperity: For this grid, choose Citrine, Green Aventurine, and Tiger's Eye. Arrange them in a circle on a green cloth, symbolizing growth and abundance. Place the Citrine in the center, representing the manifestation of wealth. Position the Green Aventurine and Tiger's Eye around the Citrine, their energies enhancing the abundance-attracting power of the central crystal. Focus on your intention of attracting financial abundance and prosperity into your life.

Grid for Healing and Emotional Well-being: For this grid, utilize Rose Quartz, Amethyst, and Clear Quartz. Arrange them in a heart shape, reflecting the intention of emotional healing and self-love. Place the Rose Quartz in the center, representing compassion and healing. Place the Amethyst on the left, promoting emotional release and spiritual comfort, and the Clear Quartz on the right, amplifying the healing energy of the entire grid. Focus your intention on healing emotional wounds and restoring emotional balance.

Grid for Protection and Safety: For this grid, select Black Tourmaline, Clear Quartz, and Selenite. Arrange them in a square, representing stability and grounding. Place the Black Tourmaline in each corner, acting as protective shields against negative energy. Place the Clear Quartz in the center, amplifying the protective energy and enhancing clarity. Place the Selenite in the middle of each side, for purification and cleansing. Focus your intention on shielding yourself and your space from negativity and promoting feelings of safety and security.

Grid for Enhanced Creativity: For this purpose, use Carnelian, Sunstone, and Orange Calcite. Arrange them in a triangle, symbolizing growth and manifestation. Place the Carnelian at the apex, stimulating creative energy and self-expression. Place the Sunstone and Orange Calcite at the base, enhancing creativity and promoting self-confidence. Focus your intention on unlocking your creative potential and expressing yourself freely and authentically.

Grid for Spiritual Growth: Use Amethyst, Clear Quartz, and Selenite. Arrange them in a circle. Place the Amethyst at the top of the circle for spiritual awareness and intuition. The Clear Quartz in the center amplifies the spiritual energy. The Selenite can be placed at the bottom of the circle for purification and enhanced connection to higher consciousness. Focus your intention on deepening your spiritual connection and expanding your awareness.

Remember, these are just examples. Feel free to experiment with different crystal combinations and grid designs, allowing your intuition to guide you. The most important aspect is your intention and the energy you infuse into the process. Crystal grids are powerful tools for manifesting your desires and enhancing your well-being; treat them with respect and intention, and allow their transformative energy to support you on your journey. As you gain experience, you'll find yourself becoming more attuned to the subtle energies of the crystals and refining your ability to create powerful and effective grids to support your spiritual growth and manifestation. Embrace the journey, trust your intuition, and watch as the energy of the crystals helps you bring your visions to life. The power of crystal healing truly blossoms when integrated with other energy healing modalities. It's like adding vibrant colors to a masterpiece, deepening its impact and creating a richer, more resonant experience. Think of it as a symphony of energies, each instrument – Reiki, chakra balancing, meditation, and crystal healing – playing its part to create a harmonious and transformative whole. The result is a holistic approach that addresses the individual on multiple levels, fostering profound healing and personal growth.

One particularly potent combination is crystal healing and Reiki. Reiki, a Japanese energy healing technique, channels universal life force energy to promote relaxation, balance, and healing. When combined with crystals, the Reiki energy is amplified and directed with greater precision. For instance, during a Reiki session, placing amethyst on the third eye chakra can enhance intuition and spiritual awareness, while simultaneously allowing the Reiki energy to flow more freely through that area. Similarly, using rose quartz during a Reiki session can amplify the energy of love and compassion, facilitating deeper emotional healing. The practitioner can consciously direct the Reiki energy through specific crystals to target particular chakras or areas of the body needing attention. This synergistic approach offers a profound and nuanced healing experience, exceeding the limitations of either modality alone. The interplay between crystal healing and chakra balancing is another powerful synergy. Each chakra, an energy center within the body, corresponds to specific emotional, mental, and spiritual states. Crystals, with their unique vibrational frequencies, can help to balance and harmonize these chakras. For example, placing a carnelian on the sacral chakra, which governs creativity and sexuality, can help to unlock blocked energy and promote vitality. Similarly, using lapis lazuli on the throat chakra can enhance communication and self-expression. Combining crystal placement with chakra-balancing techniques like meditation or breathwork further amplifies the effects, creating a potent and transformative experience. Imagine visualizing the specific chakra, feeling its energy, and then placing the corresponding crystal on the area, intensifying the visualization and allowing the crystal's energy to work in conjunction with your intention.

Meditation, a cornerstone of many holistic practices, synergizes beautifully with crystal healing. Holding a crystal during meditation can enhance focus, deepen relaxation, and amplify the meditative experience. For example, using a clear quartz crystal can amplify your intention during meditation, helping you connect more deeply with your inner self. Amethyst, known for its calming properties, can enhance a meditative state and promote relaxation. Selenite, with its high vibrational energy, can facilitate spiritual connection and heightened awareness during meditation. The crystal acts as a focal point, anchoring your attention and enhancing your ability to access deeper states of consciousness. The synergistic effect allows for more profound introspection, leading to a deeper understanding of oneself and facilitating greater self-acceptance and self-compassion.

The integration of crystal healing doesn't stop at Reiki, chakra balancing, and meditation. It extends to various other holistic modalities, such as aromatherapy and sound healing. The combination of crystals and essential oils can create a powerful sensory experience that promotes deep relaxation and healing. For instance, combining rose quartz with rose essential oil can amplify the soothing and heart-opening effects of both. Likewise, combining amethyst with lavender essential oil can enhance relaxation and reduce stress. These combined approaches work on multiple levels simultaneously – through the energy of the crystals, the aroma of the oils, and the overall sensory experience. The carefully curated combination stimulates the senses in a holistic way, promoting a deeper healing experience. Sound healing, another complementary practice, involves using various instruments, such as singing bowls, to create vibrational frequencies that resonate with the body's energy field. Combining crystal healing with sound healing can enhance the healing process. For example, using specific crystals during a sound healing session can amplify the vibrational frequencies and direct them to specific areas of the body needing attention. The combined effects create a powerful and immersive experience that can lead to deep relaxation, stress reduction, and enhanced well-being. The vibrational frequencies from the sound instruments and the crystals combine and resonate within the body, creating a synergistic healing effect surpassing the power of each therapy used independently.

The effective integration of crystal healing with other energy healing modalities requires a nuanced understanding of each practice and their potential synergies. It's a creative process, where the practitioner intuitively chooses crystals and modalities to best support the individual's specific needs and goals. This intuitive approach guides the practitioner to select the most suitable crystals and modalities to achieve the intended outcome. The practitioner's intention plays a vital role in guiding the energy flow and maximizing the effects of the combined modalities.

Consider a case where a client is experiencing both physical pain and emotional distress. A holistic practitioner might use a combination of modalities to address both issues simultaneously. Reiki might be used to release stagnant energy, while specific crystals – like amethyst for emotional healing and clear quartz for amplification – could be placed on relevant chakras to enhance the Reiki's effect. Simultaneously, aromatherapy with calming essential oils could further enhance relaxation and reduce stress. This integrated approach offers a more comprehensive and impactful healing journey. The practitioner's awareness of the client's energy field informs the strategic application of different modalities and crystal selection. The entire process is informed by a holistic perspective, addressing the client's physical, emotional, and spiritual well-being.

Another example involves a client struggling with creative block. A practitioner might use a combination of crystal healing and meditation to unlock their creative potential. Carnelian, known for its ability to stimulate creativity, could be placed on the sacral chakra, while clear quartz could amplify the energy and intention during meditation. The combined effect enhances the meditative state, allowing the client to connect with their inner creative source and overcome the block. The synergistic effect amplifies the benefits, allowing for a richer and more profound healing experience than either method alone. The client will experience a more potent and comprehensive healing effect from the combined synergistic energy.

The combination of crystal healing and other energy modalities isn't just about adding practices together; it's about creating a harmonious synergy that amplifies the healing process. It's a holistic approach that addresses the interconnectedness of the mind, body, and spirit, leading to more profound and lasting transformation. As a practitioner, one must embrace intuition and tailor the combination of modalities to each individual's unique needs and energy signature. The practitioner becomes a conductor, orchestrating a symphony of energies that brings balance and harmony to the individual. This artful integration leads to a profound and lasting impact, leading to enhanced well-being and self-discovery. **The ability to intuitively blend these energy modalities is a hallmark of a skilled and compassionate holistic healer.**

Chapter 7: Creating a Holistic Wellness Routine

Developing a **personalized daily practice** is the cornerstone of sustained holistic well-being. Think of it as cultivating a garden – you wouldn't expect a bountiful harvest without consistent tending. Similarly, the profound benefits of Reiki, crystal healing, numerology, and astrology unfold not through sporadic bursts of activity, but through consistent, nurturing daily practice. This isn't about rigid schedules or overwhelming commitments; rather, it's about integrating these practices seamlessly into your life, creating a rhythm of self-care that nourishes your mind, body, and spirit.

The beauty of a personalized daily routine lies in its *adaptability*. There's no one-size-fits-all approach. What resonates deeply with one individual might feel forced or ineffective for another. The key is to experiment, to discover what practices bring you joy, energy, and a sense of connection to your inner self. Start small, focusing on one or two practices initially, and gradually incorporate more as you feel comfortable. Remember, consistency is more crucial than intensity. A five-minute mindful meditation each morning is far more beneficial than a strenuous hour-long session once a week, only to be abandoned due to feelings of overwhelm.

Let's begin by considering the foundational elements. Many find starting their day with a few minutes of mindful breathing incredibly beneficial. This can be as simple as sitting comfortably, closing your eyes, and focusing on the natural rhythm of your breath. Feel the air entering your nostrils, expanding your lungs, and then gently exhaling. This simple act can center you, calming the mind and preparing you for the day ahead. You might choose to incorporate a short affirmation or intention, setting the tone for a positive and productive day. For example, you could affirm, "Today, I embrace peace and harmony within myself and all around me," or "Today, I am open to receiving guidance and blessings from the universe." After mindful breathing, you might incorporate a short crystal meditation. Choose a crystal that resonates with your intention for the day. For example, if you need focus and clarity, select a clear quartz. If you seek emotional healing, choose a rose quartz. Hold the crystal in your hand, visualize its energy, and focus on your intention. Allow the crystal's energy to amplify your meditative state, guiding you into a deeper connection with your inner self. Even five minutes of this focused practice can make a significant difference in your day.

Numerology can also be seamlessly woven into your daily practice. Consider your birth number or a number significant to your current journey. Reflect on the qualities associated with that number – are they qualities you want to nurture or aspects you might need to address? This reflection can offer valuable self-awareness and guide your intentions for the day. For instance, if your birth number suggests a need for greater self-expression, you could consciously focus on communicating your thoughts and feelings more openly and honestly. Astrology provides another layer of guidance. Pay attention to the daily planetary transits. Understanding the current energetic influences can help you navigate challenges with greater ease and align yourself with the prevailing energies. For example, if the planets suggest a day of heightened emotional sensitivity, you might schedule more downtime for self-care and avoid stressful situations. Conversely, if the astrological forecast indicates a day of heightened energy and creativity, you might schedule tasks requiring focus and inspiration. This conscious awareness empowers you to work *with* the cosmic energies, rather than against them.

Reiki self-healing is another powerful tool for your daily practice. Even a brief self-Reiki session of five to ten minutes can make a profound difference in your energy levels and overall well-being. Focus on your hands, visualizing the flow of Reiki energy. Direct the energy to areas of your body that feel tense or unbalanced. This practice can help to release blockages, promoting relaxation and rejuvenation.

As you integrate these various practices, remember the importance of *self-compassion*. Some days, you might feel energized and engaged; other days, you might find yourself needing more rest and less structured activity. Don't judge yourself for days when you don't adhere perfectly to your routine. Flexibility and self-acceptance are essential components of a sustainable, holistic wellness routine. View your daily practice as an ongoing journey of self-discovery, not a rigid performance.

Consider creating a journal to document your daily practice. Note what practices you engaged in, how you felt during and after each practice, and any insights or synchronicities you experienced. This journal will become a valuable tool for tracking your progress, identifying what works best for you, and refining your routine over time.

Here's an example of a personalized daily routine:

Morning (5-15 minutes): Mindful breathing and a short affirmation focusing on gratitude. A brief crystal meditation with a clear quartz or amethyst.

Midday (10 minutes): A quick Reiki self-healing session, focusing on releasing stress and promoting energy flow.

Evening (15-20 minutes): Journaling about your day, reflecting on your experiences and setting intentions for the following day. A short numerology reflection, focusing on your birth number or a significant number from the day.

Throughout the day: Consciously carry a protective crystal, such as black tourmaline, to ground and protect your energy. Pay attention to the astrological influences of the day and adjust your activities accordingly.

Remember, this is just a template. Feel free to adjust it based on your personal needs, preferences, and available time. The most important aspect is consistency and self-compassion. Gradually incorporate new practices as you feel comfortable, allowing your daily routine to evolve organically. Celebrate your progress, and remember that your journey toward holistic well-being is a continuous process of growth and self-discovery. Embrace the process, and enjoy the journey! The ultimate aim isn't to achieve perfection, but to cultivate a nurturing and empowering relationship with yourself and the universe.

Don't be afraid to experiment with different combinations of practices and different times of day. If morning doesn't work for you, perhaps evening is better suited to your rhythm. If you find yourself struggling with a particular practice, don't force it; instead, explore other options that resonate with you more deeply. The key is to find practices that bring you joy, nourishment, and a stronger sense of connection to your inner self and the universe. Trust your intuition; it's your wisest guide on this path.

Consider incorporating *movement* into your routine. Even a short walk in nature can be incredibly restorative. Connect with the earth's energy, feel the sun on your skin, and allow the natural world to soothe your mind and body. Yoga, Tai Chi, or Qi Gong are other options that blend physical movement with mindfulness, promoting both physical and energetic well-being. These practices can help to release physical tension and improve flexibility, while also calming the mind and promoting a deeper sense of self-awareness.

Another element to consider is *healthy nutrition*. Pay attention to the foods you consume, choosing options that nourish your body and provide sustained energy. Limit processed foods, refined sugars, and excessive caffeine, opting instead for fresh fruits, vegetables, whole grains, and lean protein. Hydration is also vital; ensure you are drinking plenty of water throughout the day. Your body is a temple; nourish it with love and respect.

Adequate sleep is another essential pillar of a holistic wellness routine. Aim for seven to eight hours of quality sleep each night. Create a relaxing bedtime routine, such as taking a warm bath, reading a book, or listening to calming music. Avoid screen time before bed, as the blue light emitted from electronic devices can interfere with sleep quality. A well-rested body and mind are better equipped to handle the challenges of daily life and to embrace the opportunities for growth and transformation.

Finally, remember the importance of *connecting with your community*. Nurture your relationships with loved ones, engaging in activities that bring you joy and connection. Spend time with people who uplift and inspire you. Human connection is vital for emotional and spiritual well-being. A strong support system can provide encouragement, understanding, and a sense of belonging, strengthening your resilience and ability to navigate life's challenges. This holistic approach, encompassing physical, emotional, mental, and spiritual elements, creates a powerful foundation for sustained well-being and a life filled with purpose and joy. The journey to holistic well-being is a continuous evolution, a dance between intention and adaptation, self-compassion and unwavering commitment to your own growth. Enjoy the process!Incorporating movement into our holistic wellness routine isn't merely about physical fitness; it's about cultivating a mindful connection between our bodies and our energy systems. Think of your body as a finely tuned instrument—to play it beautifully, you need to regularly tune and exercise it. Just as stagnant water becomes foul, so too can our energy become sluggish without the flow that physical activity provides. Movement unlocks the channels of energy, allowing prana (life force) to circulate freely, revitalizing both our physical and spiritual selves.

Many ancient traditions recognized the intimate connection between physical movement and spiritual well-being. **Yoga**, for instance, is not simply a series of poses; it's a holistic practice that unites the mind, body, and spirit. Each asana (pose) is designed to stretch and strengthen the physical body, while simultaneously stimulating the flow of energy through the chakras. Certain poses, like downward-facing dog or cobra pose, are particularly effective in opening energy channels and releasing blockages. As you move through the sequences, focus on your breath, allowing it to guide your movements and deepen your connection to your inner self. The intentionality of the movement becomes as crucial as the movement itself, transforming a physical exercise into a spiritual practice.

Tai Chi Chuan, another ancient practice originating in China, elegantly blends graceful movements with deep meditative principles. The slow, flowing movements promote balance, coordination, and flexibility, while simultaneously calming the mind and fostering inner peace. The gentle, circular motions are believed to enhance the flow of Qi (vital energy), harmonizing the body's energy fields and promoting overall well-being. Practicing Tai Chi in a natural setting, such as a park or garden, further enhances the experience, grounding you in the earth's energy and allowing nature's rhythm to harmonize your own.

Even something as simple as a daily walk can significantly contribute to your holistic wellness. Walking in nature, surrounded by trees and greenery, is particularly beneficial. The earth's energy, or "grounding," can be powerfully restorative, counteracting the stresses of modern life. As you walk, focus on your breath, the rhythm of your steps, and the sensations in your body. Pay attention to the sights, sounds, and smells around you; allow yourself to be fully present in the moment. A mindful walk can become a meditative practice, helping you to quiet the incessant chatter of your mind and connect with the natural world around you.

For those seeking a more vigorous form of movement, consider activities like dancing, swimming, cycling, or hiking. These activities not only improve cardiovascular health and strengthen muscles but also provide opportunities for joyful self-expression. Let go of inhibitions and allow your body to move freely, expressing emotions and releasing pent-up energy. The feeling of exhilaration and freedom that accompanies these activities can be incredibly uplifting, promoting both physical and emotional well-being.

Remember to choose activities that you enjoy and that fit your physical capabilities. There's no need to push yourself beyond your limits; gentle, consistent movement is far more effective than sporadic bursts of intense activity. Listen to your body, and respect its limitations. If you experience pain, stop and rest. The goal is to nourish your body and enhance energy flow, not to inflict harm.

Mindful movement is key. Whether you are practicing yoga, Tai Chi, walking, or another form of exercise, bring awareness to your body and your breath. Pay attention to the sensations in your muscles and joints; notice how your body feels as you move. This mindful approach helps to deepen your connection to your body, fostering a greater sense of self-awareness and appreciation. It also allows you to identify any areas of tension or imbalance, potentially addressing physical and energetic blockages before they become major issues. Incorporating mindful movement into your daily routine can be as simple as taking the stairs instead of the elevator, walking or cycling instead of driving short distances, or incorporating stretching into your workday. These small changes, when consistently applied, can have a profound impact on your overall well-being. They not only improve your physical health but also enhance your energy levels, reduce stress, and promote a deeper connection to your body and your inner self.

The connection between movement and energy flow is deeply significant within the context of chakra balancing. Each chakra, representing a specific energy center in the body, is associated with different physical postures and movements. For example, poses that stretch and open the hips are beneficial for the sacral chakra (second chakra), which governs creativity, sexuality, and emotional expression. Forward bends can help to ground and stabilize the root chakra (first chakra), enhancing feelings of security and stability. Backbends can open the heart chakra (fourth chakra), promoting feelings of love, compassion, and connection. Understanding this link allows you to tailor your movement practices to address specific energetic imbalances. If you're feeling emotionally blocked, incorporate poses that open the heart and sacral chakras. If you're feeling ungrounded or anxious, focus on poses that stimulate the root chakra. Through mindful movement, you can consciously influence your energy flow, bringing balance and harmony to your entire system.

Beyond the physical and energetic benefits, movement also provides a powerful opportunity for *self-reflection*. As you move your body, allow your thoughts and feelings to surface. Don't judge them; simply observe them. This mindful awareness can provide valuable insights into your inner world, helping you to identify patterns, beliefs, and emotions that might be contributing to imbalances in your life.

Incorporating movement into your holistic wellness routine is not about striving for perfection or achieving unrealistic fitness goals. It's about nurturing your body, enhancing energy flow, and fostering a deeper connection with yourself. Begin with small, manageable changes, and gradually incorporate more movement into your daily life. Listen to your body, respect its limitations, and celebrate your progress. The journey is the destination; embrace each step with joy and mindful awareness. This holistic approach to movement, combined with the other practices discussed earlier, will create a vibrant and harmonious foundation for sustained well-being and a life filled with energy, purpose, and joy. Remember to listen to your body; rest is just as important as movement. Don't be afraid to adjust your routine based on your energy levels and needs. Self-compassion is crucial. The goal is to create a sustainable practice that brings you joy and supports your overall well-being, not to create another source of stress or pressure. Celebrate your achievements, no matter how small, and embrace the ongoing journey of self-discovery. Your body is your temple; treat it with respect and love. Nourishment is the cornerstone of a vibrant life, a fundamental aspect of holistic well-being often overlooked amidst the flurry of energy work and spiritual practices. Just as a finely tuned instrument requires proper maintenance, our physical bodies need the right fuel to function optimally and support our energetic systems. The food we consume directly impacts our energy levels, emotional stability, and even our spiritual clarity. Mindful eating, therefore, transcends mere sustenance; it becomes a sacred act of self-care, a way to nurture our bodies and honor our connection to the earth.

Our bodies are complex ecosystems, constantly working to maintain balance and harmony. When we nourish them with vibrant, whole foods, we provide the building blocks for optimal functioning. These foods are rich in vital nutrients—vitamins, minerals, antioxidants, and phytonutrients—that support cellular health, bolster our immune systems, and enhance energy production. Conversely, a diet laden with processed foods, excessive sugar, and artificial ingredients creates an imbalance, disrupting the delicate harmony within our bodies and affecting our energy systems.

Think of your chakras as energy vortexes that require a consistent flow of vital energy. A diet rich in refined sugars and processed foods can clog these channels, creating blockages that lead to imbalances in your physical, emotional, and spiritual well-being. Refined sugars, in particular, create a surge of energy followed by a drastic crash, mirroring the erratic energy fluctuations we often experience when our chakras are out of balance. This instability can manifest as mood swings, fatigue, and a general sense of unease.

A balanced diet, on the other hand, provides a steady stream of sustained energy, supporting the smooth flow of prana through your chakras. This balance translates into increased vitality, emotional resilience, and mental clarity. Just as crystals amplify and direct energy, certain foods possess unique energetic properties that can help to cleanse, balance, and revitalize specific chakras.

Consider the root chakra, the foundation of our being, associated with feelings of security and stability. Root vegetables like carrots, beets, and sweet potatoes are grounding and nourishing, literally anchoring us to the earth's energy. Their rich earthy flavors and grounding properties are reflected in their energetic qualities, supporting the root chakra's function. Similarly, foods rich in iron, such as leafy greens and legumes, support the healthy functioning of the blood, strengthening the connection to the earth and enhancing feelings of security and stability.

The sacral chakra, associated with creativity, sexuality, and emotional expression, thrives on vibrant, juicy fruits like oranges, mangoes, and berries. Their bright colors and sweet flavors reflect their life-giving energy, stimulating creativity and emotional fluidity. Foods rich in omega-3 fatty acids, such as salmon and flaxseed, are also beneficial for the sacral chakra, supporting healthy hormone production and emotional balance.

The solar plexus chakra, our center of personal power, benefits from foods that are warming and energizing, such as ginger, turmeric, and cinnamon. These spices are not only delicious but also possess potent medicinal properties that boost digestion, improve circulation, and enhance vitality. They metaphorically ignite our inner fire, supporting personal power and self-confidence. Proteins, particularly those from lean meats or legumes, are also crucial for building and maintaining the vitality necessary for expressing our inner power.

The heart chakra, the center of love and compassion, thrives on foods rich in magnesium and potassium, such as avocados, bananas, and leafy greens. These nutrients support healthy heart function, mirroring the heart chakra's role in promoting love and compassion. Foods rich in antioxidants, like berries and dark chocolate (in moderation!), also protect against cellular damage and support emotional well-being.

The throat chakra, associated with communication and self-expression, benefits from foods that are light and airy, such as salads, leafy greens, and clear broths. These foods are easily digested and support clear communication, ensuring that your voice is heard and understood. Foods rich in Vitamin C, such as citrus fruits and bell peppers, support a healthy immune system, vital for effectively conveying your messages.

The third eye chakra, the center of intuition and insight, benefits from foods that enhance mental clarity and focus, such as blueberries, walnuts, and oily fish. These foods are rich in omega-3 fatty acids, antioxidants, and other nutrients that support brain function and cognitive clarity. Meditation and mindful practices combined with these nourishing foods can assist in unlocking greater intuition and insight.

Finally, the crown chakra, our connection to the divine, benefits from foods that are pure and spiritually uplifting, such as herbs and spices, particularly those associated with spiritual practices in various cultures. Sage, for instance, is a common herb used in cleansing and purification rituals. Mindful consumption of these foods, coupled with spiritual practices, can enhance your connection to a higher power and promote inner peace.

Beyond the specific energetic benefits of certain foods, mindful eating is equally important. Eating slowly, savoring each bite, and paying attention to the flavors, textures, and aromas of your food cultivates a deeper connection to your body and your nourishment. This practice fosters gratitude for the gifts of nature, enhancing both physical and spiritual well-being. It allows us to appreciate the energy and life force imbued in the food we consume. Chewing thoroughly allows for better digestion and nutrient absorption, further enhancing the body's ability to utilize the energy from food.

Avoid distractions while eating, such as television or mobile phones. Create a sacred space for your meals, free from stress and interruptions. This intentional approach transforms the act of eating into a meditative practice, allowing you to connect with your inner self and nourish your body and spirit simultaneously.

Incorporating these principles into your daily life may involve gradual changes. Begin by reducing your intake of processed foods, refined sugars, and artificial ingredients. Increase your consumption of fresh fruits, vegetables, whole grains, and lean proteins. Experiment with different foods to discover which ones resonate with you and support your energetic balance.

Remember, nutrition is not about restrictive diets or deprivation; it's about nourishing your body with love and intention. It's about listening to your body's signals and choosing foods that support your overall well-being. A holistic wellness routine is incomplete without mindful attention to nutrition, forming a harmonious partnership between your physical and spiritual selves. By consciously choosing the foods we consume, we actively participate in the creation of a healthy, vibrant, and energized life. This mindful approach to eating, integrated with the other holistic practices, lays a robust foundation for long-term health and a life brimming with vitality, joy, and purpose. The journey towards optimal wellness is a personal one, requiring self-awareness, patience, and consistent effort. There is no one-size-fits-all approach, and experimentation is key to discovering what works best for your unique body and energy system. Trust your intuition, listen to your body, and enjoy the process of nurturing your physical and spiritual well-being.Sleep. The very word evokes images of peaceful slumber, a retreat from the day's demands. Yet, in our relentlessly busy lives, sleep often takes a backseat, becoming a luxury rather than a necessity. This is a tragic oversight, for quality sleep isn't merely a restorative period; it's a fundamental pillar of holistic well-being, inextricably linked to our physical, emotional, and spiritual health. Without adequate rest, our energy systems become depleted, our chakras falter, and our ability to heal and thrive diminishes.

Think of sleep as a nightly reset for your energetic body. During this time, your body performs crucial repair and rejuvenation processes. Your cells regenerate, toxins are eliminated, and your energy meridians recalibrate, preparing you for the next day's challenges. A lack of sleep disrupts this vital process, leading to a buildup of energetic blockages and an imbalance in your chakras. This imbalance manifests in various ways, from fatigue and irritability to diminished intuition and decreased emotional resilience.

Imagine your chakras as spinning wheels of energy, each contributing to your overall well-being. When you're well-rested, these wheels spin smoothly and harmoniously, allowing energy to flow freely throughout your system. But when you deprive yourself of sleep, these wheels slow down, become sluggish, and eventually stall. This stagnation leads to energetic blockages, creating imbalances that manifest as physical ailments, emotional turmoil, and spiritual stagnation. A depleted energy field weakens your ability to perform energy healing, hindering your progress on your path to self-mastery.

The connection between sleep and energy healing is profound. Many energy healing modalities, including Reiki, emphasize the importance of rest and relaxation in enhancing the healing process. Adequate sleep allows your body to absorb and integrate the healing energy more effectively. It strengthens your energy field, making you more resilient to stress and illness, and amplifies your ability to channel and utilize healing energy. Think of it as charging your batteries before embarking on a spiritual journey; you can't effectively help others or perform energy healing effectively without first tending to your own well-being. Improving your sleep quality isn't about simply spending more hours in bed; it's about cultivating a sleep sanctuary, a space conducive to deep, restorative rest. This begins with creating a calming bedtime routine, a ritual that signals to your body and mind that it's time to unwind. This could involve a warm bath infused with Epsom salts and lavender essential oil—both known for their relaxing properties—followed by gentle stretching or yoga. Avoid vigorous exercise close to bedtime, as this can stimulate your nervous system and make it difficult to fall asleep.

Consider the power of aromatherapy. Lavender, chamomile, and sandalwood are known for their calming effects, and diffusing these scents in your bedroom can create a peaceful and soothing atmosphere. Similarly, the right lighting is crucial; dim, warm lighting helps to regulate your melatonin production, a hormone that regulates sleep-wake cycles. Avoid bright screens before bed, as the blue light emitted from electronic devices interferes with melatonin production, making it harder to fall asleep.

Your *sleep environment* plays a crucial role in the quality of your rest. A cool, dark, and quiet room is ideal for promoting deep sleep. Invest in comfortable bedding, ensuring that your mattress, pillows, and blankets support proper spinal alignment and provide optimal comfort. If noise is a problem, consider using earplugs or a white noise machine to create a peaceful soundscape. Pay attention to the energy in your bedroom. Clutter can disrupt the flow of energy, making it difficult to relax and fall asleep. Clear your space of unnecessary items, and consider placing crystals known for their calming properties, such as amethyst or selenite, in your bedroom to promote tranquility and rest.

Numerologically, the number of hours you sleep significantly impacts your life path. Consider the numerical vibrations associated with your sleep cycle and how it interacts with your birthdate. A balanced number signifies better overall wellness. For example, if your life path number points towards creativity and you constantly sacrifice sleep, it may lead to a sense of imbalance, ultimately reducing your creative output. Understanding the subtle numerical connections that underpin your life can guide you in making conscious choices about your sleep patterns.

Astrology also offers insights into optimizing your sleep habits. Understanding your astrological sign and its planetary influences can help you identify patterns in your sleep cycles and address any potential imbalances. For example, certain astrological alignments might exacerbate anxiety or restlessness, making it more challenging to fall asleep. By understanding these cosmic influences, you can take proactive measures to create a sleep-conducive environment that counters these potential challenges. For instance, if you find yourself restless during certain planetary configurations, you may want to consider incorporating calming rituals into your bedtime routine.

Beyond the practical strategies for improving sleep quality, it's equally important to cultivate self-compassion. We often judge ourselves harshly for not getting enough sleep, creating a cycle of negativity that further impedes rest. Instead, approach sleep challenges with kindness and understanding. Acknowledge the pressures of daily life and remember that prioritizing rest is not a sign of weakness; it's a testament to your self-awareness and commitment to holistic well-being. Celebrate small victories, recognizing the progress you make in establishing healthy sleep habits. This self-compassion fosters a positive internal environment, making it easier to fall asleep and stay asleep.

Regular rest, beyond just nighttime sleep, is equally crucial. Incorporate short periods of rest throughout the day. A brief nap, a few moments of meditation, or simply sitting quietly to gather your thoughts can do wonders for your energy levels and emotional stability. These mini-breaks help you avoid burnout and maintain a balanced state of being. This is especially relevant during times of significant stress or intense energy work. Short periods of rest facilitate the integration of energy, assisting in resolving blockages and maintaining the balance of your chakras.

Remember, sleep is not a luxury; it's a fundamental necessity for optimal health and spiritual growth. Prioritize sleep and rest; they are the cornerstones of holistic wellness. By integrating these principles into your daily routine, you create a solid foundation for your journey of self-discovery and healing, allowing your chakras to spin freely, enabling your journey towards vibrant health and deep spiritual connection. Nourishment, rest, and mindfulness work in concert; one cannot thrive without the others. Your holistic wellness journey is a tapestry woven from these essential threads. The foundation of holistic wellness rests not just on sufficient rest and nourishment, but also on our ability to navigate the inevitable stresses of life with grace and mindfulness. Modern life, with its relentless demands and constant connectivity, often leaves us feeling overwhelmed and depleted. Chronic stress acts like a relentless drain on our energy reserves, disrupting the delicate balance within our chakra system and hindering our ability to heal and thrive. Unmanaged stress can manifest physically as headaches, digestive issues, and weakened immunity, while emotionally it can lead to anxiety, irritability, and depression. Spiritually, prolonged stress can disconnect us from our intuition and our sense of inner peace.

Fortunately, cultivating mindfulness and incorporating stress-management techniques into our daily routine can profoundly impact our overall well-being. Mindfulness, at its core, is the practice of paying attention to the present moment without judgment. It's about acknowledging our thoughts and feelings without getting swept away by them. It's about observing the breath, the sensations in our body, and the world around us with a sense of gentle awareness. This simple act of presence can be incredibly powerful in reducing stress and promoting emotional regulation.

One of the most accessible mindfulness practices is meditation. While the image of a serene monk sitting cross-legged may come to mind, meditation can be adapted to fit any lifestyle. Even five minutes of focused attention on the breath can make a significant difference. Find a quiet space, sit comfortably, close your eyes, and simply observe your breath as it enters and leaves your body. Notice the rise and fall of your chest or abdomen. When your mind wanders, which it inevitably will, gently guide your attention back to your breath. There's no right or wrong way to meditate; the key is to be present and kind to yourself.

Deep breathing exercises are another powerful tool for stress management. Our breath is intimately connected to our nervous system. When we're stressed, our breathing becomes shallow and rapid, triggering the body's fight-or-flight response. Deep, conscious breathing helps to activate the parasympathetic nervous system, which calms the body and reduces stress hormones. Try this simple exercise: inhale deeply through your nose, filling your lungs completely, hold for a few seconds, and then exhale slowly and completely through your mouth. Repeat this several times, focusing on the sensation of your breath moving through your body.

The power of mindful movement shouldn't be underestimated. Yoga, Tai Chi, and Qi Gong are excellent examples of practices that combine physical movement with mindfulness. These practices not only improve physical flexibility and strength but also promote a sense of calm and centeredness. As you move your body, pay attention to the sensations in your muscles and joints. Notice the rhythm of your breath and the flow of energy through your body. Even a short walk in nature can be incredibly restorative, allowing you to connect with the natural world and escape the stresses of daily life.

Beyond these formal practices, mindfulness can be integrated into every aspect of our daily lives. Instead of rushing through our meals, we can practice mindful eating, savoring each bite and paying attention to the textures, flavors, and aromas of our food. We can practice mindful listening, giving our full attention to the person we're speaking with, without interrupting or thinking about our next response. We can even practice mindful showering, noticing the temperature of the water on our skin and the sensation of the soap lathering. These small acts of presence can transform our daily experiences, making them more enjoyable and less stressful.

The use of crystals can also enhance your mindfulness practice. Certain crystals are known for their calming and grounding properties, such as amethyst, rose quartz, and clear quartz. Holding a crystal during meditation or placing it near your workspace can help to create a peaceful and focused environment. Amethyst, in particular, is often associated with spiritual awareness and tranquility, while rose quartz promotes feelings of love, compassion, and emotional healing. Clear quartz amplifies energy and intentions, making it a versatile tool for enhancing any meditative practice. Remember to cleanse your crystals regularly to maintain their energetic purity.

Numerology can offer insights into our individual predispositions to stress and how we might best manage it. Your life path number, calculated from your birthdate, reveals inherent traits and challenges. Understanding these can help you identify patterns of stress in your life and develop strategies tailored to your personality. For instance, those with a life path number associated with ambition might be prone to overworking and burnout, requiring conscious effort to prioritize rest and relaxation.

Astrology also provides a valuable perspective on stress management. Understanding your astrological chart can highlight periods of heightened stress and offer guidance on navigating these times. By being aware of planetary transits and their potential impact on your emotional state, you can proactively implement stress-reduction techniques during challenging periods. For example, if you're particularly sensitive to lunar cycles, you might schedule more downtime during the full moon, known for its intensifying energies. Incorporating these practices into a daily routine is crucial for sustained stress reduction and improved well-being. Start small, choosing one or two techniques to focus on, and gradually add more as you become more comfortable. Consistency is key. Even a few minutes of daily mindfulness can have a significant impact over time. Consider creating a dedicated space for your mindfulness practice—a quiet corner in your home, or a spot in nature—where you can disconnect from the demands of daily life and reconnect with yourself.

Remember, the journey towards holistic wellness is not a race but a process. Be patient and compassionate with yourself, acknowledging that there will be days when you feel more stressed than others. Don't beat yourself up over setbacks; simply acknowledge them and gently guide yourself back to your practice. The goal isn't to eliminate stress altogether, which is often impossible, but to develop a healthy relationship with stress, learning to manage it effectively and cultivate inner peace amidst the challenges of life. This mindful approach, combined with your understanding of chakras, energy healing, and the cosmic influences affecting your life path, will help create a robust and resilient foundation for your overall well-being. The synergy between these seemingly disparate practices creates a holistic approach that empowers you to navigate life's complexities with greater ease and joy. Embrace the journey, and trust in your innate ability to heal and thrive.

Chapter 8: Deepening Your Spiritual Connection

Having established a strong foundation of mindfulness and stress management, we now embark on a deeper exploration of spiritual practices that can further enhance your connection to your inner self and the universe. This journey isn't about adhering to a rigid dogma or subscribing to a single belief system, but rather about *discovering the practices that resonate most deeply with your soul and support your unique path toward holistic wellness*. Remember, the path to spiritual growth is deeply personal, and what works for one individual may not work for another. The key is to approach this exploration with an open heart and a willingness to experiment.

Meditation, as previously mentioned, is a cornerstone of many spiritual traditions. However, its benefits extend far beyond stress reduction. Regular meditation cultivates a deeper connection with your intuition, enhances self-awareness, and fosters a sense of inner peace that transcends the fluctuations of daily life. Beyond the simple breath-focused meditation, explore different forms of meditation, such as walking meditation, mantra meditation, or guided meditation. Walking meditation involves paying close attention to the sensations of your feet on the ground as you walk, bringing awareness to each step. Mantra meditation utilizes the repetition of a sacred word or phrase to quiet the mind and focus your attention. Guided meditations, often available through apps or recordings, can lead you through visualizations and affirmations, guiding your mind toward specific intentions or states of being.

Prayer, in its broadest sense, is a form of communication with a higher power, whether that be a deity, the universe, or your own higher self. Prayer can take many forms, from formal liturgical prayers to spontaneous expressions of gratitude or supplication. It is a powerful tool for connecting with something larger than oneself, fostering a sense of belonging and grounding. Experiment with different forms of prayer to discover what resonates with you. Consider journaling your prayers, using them as a way to clarify your thoughts and intentions. Even simple expressions of gratitude, spoken aloud or written down, can have a profound impact on your emotional and spiritual well-being.

Visualization is another powerful spiritual practice that taps into the creative power of your mind. By vividly imagining a desired outcome or state of being, you can begin to manifest it in your reality. This isn't about wishful thinking, but rather about aligning your intentions with the universal energy that supports creation. Visualization is often used in conjunction with other practices, such as meditation or affirmation. For example, you might visualize yourself radiating vibrant energy while meditating, or visualize yourself achieving a specific goal while repeating affirmations.

Connecting with nature is a profoundly grounding and restorative spiritual practice. Spending time outdoors, whether in a forest, by the ocean, or even in a city park, helps to reconnect you with the natural rhythms of life and reduces feelings of stress and isolation. Engage all your senses as you connect with nature: feel the earth beneath your feet, breathe in the fresh air, listen to the sounds of birdsong, observe the colors of the flowers, and appreciate the beauty of the natural world. Consider incorporating practices like forest bathing (shinrin-yoku), a Japanese practice of spending time in a forest to enhance well-being, or simply taking a mindful walk in nature.

Engaging with different spiritual traditions can broaden your understanding and appreciation of diverse perspectives. Research and explore traditions such as Buddhism, Hinduism, Christianity, Taoism, Shamanism, and many others. Read books, attend workshops, or participate in ceremonies to gain a deeper understanding of their practices and philosophies. Remember, this exploration is not about converting to a particular religion but about appreciating the wisdom and insights that different traditions offer. However, always approach this with respect and a deep understanding of the cultural context in which these traditions exist. Avoid appropriating elements without understanding their true significance. Working with crystals can enhance your spiritual practices. Each crystal carries a unique vibrational frequency that can influence your energy field and emotional state. Amethyst, known for its calming and spiritual properties, can facilitate meditation and enhance intuition. Rose quartz promotes self-love and compassion, while clear quartz amplifies energy and intentions. Experiment with different crystals to discover which ones resonate most strongly with you, and incorporate them into your meditation practice or place them strategically around your home to create a calming and uplifting atmosphere. Remember, consistent cleansing and charging of your crystals is essential to maintaining their energetic integrity.

The practice of *yoga*, beyond its physical benefits, offers a profound pathway to spiritual connection. The poses themselves, or asanas, work to open energy channels within the body, while the breathwork, or pranayama, cultivates a state of mindfulness and inner stillness. Different styles of yoga, from Hatha to Vinyasa, offer various approaches to achieving this balance. Exploring different styles of yoga will allow you to find what best suits your personal style and energy level. Many yoga studios offer classes that incorporate mindfulness and spiritual teachings, offering a deeper level of connection during practice.

Sound healing, a practice that utilizes the power of vibrations to promote healing and balance, offers another avenue for spiritual exploration. Various sound healing modalities exist, including singing bowls, tuning forks, and chanting. The resonant frequencies of these tools are believed to harmonize energy flow within the body, releasing blockages and promoting deep relaxation. Sound healing can be experienced individually or in group settings, providing a deeply immersive and transformative experience.

The exploration of your ancestral heritage can unveil profound insights into your spiritual path. Connecting with your roots can provide a sense of belonging, grounding, and understanding of your family's history and traditions. Researching your family tree and exploring historical records can reveal stories and practices that may resonate deeply with you, and may add depth to your own spiritual practices.

While exploring these different paths, remember the importance of self-reflection and journaling. Regularly reflecting on your experiences, noting the emotions evoked, and recording your insights, creates a chronicle of your spiritual journey. This process allows you to identify patterns, celebrate successes, and learn from challenges, deepening your self-awareness and guiding your practice.

Ultimately, the most effective spiritual practice is the one that you find most meaningful and authentic. Do not feel pressured to adopt any particular practice or belief system. Rather, experiment with various techniques, paying attention to how they make you feel. Trust your intuition and allow yourself to be guided by your inner wisdom. The journey of spiritual exploration is ongoing, a continuous process of self-discovery and growth. Embrace the unfolding of your spiritual journey with patience, compassion, and a deep sense of gratitude for the opportunities it presents. This deeper connection with yourself and the universe will enrich every aspect of your life, fostering a sense of purpose, joy, and profound well-being. The synergy between these practices and your understanding of chakras, energy healing, numerology, and astrology will create a powerful and harmonious integration, paving the way for a truly fulfilling and authentic life.Connecting with nature isn't merely a pleasant pastime; it's a potent spiritual practice, a deep communion with the Earth's life force. Our modern lives, often confined within concrete jungles, have severed us from this vital connection, leaving many feeling disconnected and depleted. Re-establishing this link is crucial for holistic well-being, recharging our energy reserves, and fostering a profound sense of peace. The Earth, in its raw, untamed beauty, pulsates with an energy that resonates deeply within our own energetic bodies. This energy, often referred to as "grounding energy" or "earth energy," provides a stabilizing and anchoring force, counteracting the chaotic energies that can overwhelm us in daily life. Imagine the vastness of the ocean, the towering majesty of mountains, or the silent wisdom of ancient forests – these are not just physical landscapes; they are expressions of powerful, life-giving energy, readily available to those who seek to connect.

One of the simplest yet most effective ways to connect with this energy is through grounding exercises. These techniques help to anchor your energy to the Earth, stabilizing your emotional and energetic state. Find a quiet spot outdoors, preferably on bare earth—grass, sand, or soil. Remove your shoes and feel the earth beneath your feet. Notice the texture, the temperature, the subtle variations in the ground. Imagine roots growing from your feet, extending deep into the earth, drawing up its life-giving energy. Feel this energy flowing up your legs, through your body, filling you with a sense of stability and security. Visualize this energy as a grounding cord, connecting you to the heart of the Earth.

Spend time in nature. This doesn't necessarily mean embarking on a strenuous hike; even a few minutes in a park, garden, or by a tree can make a significant difference. Let nature envelop you. Breathe in the fresh air, feel the sun on your skin, listen to the sounds of birds singing, the wind rustling through leaves, the gentle murmur of a stream. Engage all your senses – taste the rain, smell the earth, feel the texture of bark against your hand. Allow yourself to be present in the moment, fully absorbed in the beauty and wonder of the natural world.

Forest bathing, or Shinrin-yoku, a Japanese practice that involves spending time in a forest, offers profound benefits for both physical and mental well-being. Studies have shown that spending time amongst trees can lower blood pressure, reduce stress hormones, boost the immune system, and improve mood. The practice isn't about achieving a specific goal or pushing yourself physically; it's about slowing down, being present, and allowing the forest to nurture you. Walk slowly and mindfully, paying attention to every detail of your surroundings. Observe the light filtering through the trees, the intricate patterns of leaves, the delicate dance of butterflies. Listen to the sounds of the forest – the chirping of crickets, the rustling of leaves, the gentle breeze whispering through the branches. Take deep, slow breaths, allowing the fresh, clean air to fill your lungs. Feel the energy of the trees, their strength and resilience, their connection to the earth. Let yourself be soothed and rejuvenated by their presence.

Beyond forest bathing, explore other nature-based activities that resonate with you. Go for a walk on the beach, feeling the sand between your toes and the invigorating sea breeze on your face. Spend time by a lake or river, observing the calm waters and the reflection of the sky. Climb a mountain, enjoying the panoramic views and the sense of accomplishment. Even gardening can be a deeply spiritual practice, nurturing life and connecting with the earth's energy. The key is to engage with nature mindfully, appreciating its beauty and its power to heal and restore.

Consider the impact of different natural elements. Water, for instance, symbolizes purification and cleansing. Spending time near a waterfall, ocean, or lake can be incredibly restorative, washing away negative energies and promoting emotional clarity. Mountains represent strength, stability, and grounding. Spending time in mountainous regions can instill a sense of groundedness and resilience. Forests offer tranquility, serenity, and a deep connection with nature's wisdom. Spending time in forests can facilitate meditation and promote a sense of peace. Each natural element holds unique energy, offering its own unique gifts to those who seek to connect.

The subtle energies of nature are not merely symbolic; they are palpable and powerful. Imagine standing beneath a towering redwood tree, its ancient energy flowing through you. Feel the sun's warmth energizing your body, its life-giving rays revitalizing your cells. Notice the moon's gentle glow, its ethereal energy influencing the tides of emotion within you. These are not merely sensations; they are interactions with subtle energies, shaping your energetic field and influencing your overall well-being.

Through this deep connection with nature, you begin to perceive the interconnectedness of all things. You understand that you are not separate from the natural world, but an integral part of it. Your well-being is directly linked to the health of the planet, and your actions have a ripple effect on the entire ecosystem. This understanding fosters a sense of responsibility and compassion, encouraging you to live in harmony with nature and protect its beauty.

Remember the importance of reciprocity. When you receive the gifts of nature, it's essential to give back. Practice responsible environmental stewardship. Reduce your carbon footprint, conserve water, and support environmental protection efforts. Show gratitude for the Earth's generosity by protecting its beauty and preserving its resources.

Connecting with nature is a continuous process of learning, discovery, and deepening understanding. Allow yourself to be a student of the natural world, observing its cycles, appreciating its rhythms, and marveling at its breathtaking beauty. As you connect more deeply with the Earth's energy, you'll experience a profound sense of peace, purpose, and belonging. This connection will strengthen your spiritual practice, nurturing your soul and grounding your spirit, allowing you to blossom into a more vibrant and fulfilled version of yourself. The Earth's energy is a constant source of support, renewal, and deep spiritual nourishment, available to all who seek to embrace its boundless gifts. Allow this profound connection to enrich every aspect of your life, creating a harmonious and deeply fulfilling journey of spiritual growth and holistic wellness.Beyond the grounding energy of the Earth lies a vast, interconnected realm of spiritual beings—guides and angels—who are eager to assist us on our journey. These are not mythological figures confined to the pages of ancient texts but rather subtle energies, conscious presences that offer support, guidance, and unconditional love. Connecting with these benevolent beings can profoundly enrich our spiritual lives, providing clarity, direction, and a deeper sense of purpose.

The key to connecting with spirit guides and angels lies in cultivating an open and receptive heart. This involves quieting the incessant chatter of the mind and tuning into the subtle whispers of your intuition. Your intuition is not some mystical, elusive force; it's the quiet, inner knowing that resides within your heart, a direct connection to your higher self and the spiritual realm. Trusting your intuition is paramount in navigating the subtle energies and receiving clear guidance.

Before embarking on any communication with your guides, it is essential to establish a clear and focused intention. Ask yourself: What specific guidance do I seek? What challenges am I facing? What support do I need? Having a clear intention helps to focus your energy and attract the appropriate guidance.

One of the most effective methods for connecting with your guides is through meditation. Find a quiet space where you can relax and unwind, free from distractions. Sit or lie down comfortably, close your eyes, and begin to focus on your breath. As you breathe deeply, visualize a soft, white light surrounding you, purifying your energy field and preparing you for communication.

As you settle into a meditative state, visualize your guides as beings of light, love, and wisdom. Picture them as beings who are there to support and guide you unconditionally. There's no one "right" way to visualize them; trust your intuition to guide you. They may appear as luminous figures, orbs of light, or simply as a feeling of warmth and peace. Once you feel connected, begin to communicate with your guides. You can do this silently, through your thoughts, or aloud, speaking your intentions and questions clearly and concisely. Be patient and listen attentively. The answers may not always come in a dramatic fashion; they may be subtle, a feeling, an insight, or a gentle nudge in a certain direction. Pay close attention to your intuition. Your guides often communicate through subtle signs and synchronicities, such as a recurring image, a particular song, or a chance encounter. These synchronicities are not coincidences; they are messages from your guides, offering guidance and reassurance. Keep a journal to record any messages or insights you receive during your meditations or throughout your day.

Discernment is crucial when working with spiritual guides. Not all communication comes from benevolent sources. It's essential to discern between genuine guidance and messages that may not be in your best interest. Your intuition will be your most reliable guide in this process. If something feels off, uneasy, or manipulative, trust your instincts and discontinue the communication.

Remember, your guides are there to support you, not to control you. They will not dictate your choices or tell you exactly what to do. Instead, they offer guidance and encouragement, empowering you to make your own decisions and chart your own course.

Another effective method for connecting with spirit guides and angels is through journaling. Express your concerns, fears, and aspirations in writing. Ask your guides for guidance and wisdom. Then, allow yourself time to reflect on what emerges. Pay close attention to recurring themes or insights.

Incorporating crystal healing can enhance your connection with the spiritual realm. Certain crystals, such as amethyst, selenite, and clear quartz, are known to amplify spiritual energy and facilitate communication with guides. Hold the crystal as you meditate, visualize its energy cleansing and harmonizing your aura, opening you to receiving higher guidance. Astrology can also illuminate your connection with your spirit guides. The planets and celestial bodies influence our lives, and understanding your astrological birth chart can help you discover which guides and angels are most aligned with your soul's journey. For instance, the position of certain planets could reveal which archetypal energies or qualities resonate most strongly with your guides.

Numerology, too, can provide valuable insights into your connection with the spiritual realm. Your life path number, for instance, can reveal the overall energies and life lessons aligned with your spiritual path, attracting certain types of guides to assist you. The numbers appearing around you might contain coded messages from your guides. Pay attention to recurring numbers and their symbolism.

Beyond meditation and journaling, simply expressing gratitude is a powerful way to invite the presence and support of your guides and angels. Acknowledge their assistance and express appreciation for their guidance. This simple act strengthens your connection and opens a channel for more profound communication.

However, remember that establishing a strong connection with spiritual guides is a journey, not a destination. It's a gradual unfolding of awareness and receptivity. Be patient and persistent, allowing the connection to deepen over time. Don't expect dramatic manifestations or immediate answers. Instead, cultivate an attitude of openness and trust. Embrace the subtle signs and synchronicities that guide you along the path.

Setting healthy boundaries is essential when working with guides. You're not surrendering your free will; you're collaborating with higher forces. Trust your own intuition and discernment. Don't allow any communication to override your own sense of self or inner wisdom. Maintain a sense of self-awareness and groundedness throughout your interactions. Remember, you have agency in your life, and your guides are there to support you, not to take control.

Remember, your guides are not distant, ethereal beings; they are extensions of your own inner wisdom and divine connection. They are there to support you in achieving your highest potential and navigating the challenges of life. By embracing these methods of connection and fostering an environment of trust and openness, you invite a profound and enriching partnership that will guide you toward a more fulfilling and meaningful life. As you deepen this relationship, you'll discover a level of support, wisdom, and unconditional love that will transform every aspect of your existence, shaping you into a more spiritually aware and grounded individual. This journey of connection will not only enhance your spiritual practices but also deepen your overall well-being, leading you toward a more vibrant, balanced, and harmonious life. Embrace the journey, trust your intuition, and allow your heart to open to the boundless love and support available to you in the spiritual realm. This connection is a continual process of growth, learning, and deepening your understanding of yourself and the universe. The more you cultivate this relationship, the richer and more fulfilling your life becomes.Developing a strong intuition isn't about suddenly acquiring psychic abilities; it's about cultivating a deep listening to the quiet wisdom within. It's the gentle whisper of your soul, often drowned out by the constant noise of daily life – the anxieties, the to-do lists, the external pressures. Learning to trust your intuition is a process of reclaiming this inner voice, a journey of self-discovery that intertwines deeply with your spiritual growth. It's about recognizing the subtle cues, the gut feelings, the flashes of insight that emerge from the depths of your being.

One effective way to begin honing your intuition is through mindful observation. Pay attention to your physical sensations. Does a particular situation leave you feeling energized and excited, or drained and apprehensive? These physical responses often serve as invaluable indicators of your inner knowing. A racing heart, a knot in your stomach, or a sudden chill might signal a warning or a need for caution. Conversely, a feeling of warmth, lightness, and ease often indicates that you're on the right path.

Beyond physical sensations, notice your emotional responses. Do certain people or situations consistently evoke feelings of discomfort or unease? These feelings can reflect a deeper intuition about the situation or the individual. Similarly, moments of profound joy, peace, or contentment may indicate alignment with your soul's purpose. These seemingly minor emotional fluctuations hold a wealth of information, offering subtle clues about your intuition's guidance.

Practice active listening to your inner voice. This means silencing the incessant mental chatter and creating space for the quiet whispers of your intuition to be heard. Meditation is a powerful tool for this. Find a quiet space, close your eyes, and focus on your breath. As you breathe deeply, allow your mind to settle, gently releasing any thoughts or worries that arise. In this quiet space, you can begin to listen for the subtle nudges of your intuition, those intuitive insights that might come as a sudden thought, a fleeting image, or a feeling of knowing.

Journaling can further enhance your intuitive development. Regularly record your thoughts, feelings, and observations throughout the day. Pay attention to recurring themes or patterns that emerge. These patterns can reveal underlying messages, showing you where your intuition is guiding you. Journaling creates a space for reflection, allowing you to process your experiences and discern the subtle signals your intuition is sending.

Engage in activities that cultivate mindfulness. Simple practices like paying attention to your senses while eating, savoring the taste and texture of your food, or noticing the feeling of the sun on your skin can enhance your awareness of your inner world. These practices train your mind to focus on the present moment, creating a receptive space for your intuition to surface. Mindful walking in nature, where you focus on the sights, sounds, and sensations surrounding you, can be particularly effective.

Trusting your intuition requires self-belief and self-acceptance. It involves recognizing that you possess an inner wisdom that guides you towards your highest good. Embrace the uncertainty, the moments of doubt and confusion, as part of the process. Intuition isn't always a clear, definitive voice; it often comes as a feeling, a hunch, or a gut instinct. Learn to trust these subtle cues, even when they contradict logic or reason.

Challenge self-limiting beliefs that hinder your intuition. Do you often dismiss your instincts as mere coincidence or overactive imagination? Recognize and challenge these beliefs. Remind yourself that you have an innate ability to access inner wisdom, and trust that your intuition is a valuable guide. Affirmations can be incredibly helpful in reinforcing this self-belief. Repeat affirmations like "I trust my intuition," "I am guided by my inner wisdom," and "I am confident in my ability to make wise choices," until they resonate deeply within you. Visualizations can enhance your connection with your intuition. Imagine a bright, clear light emanating from your heart center, symbolizing your intuition. Visualize this light growing stronger and brighter, illuminating your path and guiding your decisions. Imagine yourself effortlessly tuning into the subtle whispers of your inner voice, receiving clear and confident guidance. Regular visualization practices can strengthen your intuitive abilities and deepen your trust in your inner knowing.

Numerology, with its symbolic associations and number patterns, can surprisingly enhance your intuition. Pay attention to recurring numbers that appear in your life – on license plates, clocks, receipts. These may not be random occurrences; instead, they might be messages from your higher self, guiding you towards a certain direction or providing reassurance. Research the symbolism of these numbers, exploring their energetic vibrations and meanings. Understanding the underlying energy of these numbers can enhance your intuitive understanding of events and situations.

Similarly, the practice of Astrology can provide insightful clues. By understanding your astrological birth chart, you can gain a better understanding of your personality traits, strengths, and weaknesses. By recognizing your innate tendencies, you can identify patterns in your life and learn to trust your intuitive responses more readily. Understanding your planetary placements can reveal your natural inclinations and predispositions, enhancing your ability to interpret the subtle messages of your intuition.

Crystal healing can also augment your intuitive abilities. Crystals, with their unique vibrational properties, can enhance clarity and focus, facilitating a deeper connection with your inner wisdom. Specific crystals, such as amethyst, selenite, or clear quartz, are particularly helpful in amplifying spiritual energy and improving intuitive perception. Hold the crystal during meditation, visualize its energy cleansing and harmonizing your energy field, and open yourself to receiving intuitive guidance.

As you cultivate your intuition, remember that trusting your inner voice is an ongoing process. It's a journey of self-discovery and self-empowerment, requiring patience, persistence, and a willingness to embrace the unknown. There will be times when your intuition is clear and strong, and times when it is more subtle and elusive. Accept these variations as natural aspects of the journey. The more you practice listening to and trusting your intuition, the stronger and more reliable it becomes.

Through consistent practice and a commitment to self-trust, you'll discover that your intuition is a powerful tool for navigating life's complexities, making informed decisions, and living a more fulfilling and spiritually aligned life. It becomes a reliable compass, guiding you towards your true purpose, helping you to discern what aligns with your values and what does not. As your intuition grows stronger, so too does your self-belief, creating a powerful synergy that enhances your overall sense of well-being. It's a beautiful reciprocal relationship: the more you trust your intuition, the more it unfolds, revealing its deeper wisdom and guidance. This journey of deepening intuition not only leads to a more harmonious life but also strengthens your spiritual connection, bringing you closer to the true essence of who you are. Embrace the journey, and trust the whispers of your heart. They hold the key to unlocking your full potential.The journey towards a deeper spiritual connection isn't solely about mastering esoteric practices; it's also about cultivating a profound appreciation for the present moment and all that it holds. Gratitude, often overlooked in our busy lives, serves as a powerful catalyst for spiritual growth. It acts as a bridge, connecting us to the inherent goodness and abundance in our existence, regardless of external circumstances. This feeling of thankfulness isn't simply a fleeting emotion; it's a conscious practice, a way of shifting our perception from lack to abundance, from negativity to positivity. The more we cultivate gratitude, the more we open ourselves to the subtle energies of the universe, enhancing our spiritual sensitivity and intuition.

Think of gratitude as a spiritual muscle. The more you exercise it, the stronger it becomes. Initially, expressing gratitude might feel forced, or even disingenuous. But with consistent practice, it transforms into a genuine expression of appreciation, deeply enriching your inner landscape. This isn't about suppressing negative feelings or pretending that everything is perfect; it's about acknowledging the good amidst the challenges, finding the silver lining in the clouds.

The benefits of practicing gratitude are far-reaching and profound. On an emotional level, it acts as a potent antidote to negativity, anxiety, and depression. When we focus on what we are grateful for, we shift our attention away from what's lacking, reducing stress and fostering a sense of contentment. Studies have shown that regularly expressing gratitude can lead to improved mood, increased self-esteem, and a greater sense of overall well-being. Mentally, gratitude enhances clarity and focus. By consciously appreciating the positive aspects of our lives, we train our minds to recognize and amplify these experiences. This enhances our ability to problem-solve, make better decisions, and approach life's challenges with a more resilient mindset. The act of gratitude itself is a form of mindfulness, grounding us in the present moment and preventing our minds from wandering into unproductive thoughts of worry and anxiety.

Spiritually, gratitude fosters a deeper connection to something larger than ourselves. It reminds us that we are not alone in this journey, that there is a benevolent force guiding and supporting us. By expressing gratitude, we acknowledge the blessings in our lives – both big and small – recognizing that they stem from a source of abundance beyond our individual efforts. This sense of interconnectedness nourishes our spiritual growth, fostering a feeling of peace, purpose, and belonging.

So, how do we cultivate this profound sense of gratitude? The answer lies in conscious practice and mindful integration into our daily lives. One of the most effective methods is keeping a gratitude journal. Each day, take a few moments to jot down three to five things you are grateful for. These don't have to be monumental events; they can be as simple as the warmth of the sun on your skin, the kindness of a stranger, or the taste of your morning coffee. The act of writing these things down reinforces the feeling of appreciation, strengthening the neural pathways associated with gratitude.

Another powerful technique is to express gratitude verbally. Take the time to tell someone you appreciate them. A simple "thank you" can have a profound impact, not only on the recipient but also on the giver. Expressing gratitude to your loved ones, friends, and even colleagues can strengthen relationships and create a more positive and supportive environment around you. This can extend to expressing gratitude for seemingly insignificant things, like the smooth functioning of public transportation or the availability of clean water. Incorporating gratitude into your spiritual practices enhances their effect. During meditation, focus on the feeling of gratitude for your health, your loved ones, and the opportunity to engage in spiritual growth. This can be integrated into any meditation technique, whether it's focused breathing, body scan meditation, or guided imagery. Infuse your prayers with gratitude, thanking the divine source for all the blessings in your life.

Engage in *acts of service and kindness*. Helping others is a powerful way to cultivate gratitude. When we offer our time, energy, or resources to someone in need, we shift our focus from ourselves to others, fostering a sense of empathy and appreciation for all that we have. Volunteering at a local charity, assisting an elderly neighbor, or simply offering a helping hand to someone in need can be a deeply rewarding experience, cultivating both gratitude and a deeper sense of spiritual purpose.

Mindful appreciation is another key element. Slow down and savor the simple pleasures of life. Pay attention to the details: the beauty of nature, the taste of your food, the warmth of human connection. By actively appreciating these moments, we cultivate a greater awareness of the abundance that surrounds us, fostering a deeper sense of gratitude. Take your time eating a meal, appreciating the flavors and textures. Take a mindful walk in nature, appreciating the sights, sounds, and smells around you.

Throughout the day, make a conscious effort to notice and appreciate the small blessings that often go unnoticed. A sunny day, a kind word from a friend, a successful completion of a task – all of these contribute to a feeling of overall well-being. By acknowledging these moments, we train our minds to focus on the positive aspects of our lives, shifting our perspective from one of scarcity to one of abundance. This constant awareness helps to foster a deep, consistent gratitude that pervades all aspects of our lives.

Consider using crystals to amplify your feelings of gratitude. Crystals like Rose Quartz, known for its gentle and loving energy, can enhance compassion and appreciation. Citrine, with its bright and sunny energy, promotes abundance and joy, encouraging feelings of thankfulness. Keep these crystals nearby as a reminder to practice gratitude, or incorporate them into your meditation practices to enhance the experience. Visualize the energy of the crystal flowing through you, amplifying your feelings of gratitude and appreciation.

Numerology can also play a role. Pay attention to recurring number patterns in your life. If you find yourself frequently encountering the number 3, for example, research its numerological significance. The number 3 often represents joy, creativity, and optimism – all attributes that support a feeling of gratitude. Understanding the symbolic meaning of recurring numbers can deepen your understanding of the universe's messages, encouraging a greater sense of appreciation for the synchronicities in your life.

Similarly, astrology can provide insightful guidance. Understanding your astrological birth chart can help you identify planetary influences that might impact your capacity for gratitude. For instance, if you have a strong emphasis on Venus in your chart, you might naturally possess a heightened sense of appreciation for beauty and harmony. Understanding your astrological predispositions can help you cultivate this inherent capacity for gratitude and enhance your spiritual connection.

By consciously integrating gratitude into your daily life, you are not merely expressing thankfulness; you are actively participating in creating a more positive and fulfilling reality. It's a form of spiritual alchemy, transforming your perspective and opening you to the limitless possibilities of the universe. Gratitude isn't about ignoring the challenges; it's about finding the strength and resilience to overcome them, appreciating the lessons learned, and recognizing the blessings that often come disguised as difficulties. Cultivate this spiritual muscle, and you'll discover a profound shift in your perspective, leading to a richer, more meaningful, and spiritually aligned life. The path to a deeper spiritual connection is paved with gratitude, and each step taken on this path brings us closer to our true selves and the infinite abundance of the universe.

Chapter 9: Overcoming Challenges and Obstacles

The journey of self-healing is often paved with unexpected obstacles, and one of the most significant hurdles we encounter is the presence of limiting beliefs. These deeply ingrained thought patterns, often formed in childhood or through past experiences, act as invisible chains, restricting our potential for growth and well-being. They whisper doubts, stifle our aspirations, and prevent us from fully embracing our innate capacity for healing and transformation. Recognizing and dismantling these limiting beliefs is crucial for unlocking our true potential and embarking on a path towards genuine self-discovery.

Identifying these beliefs can be challenging, as they often operate subconsciously, subtly influencing our thoughts, emotions, and behaviors. They manifest as negative self-talk, recurring patterns of self-sabotage, or a persistent feeling that we are somehow "not enough." Perhaps you find yourself constantly comparing yourself to others, believing you'll never achieve their level of success or happiness. Maybe you're plagued by fears of failure, preventing you from taking risks and pursuing your dreams. Or perhaps you hold onto beliefs about your unworthiness, believing you don't deserve love, abundance, or happiness. These are just a few examples of how limiting beliefs can manifest, hindering our progress on the path to holistic wellness.

One powerful tool for identifying these beliefs is *introspection*. Spend time in quiet contemplation, reflecting on your recurring thoughts and feelings. Pay attention to the internal dialogue—that relentless stream of commentary that plays constantly in your mind. What are the recurring themes? Are you constantly criticizing yourself, focusing on your flaws and shortcomings? Do you frequently engage in negative self-comparison? Journaling can be an invaluable aid in this process, providing a safe space to explore your thoughts and emotions without judgment. Write down your thoughts, feelings, and experiences, paying close attention to recurring patterns and themes. This process can unearth hidden beliefs that are silently shaping your reality.

Another approach is to pay attention to your *body's signals*. Limiting beliefs often manifest physically as tension, discomfort, or pain. Notice any physical sensations associated with specific thoughts or situations. Do you experience tightness in your chest when thinking about a particular challenge? Do you feel a knot in your stomach when faced with a specific fear? These physical cues can provide valuable insights into the underlying beliefs that are affecting your well-being. Consider using energy healing modalities like Reiki to help release blocked energy associated with these limiting beliefs. The gentle energy flow of Reiki can help to dissolve energetic blockages and promote a sense of balance and harmony within your energy system.

Once you've identified your limiting beliefs, the next step is to challenge and transform them. This is not about simply wishing them away; it's about actively engaging in a process of cognitive restructuring—rewiring your neural pathways to create new, more empowering beliefs. Start by questioning the validity of these limiting beliefs. Are they truly accurate reflections of reality, or are they based on past experiences, assumptions, or fears? Consider the evidence both for and against these beliefs. Often, we find that the evidence supporting the limiting belief is minimal, while the evidence against it is far more substantial. Affirmations are a powerful tool for challenging limiting beliefs. Affirmations are positive statements that repeat desired beliefs, helping to reprogram your subconscious mind. For instance, if you believe you're not worthy of love, you can counter this with affirmations like, "I am worthy of love and acceptance," or "I am lovable and deserving of happiness." Repeat these affirmations regularly, ideally in conjunction with visualization techniques. Visualize yourself embodying these new beliefs, experiencing the feelings of self-worth, confidence, and self-love. The combination of affirmations and visualization creates a powerful synergy, helping to embed these positive beliefs deeply within your subconscious mind.

Cognitive restructuring involves actively challenging and replacing negative thought patterns with more positive and realistic ones. When you catch yourself engaging in negative self-talk, gently challenge those thoughts. Ask yourself, "Is this thought truly helpful? Is it based on fact or fear?" Then, actively replace the negative thought with a more positive and empowering one. For example, if you catch yourself thinking, "I'm going to fail," you might reframe this thought as, "I'm going to give it my best shot, and even if I don't succeed, I will learn from the experience."

Visualization can be incredibly powerful in this process. Imagine yourself effortlessly overcoming the challenges you face, embodying the qualities you aspire to possess. Feel the emotions associated with these positive outcomes—the sense of accomplishment, joy, and self-confidence. This helps to solidify these new beliefs within your subconscious mind, creating a powerful foundation for positive change.

Incorporating crystal healing into your practice can further enhance the process of transforming limiting beliefs. Certain crystals are known for their ability to enhance self-esteem, promote emotional healing, and facilitate spiritual growth. Amethyst, for instance, is known for its calming and purifying properties, helping to clear away negative energy and promote inner peace. Rose quartz, with its gentle and loving energy, encourages self-acceptance and fosters feelings of compassion and self-love. By holding or meditating with these crystals, you can amplify the effectiveness of your affirmations and visualizations, fostering a deeper sense of self-acceptance and empowerment.

Numerology can also provide valuable insights into your limiting beliefs. Understanding your life path number and other numerological aspects of your birth date can help you identify patterns and themes that contribute to these beliefs. For example, if you have a life path number associated with challenges related to self-esteem, this knowledge can provide valuable context for understanding the root causes of your limiting beliefs. By understanding this numerological insight, you can work more effectively to address these underlying issues. Astrology, too, can offer a unique perspective. Examining your natal chart can reveal planetary influences that might be contributing to your limiting beliefs. For instance, certain planetary placements might indicate a predisposition towards self-doubt or fear of failure. Understanding these influences can provide valuable insights into your challenges and help you develop strategies for overcoming them. The astrological insights can illuminate the deeper patterns at play, making it easier to pinpoint the origin of these limiting beliefs and develop effective strategies for transforming them.

Remember, this is a process, not a destination. Be patient with yourself, acknowledging that change takes time and effort. Celebrate your progress, no matter how small, and don't be discouraged by setbacks. Each step you take towards identifying and challenging your limiting beliefs brings you closer to living a more authentic, fulfilling, and empowered life. The journey towards self-discovery and healing is often a winding path, but the destination – a life filled with joy, purpose, and unwavering self-belief – is well worth the effort. Embrace the journey, trust in your innate capacity for healing, and remember that you are not alone on this path. The universe is supporting you, guiding you, and empowering you every step of the way. The more you work on dismantling your limiting beliefs, the more you open yourself up to the infinite possibilities that await you. The work of dismantling limiting beliefs paves the way for addressing deeper emotional wounds and traumas. Often, these deeply ingrained negative thought patterns are a direct result of past hurts and unresolved emotional pain. While challenging these beliefs is a crucial step, it's equally important to address the root causes of these beliefs – the emotional pain and trauma that have shaped them. This process requires gentleness, self-compassion, and a willingness to confront difficult emotions and experiences.

Emotional pain and trauma are not merely fleeting feelings; they are energetic imprints etched onto our energy field, subtly influencing our thoughts, behaviors, and overall well-being. They can manifest in various ways, from anxiety and depression to chronic pain and physical ailments. Unresolved trauma can create energetic blockages within our chakra system, disrupting the natural flow of energy and affecting our physical, emotional, and spiritual health.

The first step in dealing with emotional pain and trauma is *acknowledging its presence*. This can be incredibly challenging, as we often unconsciously avoid or suppress these difficult emotions. But avoidance only prolongs the healing process. Creating a safe space for yourself —a sanctuary of self-compassion—is paramount. This space could be a quiet corner in your home, a peaceful nature setting, or even a designated time set aside each day for reflection. In this space, allow yourself to feel the emotions without judgment. Don't try to suppress or analyze them; simply observe them as they arise and pass. Journaling can be a valuable tool here; pouring your emotions onto paper can help release pent-up feelings and provide a tangible record of your healing journey.

Deep breathing exercises are a powerful way to regulate your nervous system and calm the emotional turmoil. Practicing diaphragmatic breathing—breathing deeply into your belly— can help ground you in the present moment and reduce feelings of overwhelm. Combine this with mindfulness meditation, focusing your attention on the present moment without judgment. This practice helps you cultivate self-awareness, allowing you to observe your thoughts and emotions without being swept away by them.

Energy healing modalities, like Reiki, are particularly effective in addressing the energetic imbalances caused by emotional trauma. Reiki's gentle, nurturing energy helps to clear blocked energy, promoting a sense of balance and harmony within your energy field. A Reiki practitioner can help guide you through this process, providing support and guidance as you release trapped emotions and heal energetic wounds. Imagine the Reiki energy gently washing over you, dissolving the energetic knots and tension associated with your trauma. Crystal healing can complement Reiki, offering additional support during emotional healing. Crystals like amethyst are known for their calming and purifying properties, helping to soothe the nervous system and release pent-up emotions. Rose quartz, with its gentle and loving energy, fosters self-compassion and promotes emotional healing. Holding these crystals while practicing meditation or breathing exercises can amplify the healing process. Visualize the crystal's energy dissolving the emotional pain, replacing it with feelings of peace, serenity, and self-acceptance.

Numerology can provide valuable insights into your karmic patterns and the underlying causes of your emotional pain. By understanding your life path number and other numerological aspects of your birth date, you may uncover recurring themes and patterns that contribute to your emotional challenges. This understanding can provide valuable context and empower you to make conscious choices to break free from these patterns. Astrological insights can further deepen your understanding of your emotional landscape. Your natal chart provides a roadmap of your personality and karmic tendencies. By examining the planetary influences, you may identify planetary aspects that indicate emotional vulnerabilities or predispositions towards certain types of trauma. Understanding these astrological influences can help you develop coping mechanisms and strategies to navigate these emotional challenges with more grace and resilience.

Remember, the journey of healing from emotional pain and trauma is not a linear process. There will be ups and downs, moments of progress followed by periods of regression. Be patient and kind to yourself. Celebrate your small victories and acknowledge the challenges you face without judgment. Self-compassion is crucial during this process; treat yourself with the same kindness and understanding you would offer a dear friend.

While self-care practices and energy healing modalities can be incredibly beneficial, it's essential to recognize when professional help is needed. If you're struggling to cope with intense emotional pain or trauma on your own, please seek the guidance of a qualified therapist or counselor. They can provide a safe and supportive space to explore your experiences, develop coping mechanisms, and process your emotions in a healthy way. Don't hesitate to reach out for professional support – it's a sign of strength, not weakness. Incorporating these holistic approaches into your life can profoundly impact your healing journey. However, remember that healing is a personal journey, and there is no one-size-fits-all approach. Experiment with different modalities and find what resonates most with you. Trust your intuition and allow yourself to be guided by your inner wisdom.

The process of healing from emotional pain and trauma is a testament to the resilience of the human spirit. It is a journey of self-discovery, self-acceptance, and profound personal growth. Embrace the challenges, celebrate your progress, and remember that you are not alone. The universe supports you, and you possess the innate capacity to heal and thrive. Your journey towards wholeness is a testament to your strength, your courage, and your unwavering spirit. Embrace the power of self-compassion, and allow yourself the time and space to heal at your own pace. Remember, the healing process is unique to each individual, and the most important thing is to be patient with yourself and celebrate your progress along the way. The path to healing may be long and winding, but it is a path worth traveling, leading to a more authentic, joyful, and fulfilling life. By integrating the wisdom of ancient healing practices with modern therapeutic approaches, you can create a holistic healing plan tailored to your specific needs and experiences.

The integration of energy healing modalities, such as Reiki, with traditional therapy can provide a powerful synergy, allowing you to address both the energetic and psychological aspects of trauma. Reiki can help to clear energetic blockages, promoting a sense of balance and well-being, while therapy provides a safe space to process emotions and develop healthy coping mechanisms. This combined approach fosters a more comprehensive and effective healing process.

Furthermore, incorporating practices like yoga, meditation, and spending time in nature can significantly enhance your healing journey. These practices help to calm the nervous system, reduce stress, and promote a sense of grounding and connection. Connecting with nature can be particularly therapeutic, providing a sense of peace and renewal. The natural world offers a soothing balm for the soul, fostering a sense of calm and tranquility. The rhythm of the ocean, the rustling of leaves, or the warmth of the sun can all contribute to a sense of well-being and emotional healing.

Remember, the journey of healing is a marathon, not a sprint. There will be moments of progress and moments of setbacks. It's crucial to celebrate every step forward, no matter how small. Be patient and compassionate with yourself throughout the process. Embrace the journey of self-discovery and growth, knowing that you possess the strength and resilience to overcome any challenges that come your way. The path to healing is a personal one, and there is no right or wrong way to approach it. Trust your intuition, and allow yourself the freedom to explore different healing modalities and techniques until you find what resonates most deeply with you. The journey towards healing is a testament to the strength and resilience of the human spirit. It's a journey of self-discovery, self-acceptance, and profound personal growth. Embrace the challenges, celebrate your progress, and remember that you are not alone. The universe supports you, and you possess the innate capacity to heal and thrive.Navigating the complexities of human relationships can often feel like traversing a labyrinth, filled with twists, turns, and unexpected dead ends. Difficult relationships, whether with family, friends, romantic partners, or colleagues, can drain our energy, deplete our spirits, and leave us feeling emotionally exhausted. However, these challenging connections also present invaluable opportunities for growth, self-discovery, and the development of crucial life skills. Understanding the energetic dynamics at play, coupled with practical strategies, can transform these challenging interactions into pathways toward greater self-awareness and healthier connections.

One of the fundamental pillars of navigating difficult relationships is *effective communication*. Often, misunderstandings arise not from malicious intent but from a lack of clarity and open dialogue. Before engaging in a conversation with someone who consistently triggers negative emotions, take a moment to center yourself. Grounding techniques, such as deep breathing exercises or connecting with nature, can help to calm your nervous system and foster a more balanced emotional state. This will enable you to approach the conversation with greater clarity and composure, reducing the likelihood of escalating the conflict. When communicating with someone who is challenging, focus on expressing your feelings using "I" statements. Instead of resorting to accusatory language like, "You always do this," try phrasing your concerns in a way that emphasizes your own experience. For example, instead of saying, "You make me feel angry," try, "I feel angry when this happens." This approach shifts the focus from blaming the other person to expressing your own emotional state, which is generally better received and less likely to trigger defensiveness.

Active listening is equally critical. This involves not only hearing the other person's words but also paying attention to their nonverbal cues – their body language, tone of voice, and facial expressions. Reflecting back what you've heard, paraphrasing their statements to ensure understanding, shows that you are truly listening and engaging with their perspective. This can significantly de-escalate tension and foster a more collaborative dialogue. Remember that understanding someone's perspective doesn't necessarily mean agreeing with them, but it creates a space for empathy and open communication.

Setting healthy boundaries is another crucial element in managing difficult relationships. Boundaries are the limits we set to protect our emotional and energetic well-being. They define what we are and are not willing to tolerate in a relationship. Setting boundaries may involve saying "no" to requests that drain your energy, limiting contact with individuals who consistently cause stress, or establishing clear expectations for how you wish to be treated. Setting boundaries is an act of self-respect, a demonstration of your commitment to your own well-being. It is not selfish; it is essential for maintaining healthy relationships and preventing emotional depletion.

The process of setting boundaries may initially feel uncomfortable, especially if you're used to people-pleasing or avoiding conflict. However, it's vital to remember that setting boundaries isn't about controlling others; it's about taking responsibility for your own emotional and energetic well-being. This often involves aligning your actions with your intentions, ensuring that your outer expressions match your inner truth. This alignment strengthens your energy field and boosts your self-confidence, empowering you to stand firm in your boundaries.

Conflict is an inevitable part of any relationship, but *the way we handle conflict* can significantly impact the health and longevity of that relationship. Instead of viewing conflict as a battle to be won, try reframing it as an opportunity to clarify misunderstandings and strengthen the connection. Remember to approach conflict resolution with compassion and a willingness to understand the other person's perspective. However, maintain your boundaries; you don't have to endure abusive or disrespectful behavior in the name of resolution.

Effective conflict resolution often involves finding common ground, identifying shared goals, and collaboratively seeking solutions. Compromise is key, but it shouldn't come at the expense of your own well-being. If a conflict repeatedly escalates or becomes abusive, seeking professional guidance from a therapist or counselor is a wise choice. They can provide valuable support and strategies for navigating these complex situations.

Self-compassion plays a vital role in navigating difficult relationships. It's easy to blame ourselves for the challenges we face in our relationships, to believe that we're somehow responsible for the other person's behavior. However, it's essential to remember that you are not responsible for other people's actions, only for your own responses. Practice self-forgiveness, acknowledge your own imperfections, and treat yourself with the same kindness and understanding you would offer a dear friend. This self-compassion will bolster your resilience and provide the emotional strength to navigate challenging relationships.

Integrating your understanding of energy healing can further support your ability to navigate these challenging dynamics. Visualize yourself surrounded by a protective energy field, a shield against negativity and emotional manipulation. Imagine this field as a vibrant, radiant light, deflecting any harmful energy directed your way. This visualization can help you maintain a sense of emotional distance while engaging in difficult conversations. Crystals can serve as powerful allies in this process. Amethyst, known for its calming and protective properties, can help to maintain emotional equilibrium during tense interactions. Clear quartz can amplify your intentions, supporting you in communicating your needs and boundaries with clarity and confidence. Carry these crystals with you, hold them during meditation, or place them strategically in your home to create a supportive energetic environment.

Numerology can also offer valuable insights. Understanding your life path number and karmic lessons can provide context for the challenges you face in your relationships. This knowledge empowers you to approach these situations with greater awareness, understanding the recurring themes and patterns that may contribute to these difficulties. Remember that your relationships are mirrors, reflecting aspects of yourself that you might need to address.

Astrological insights can further illuminate the dynamics at play in your relationships. Examining your natal chart and the planetary aspects involved can help you understand the karmic lessons and challenges associated with certain connections. This understanding allows you to approach these interactions with more empathy and compassion, and allows for developing more skillful strategies to navigate the challenges.

The path to healthier relationships is a journey of self-discovery and personal growth. It requires courage, self-compassion, and a willingness to set boundaries and engage in authentic communication. By integrating ancient wisdom with modern techniques, you can transform your challenging interactions into opportunities for growth, leading to more fulfilling and harmonious relationships. Remember that you deserve healthy, supportive relationships that enrich your life, and you have the power to create them. Trust your intuition, embrace your inner strength, and approach each interaction with awareness and compassion. The journey may not always be easy, but the rewards of healthier relationships are immeasurable. It is a journey towards a more authentic, joyful, and fulfilling existence. Embrace the process, celebrating every step forward, and remember that the universe is always supporting you in your efforts toward growth and healing.Fear and anxiety, those unwelcome shadows that often darken our path, are universal human experiences. They are not signs of weakness, but rather signals that our survival mechanisms are at work, alerting us to perceived threats. However, when these feelings become overwhelming and persistent, they can significantly hinder our journey towards holistic well-being. The good news is that fear and anxiety are not insurmountable obstacles. By understanding their root causes and employing practical strategies, we can learn to manage them effectively and reclaim our inner peace.

One of the most powerful tools in our arsenal against fear and anxiety is meditation. Regular meditation cultivates a deeper connection to our inner selves, enabling us to observe our thoughts and emotions without judgment. It helps us to detach from the relentless stream of mental chatter that often fuels anxiety, creating space for clarity and calm. Begin with even just five minutes a day, focusing on your breath, allowing your thoughts to drift by like clouds in the sky. As you become more comfortable, gradually increase the duration of your meditation sessions.

Deep breathing exercises are incredibly effective in regulating the nervous system and reducing feelings of panic. When anxiety strikes, our breathing often becomes shallow and rapid, intensifying our feelings of distress. Conscious, deep breathing helps to slow down our heart rate, calm our minds, and restore a sense of equilibrium. Try the box breathing technique: inhale for a count of four, hold for four, exhale for four, and hold for four. Repeat this cycle several times until you feel your anxiety subside. This technique can be practiced anywhere, anytime, making it a readily available tool in your self-care toolbox. Mindfulness practices, such as paying close attention to the present moment without judgment, offer another powerful way to manage anxiety. Instead of dwelling on past regrets or future worries, mindfulness encourages us to focus on our immediate experiences: the sensation of our breath, the sounds around us, the taste of our food. This practice helps to ground us in the present, reducing the power of anxious thoughts and promoting a sense of calm. Engage in simple mindfulness exercises throughout your day: savor a cup of tea, notice the texture of the fabric on your clothes, or simply pay attention to the feeling of your feet on the ground.

Understanding the root causes of your fear and anxiety is crucial for long-term management. Journaling can be a valuable tool in this process. Write down your fears and anxieties, explore their origins, and identify any recurring patterns or triggers. This act of self-reflection can provide valuable insights into the underlying issues contributing to your emotional distress. **Ask yourself**: what specific situations or thoughts trigger my anxiety? What are the beliefs or assumptions that underpin these fears? Are there past experiences that are contributing to my present anxieties? By understanding the "why" behind your feelings, you can begin to address them more effectively.

Self-compassion is paramount in overcoming fear and anxiety. It's easy to berate ourselves for feeling anxious or afraid, adding to our emotional burden. Instead, cultivate kindness and understanding towards yourself. Recognize that everyone experiences fear and anxiety at some point in their lives. Treat yourself with the same empathy and compassion you would offer a close friend struggling with similar challenges. Remember that your feelings are valid, and you are not alone in your experience.

Addressing underlying physical factors can also significantly impact our ability to manage fear and anxiety. Ensure you're eating a healthy, balanced diet, getting sufficient sleep, and engaging in regular physical activity. Physical health is intrinsically linked to mental well-being. A diet rich in nutrients, adequate rest, and regular exercise can help to regulate hormones and neurotransmitters, reducing the likelihood of experiencing excessive anxiety. The chakra system offers a powerful framework for understanding and addressing the energetic imbalances that contribute to fear and anxiety. The root chakra, associated with security and stability, is often implicated when we experience deep-seated fears. Working with the root chakra through practices such as grounding meditations, spending time in nature, and using grounding crystals like red jasper can help to alleviate these feelings. The solar plexus chakra, related to self-esteem and personal power, also plays a vital role. When this chakra is imbalanced, we might experience feelings of inadequacy and self-doubt, contributing to anxiety. Strengthening this chakra through affirmations, setting healthy boundaries, and utilizing crystals like citrine can foster feelings of confidence and self-assurance.

The heart chakra, the center of love and compassion, is central to self-compassion, a crucial element in managing fear and anxiety. Opening the heart chakra through acts of kindness, forgiveness, and self-love can significantly reduce feelings of fear and isolation. Crystals like rose quartz can assist in this process by promoting feelings of unconditional love and acceptance. Similarly, the throat chakra, associated with self-expression, is important in overcoming fear. When we hold back our authentic self, we can experience a build-up of energy that manifests as anxiety. Engaging in creative expression, speaking your truth, and using crystals like blue lace agate can help to release this trapped energy and promote a sense of freedom and self-acceptance. Finally, the crown chakra, connected to our spiritual connection, helps us to see the bigger picture. Connecting to our spirituality through prayer, meditation, or nature can help to alleviate fear and anxiety by reminding us of our connection to something larger than ourselves.

The power of crystals in managing fear and anxiety should not be underestimated. Crystals act as energetic amplifiers and catalysts, supporting our efforts to heal and transform. Amethyst, with its calming and soothing properties, is a powerful tool for reducing anxiety. Rose quartz promotes self-love and compassion, fostering emotional resilience. Clear quartz amplifies our intentions, making our healing practices even more effective. Selenite clears away negative energy, creating space for peace and tranquility. Experiment with different crystals and find those that resonate most strongly with you.

Numerology can offer valuable insights into our life path and karmic lessons, helping us to understand the root causes of our fear and anxiety. Understanding our life path number, for instance, can reveal inherent strengths and challenges, providing context for the recurring patterns we might observe in our lives. Similarly, our birthdate and numerological chart can offer clues to our emotional tendencies and karmic patterns, aiding us in identifying and resolving underlying anxieties.

Astrology provides another lens through which we can gain deeper self-understanding. Our birth chart reveals the planetary influences that have shaped our personalities and emotional tendencies. By understanding these influences, we can gain greater self-awareness and develop strategies for managing our emotional responses. For instance, understanding planetary transits can help us prepare for potential periods of heightened anxiety or stress. This knowledge allows for pro-active measures to mitigate these challenges.

Remember that overcoming fear and anxiety is a journey, not a destination. There will be ups and downs, moments of progress, and moments of relapse. Be patient and kind to yourself, celebrating every step forward. Utilize the tools and techniques discussed in this chapter consistently, and remember that you are not alone in this journey. The universe is always supporting you, guiding you towards greater peace, resilience, and self-acceptance. Embrace this process with courage, self-compassion, and the unwavering belief in your inherent ability to heal and thrive. The path to inner peace is a journey of self-discovery, and the rewards of emotional freedom are immeasurable.Resilience isn't about never falling; it's about getting back up, stronger and wiser each time. Life, in its beautiful, chaotic dance, will inevitably throw curveballs. The unexpected job loss, the sudden illness, the shattered relationship – these are not personal failures, but rather opportunities for growth, for unveiling hidden strengths we never knew we possessed. The ability to adapt, to recalibrate, to find new pathways when the old ones crumble, is a skill as vital as breathing, as essential as the sun's warmth to a flower.

Cultivating resilience starts with self-awareness. Understand your emotional landscape. What triggers your anxieties? What patterns emerge when faced with adversity? Journaling remains a potent ally in this process. Don't simply list the events; delve into the emotions they evoked. What beliefs did these experiences challenge? What coping mechanisms did you employ (or fail to employ)? Honesty, even painful honesty, is the cornerstone of genuine self-understanding. This self-reflection illuminates your strengths and weaknesses, paving the way for targeted strategies.

Once you've identified your vulnerabilities, address them head-on. If stress triggers overeating, explore healthier coping mechanisms. Perhaps mindful eating practices, combined with regular exercise, could replace impulsive indulgence. If social isolation fuels depression, actively seek out connections. Join a club, volunteer for a cause you believe in, or simply reach out to a friend. Remember, connection is an antidote to isolation.

Embrace the power of positive self-talk. Our inner dialogue shapes our reality. Replace self-criticism with self-compassion. Instead of berating yourself for a setback, acknowledge the difficulty and affirm your ability to overcome it. Remember, setbacks are temporary; they do not define you. Use affirmations to reinforce this truth. Repeat phrases like, "I am strong," "I am resilient," "I am capable of overcoming this," until they seep into your subconscious. Building resilience also means developing a growth mindset. View challenges not as insurmountable obstacles, but as opportunities for learning and expansion. Each difficulty is a lesson in disguise, a chance to evolve, to hone your skills, and to refine your strategies. Instead of dwelling on the negative, focus on the lessons learned. What did you discover about yourself? What new skills did you acquire? What adjustments can you make in the future to navigate similar situations more effectively?

The chakra system provides a powerful framework for understanding and cultivating resilience. A balanced root chakra provides a strong foundation of security and stability, essential for navigating life's storms. Grounding practices, such as spending time in nature, practicing yoga, or utilizing grounding crystals like red jasper and hematite, reinforce this foundation. A healthy solar plexus chakra fosters self-confidence and empowers you to face challenges head-on. Affirmations of self-worth, setting clear boundaries, and using crystals like carnelian and citrine help to strengthen this vital energy center.

The heart chakra, the center of compassion and love, is crucial in times of adversity. Practicing self-compassion, extending kindness to yourself, and engaging in acts of kindness for others can help to build emotional resilience. Rose quartz, a crystal of unconditional love, is a powerful ally in opening and strengthening this chakra. The throat chakra, associated with clear communication and self-expression, allows you to voice your needs and concerns, vital for navigating challenges effectively. Crystals like blue kyanite and sodalite aid in overcoming communication blocks and fostering clear self-expression.

The third eye chakra, the center of intuition and wisdom, is critical for navigating life's complexities with greater clarity and insight. Meditation, spending time in quiet contemplation, and crystals such as amethyst and lapis lazuli help to enhance your intuition, guiding you towards wiser choices. Finally, the crown chakra, connected to spiritual understanding and acceptance, provides a broader perspective during times of adversity. Regular spiritual practices, such as meditation, prayer, and connection with nature, help to cultivate this sense of connection and acceptance, promoting inner peace and resilience. Numerology, with its insights into life paths and karmic lessons, offers a unique perspective on resilience. Understanding your life path number reveals inherent strengths and challenges, helping you anticipate and prepare for potential difficulties. Similarly, your birthdate and numerological chart can shed light on recurring patterns and karmic lessons, aiding in developing strategies to navigate challenges more effectively. By understanding the numerological blueprint of your life, you can develop a deeper understanding of your strengths and vulnerabilities.

Astrology provides another layer of understanding. Your birth chart reveals the planetary influences that shape your personality and emotional tendencies. This knowledge allows for a deeper understanding of your strengths and weaknesses, and how these tendencies might manifest during challenging times. Tracking planetary transits can help you anticipate periods of stress or challenge, enabling proactive strategies to mitigate potential difficulties. This allows you to navigate these periods with greater awareness and grace.

Incorporating crystals into your daily practice can significantly enhance your resilience. Crystals, with their inherent vibrational energies, amplify your intentions and support your efforts to heal and grow. Amethyst, known for its calming and soothing properties, can help to reduce stress and anxiety. Tiger's eye, a stone of strength and courage, empowers you to face challenges head-on. Carnelian, a stone of vitality and energy, boosts your motivation and drive. Experiment with different crystals and find those that resonate with you, creating a personalized toolkit to support your resilience journey.

Remember, developing resilience is not a one-time achievement; it's an ongoing process. It's about cultivating a mindset of strength, adaptability, and unwavering self-belief. Embrace the challenges, learn from setbacks, and celebrate your progress. Through mindful self-care, energetic alignment, and the support of these diverse holistic tools, you will not only survive life's storms, but emerge stronger, wiser, and more deeply connected to your inner strength and the boundless potential within. Your journey of self-discovery will empower you to face any obstacle with courage, compassion, and unshakeable resilience. **The path to inner strength is a lifelong journey of growth and transformation, leading to a life filled with purpose, peace, and unwavering self-belief.**

Chapter 10: Embracing Self-Compassion and Self-Love

Self-compassion, often misunderstood as mere self-indulgence, *is a profound act of self-love that fuels healing and fosters well-being on a deep, transformative level*. Unlike self-esteem, which fluctuates based on external validation and achievements, self-compassion is a constant, unwavering source of inner support. It's the ability to treat yourself with the same kindness, understanding, and patience you would offer a dear friend facing hardship. It's acknowledging your imperfections not with judgment, but with acceptance and a gentle nudge towards growth.

Imagine a friend confiding in you about a mistake they made, a failure they experienced. Would you berate them, criticize their flaws, and diminish their worth? Unlikely. Most likely, you'd offer empathy, understanding, and reassurance. You'd acknowledge their pain, validate their feelings, and encourage them to learn from the experience. Self-compassion mirrors this response; it's extending that same compassionate understanding to yourself.

The absence of self-compassion *creates a fertile ground for self-criticism*, leading to a vicious cycle of negativity that undermines your emotional well-being. This constant inner critic can manifest as harsh self-judgment, feelings of inadequacy, and a relentless pursuit of perfection —an impossible standard that leaves you perpetually feeling inadequate. This inner critic fuels anxiety, depression, and a profound sense of disconnect from your true self. It prevents you from celebrating your strengths and learning from your mistakes.

Cultivating self-compassion involves three core components**: self-kindness, common humanity, and mindfulness.** Self-kindness replaces self-criticism with understanding and self-acceptance. It acknowledges that everyone makes mistakes, experiences setbacks, and faces challenges. It's about recognizing your imperfections without labeling yourself as a failure. Instead of dwelling on your shortcomings, focus on your inherent worthiness, regardless of your mistakes.

Common humanity reminds us that suffering and imperfection are part of the shared human experience. We are not alone in our struggles; everyone, regardless of their outward appearance, grapples with difficulties, anxieties, and self-doubt. This understanding reduces feelings of isolation and shame, fostering a sense of connection and belonging. It helps to contextualize your struggles, reminding you that you are not alone in your pain and that your experience is a normal part of being human.

Mindfulness involves observing your thoughts and emotions without judgment. It's about recognizing self-critical thoughts without getting swept away by them. It's the ability to step back from the emotional storm, observe its intensity, and gently guide yourself toward a calmer state. This doesn't mean suppressing your emotions; rather, it involves acknowledging them with acceptance, without letting them dictate your self-worth. Mindfulness allows you to respond to difficult situations with greater clarity and self-compassion.

Developing self-compassion isn't an overnight transformation; it's a practice, a conscious choice to treat yourself with kindness and understanding, even (and especially) when you stumble. Start by paying attention to your inner dialogue. When you notice self-critical thoughts, gently challenge them. Ask yourself: "Would I say this to a friend?" If not, reframe your thoughts using kinder, more compassionate language.

For instance, instead of thinking, "I'm such a failure for not completing that project on time," try, "This project was challenging, and I learned valuable lessons from the experience. I'll adjust my approach next time." This subtle shift in language can significantly impact your emotional state. Replace self-judgment with self-acceptance, acknowledging your struggles without diminishing your self-worth.

Practice self-compassionate actions. Engage in activities that bring you joy and nourish your soul. Take breaks, prioritize self-care, and forgive yourself for your imperfections. These actions are not self-indulgent; they are acts of self-love, essential for healing and well-being.

Just as you'd encourage a friend to rest and recover after a setback, extend that same compassion to yourself. Acknowledge your efforts, celebrate your small victories, and show yourself gratitude for all you do.

Visualize a compassionate figure—a teacher, a loved one, or a spiritual guide—offering you unconditional support and understanding. Imagine their gentle words of encouragement, their unwavering belief in your strength and resilience. Internalize their compassion, allowing it to permeate your being, transforming your self-perception and fostering a deeper sense of self-acceptance. This visualization can be a powerful tool for cultivating self-compassion during challenging moments.

Engage in self-compassionate journaling. Reflect on your experiences and challenges, writing as if you were offering advice to a close friend facing similar difficulties. This exercise helps to distance yourself from your self-critical thoughts, allowing you to approach your situation with greater objectivity and compassion. Note the emotional patterns that emerge, and identify areas where you may be overly critical of yourself. Focus on the lessons learned, rather than dwelling on your mistakes.

Incorporate self-compassion into your daily routine. Start your day with affirmations that reinforce your self-worth. Repeat phrases like, "I am worthy of love and compassion," "I am capable of overcoming challenges," "I am kind to myself," until these words become deeply ingrained in your subconscious mind. Use these affirmations throughout the day whenever self-criticism arises, reminding yourself of your inherent worthiness and resilience.
The chakra system offers a powerful framework for understanding and cultivating self-compassion. The heart chakra, the center of compassion and love, is particularly relevant. When this chakra is open and balanced, you're naturally more inclined towards self-compassion. Practice heart-opening exercises like yoga poses that expand the chest, meditation focused on cultivating loving-kindness, and spending time in nature. Using rose quartz, the crystal of unconditional love, can further enhance the energy flow within the heart

chakra, promoting feelings of self-love and acceptance.

Self-compassion is not about complacency or avoiding responsibility. It's about *acknowledging your imperfections without letting them define you.* It's about learning from your mistakes, accepting your shortcomings, and treating yourself with the same kindness and understanding you'd offer to someone you care about. It's a journey of self-discovery, of embracing your humanity, and of recognizing the boundless potential for growth and healing within you. By cultivating self-compassion, you unlock a wellspring of inner strength, resilience, and unwavering self-belief. You'll navigate life's challenges not with fear and self-doubt, but with compassion, understanding, and the unwavering conviction that you are worthy of your own kindness and love. This, in turn, will empower you to create a life of purpose, joy, and profound fulfillment. The journey towards self-compassion often begins with a confrontation — a direct engagement with the relentless voice of self-criticism that whispers doubts and insecurities into our minds. This inner critic, a product of past experiences, societal pressures, and ingrained beliefs, can feel like an insurmountable obstacle. But it's crucial to remember that this voice is not your true self; it's a conditioned response, a habit of thought that can be unlearned and replaced with a more nurturing inner dialogue.

Identifying this negative self-talk is the first step. Pay close attention to the language you use internally. Are you constantly judging yourself, focusing on your flaws and shortcomings? Do you employ harsh, absolute terms like "always" and "never"? Do you compare yourself relentlessly to others, magnifying their perceived strengths while minimizing your own? Listen for the patterns, the recurring themes of self-deprecation that permeate your thoughts. Keep a journal dedicated to this internal dialogue, noting down these critical thoughts whenever they surface. You'll likely be surprised by the sheer volume and intensity of the negativity you uncover. This awareness is empowering because it brings the unseen critic into the light, making it easier to challenge its pronouncements.

Once you've identified the patterns, you can begin the *process of reframing*. This isn't about denying your mistakes or ignoring your shortcomings; it's about shifting your perspective, changing the lens through which you view yourself. Instead of focusing on failure, acknowledge the lessons learned from the experience. Instead of dwelling on your perceived inadequacies, celebrate your strengths and accomplishments, no matter how small. Practice gratitude for the positive aspects of your life, your capabilities, and your resilience.

A powerful technique for reframing involves the "**cognitive restructuring**" method. This involves *consciously challenging the validity of negative thoughts*. When a critical thought arises, ask yourself: Is this thought truly accurate? Is there another way to interpret this situation? What would I say to a friend in a similar situation? Often, the answers will reveal the irrationality and negativity of your initial thought. For instance, if you find yourself thinking, "I'm a complete failure because I missed that deadline," challenge that thought. Ask yourself: Is missing a deadline truly indicative of my entire worth as a person? Are there mitigating circumstances? What steps can I take to prevent this from happening again? Furthermore, consider the source of these critical thoughts. Are they echoes of past criticisms from significant figures in your life? Are they rooted in societal expectations and unrealistic beauty standards? Identifying the origin of these negative voices can help you understand and ultimately dismantle them. These critical voices often stem from a deep-seated fear of inadequacy, a fear of not measuring up to perceived expectations. Understanding this underlying fear allows you to address it with compassion and self-acceptance.

Alongside cognitive restructuring, affirmations can be powerful tools for cultivating a more positive and compassionate inner dialogue. These are positive statements that reinforce your self-worth and challenge negative beliefs. Start your day with affirmations such as, "I am worthy of love and respect," "I am capable and strong," "I embrace my imperfections," "I am enough." Repeat these affirmations throughout the day, especially when self-criticism arises. The regular repetition of these positive statements helps to reprogram your subconscious mind, gradually replacing negative thoughts with more constructive and empowering ones. Visualization can also be a very effective method. Imagine yourself as a loving, supportive friend guiding your inner child through challenging moments. See yourself offering kindness, patience, and understanding to this younger version of yourself. Visualize this supportive figure validating your feelings and reassuring you of your inherent worth. This mental imagery can create a profound shift in your self-perception, gradually replacing self-criticism with a more compassionate response. Similarly, visualize a radiant, positive energy emanating from your heart chakra, dispelling negativity and filling you with a sense of self-love and acceptance.

The practice of self-compassion extends beyond internal dialogue. It's also about making conscious choices that prioritize your well-being. This could involve setting healthy boundaries, saying no to requests that drain your energy, and engaging in activities that bring you joy and a sense of accomplishment. Self-care isn't selfish; it's an essential act of self-love that fuels your capacity for self-compassion. Make time for activities that nourish your mind, body, and spirit, such as spending time in nature, pursuing hobbies, practicing yoga or meditation, or simply enjoying moments of quiet reflection.

Another powerful technique is self-compassionate journaling. Write down the negative self-talk you experience. Once you have it on paper, you can then systematically challenge and reframe each negative thought. Ask yourself: What evidence do I have to support this negative belief? What is another way of looking at this situation? What would a compassionate friend say to me? Journaling allows you to externalize these internal struggles, creating a space to process them with greater clarity and objectivity. It also allows you to track your progress and celebrate your successes, reminding you that you are on a journey of continuous growth and transformation.

Numerology can also add a layer of self-understanding. Your life path number, calculated from your birthdate, can offer insight into your innate strengths and challenges. Understanding these inherent tendencies can help you develop self-compassion in areas where you might naturally struggle. For example, if your life path number suggests a tendency toward self-criticism, you can actively work on incorporating self-compassionate practices into your daily routine. Similarly, understanding your numerological profile can provide clarity and perspective, helping you navigate challenges with more empathy and understanding for yourself.

Astrology can also contribute. Your astrological birth chart provides a map of your personality, strengths, and challenges. Understanding your planetary placements can illuminate underlying patterns of self-criticism and offer insights into strategies for cultivating self-compassion. For example, if you have strong placements in critical signs, you may naturally be more inclined toward self-judgment. Recognizing this tendency allows you to develop targeted techniques to counteract this pattern, cultivating a more compassionate and forgiving relationship with yourself.

Crystal healing provides another avenue for promoting self-compassion. Crystals are believed to amplify intentions and facilitate energy flow. Rose quartz, the quintessential crystal of unconditional love, can be a powerful tool for opening the heart chakra, the center of compassion and self-love. Holding or meditating with rose quartz can help facilitate feelings of self-acceptance and encourage a more nurturing inner dialogue. Other crystals like amethyst, known for its calming and soothing properties, can also be beneficial in reducing stress and anxiety, which often fuel self-criticism.

Remember, challenging self-criticism is not a one-time fix; *it's an ongoing process of self-discovery and self-acceptance.* Be patient and kind to yourself along the way. Celebrate your progress, however small, and remember that even setbacks are opportunities for growth and learning. By consistently applying these techniques and embracing self-compassion as a daily practice, you will steadily transform your inner dialogue, fostering a more loving and accepting relationship with yourself. This, in turn, will empower you to live a more fulfilling and joyful life.The path to self-compassion is paved with the stones of self-forgiveness and self-acceptance. These aren't mere platitudes; they are active, ongoing practices that require conscious effort and unwavering commitment. For many, the hurdle of self-forgiveness feels insurmountable. The weight of past mistakes, perceived failures, and regrettable actions can feel like an anchor dragging them down, preventing them from moving forward with lightness and joy. But self-forgiveness is not about condoning harmful behaviors or neglecting accountability. It's about recognizing that everyone makes mistakes, that we are all works in progress, and that our past actions do not define our inherent worth.

Imagine your past self as a younger, less experienced version of you, navigating life with the limited knowledge and understanding they possessed at the time. Would you judge that younger self with the harshness and criticism you might reserve for your present self? Likely not. You would likely offer understanding, compassion, and a gentle reminder that everyone makes mistakes along the way. Extend that same compassion to your present self. Acknowledge your past missteps without dwelling on them, learn from them, and move forward with a renewed sense of purpose and self-compassion.

One effective method for practicing self-forgiveness is through journaling. Instead of focusing on blame or self-recrimination, write about your past mistakes with empathy and understanding. Describe the situation, the emotions you experienced, and the lessons you learned. Acknowledge the impact of your actions on yourself and others, but avoid self-flagellation. Focus on growth and healing. For example, if you made a hurtful remark to a friend, acknowledge the pain you caused, express regret, and commit to making amends and communicating more thoughtfully in the future. The act of writing it out allows you to process your feelings and gain a new perspective. It transforms the internal turmoil into a structured, manageable process.

Another helpful tool is the practice of mindful self-compassion. This involves actively cultivating kindness and understanding towards yourself, particularly during challenging moments. When faced with self-criticism or negative self-talk, pause and take a few deep breaths. Imagine yourself offering comfort and reassurance to a loved one facing a similar situation. Then, extend that same compassion to yourself. Speak to yourself with gentleness and understanding, acknowledging your pain and validating your emotions. This technique isn't about ignoring your mistakes or pretending they didn't happen; it's about approaching them with a gentler, more compassionate approach.

Self-acceptance is intricately intertwined with self-forgiveness. It involves acknowledging and embracing all aspects of yourself – your strengths, weaknesses, flaws, and imperfections. This doesn't mean you passively accept unhealthy behaviors or self-destructive patterns. Instead, it's about recognizing that you are a multifaceted individual, with a unique blend of qualities, both positive and negative. It's about accepting your imperfections not as failures, but as integral parts of your unique human experience.

One way to cultivate self-acceptance is to identify and challenge your negative self-beliefs. Often, these beliefs are deeply ingrained and stem from past experiences, societal pressures, or harsh self-criticism. Through self-reflection and mindfulness, you can begin to identify these negative patterns and challenge their validity. For example, if you believe you're inherently flawed or unworthy of love, ask yourself where this belief originates. What experiences shaped this belief? Is it truly an accurate representation of who you are? Often, you'll discover that these beliefs are rooted in unfounded assumptions or past hurts that no longer serve you.

A powerful technique for challenging negative self-beliefs is the use of affirmations. These are positive statements that reprogram your subconscious mind and reinforce your self-worth. Choose affirmations that address your specific negative self-beliefs. For example, if you struggle with self-doubt, you might use affirmations like, "I am capable and confident," "I trust my abilities," or "I believe in my potential." Repeat these affirmations daily, visualizing yourself embodying these qualities. The repetition reinforces positive beliefs and gradually replaces negative ones.

The energy healing modalities can also be invaluable aids in cultivating self-acceptance and forgiveness. Reiki, for example, can help to cleanse and balance your energy field, releasing stagnant energy associated with past hurts and negative emotions. The gentle, healing energy of Reiki can promote a sense of peace, calm, and self-acceptance. Visualizing Reiki energy flowing through your heart chakra, the center of compassion and self-love, can be particularly powerful in facilitating self-forgiveness and acceptance.

Numerology offers another perspective. Your life path number provides insights into your inherent strengths and challenges. Understanding your numerological profile can help you approach your self-acceptance journey with greater empathy and self-understanding. For instance, if your numerology suggests a tendency toward self-criticism, you can actively work on incorporating practices that counter this pattern. You might focus on self-compassion exercises, mindfulness techniques, or practices that nurture self-love.

Astrology can also shed light on your journey toward self-acceptance. Your birth chart reveals innate personality traits and patterns. Understanding your planetary placements can help you recognize areas where you may be overly critical of yourself and develop strategies for cultivating self-compassion. For example, a prominent Saturn placement might indicate a tendency toward self-doubt and perfectionism. Understanding this inherent tendency allows you to approach these challenges with increased self-awareness and compassion.

Crystal healing works in tandem with these other modalities. Crystals amplify intentions and energy flow. Rose quartz, the crystal of unconditional love, is excellent for opening the heart chakra, fostering self-love, and encouraging self-acceptance and forgiveness. Amethyst, known for its calming energy, can alleviate stress and anxiety, which often fuel self-criticism. Combining crystal healing with other self-compassion practices enhances the healing process. Remember, the journey toward self-forgiveness and self-acceptance is a process, not a destination. There will be days when self-criticism resurfaces, when old wounds reopen. But each time you gently guide yourself back to self-compassion, you strengthen your ability to embrace your imperfections and forgive yourself. Be patient, kind, and understanding toward yourself. Celebrate every step you take toward self-love, and remember that your inherent worth is not diminished by your past mistakes. You are worthy of love, compassion, and acceptance, just as you are. By embracing self-forgiveness and self-acceptance, you open yourself to a deeper sense of peace, joy, and fulfillment.Building a solid foundation of self-esteem and self-worth is crucial to the journey of self-love and compassion. It's about recognizing your inherent value, independent of external validation or achievements. This isn't about inflated ego or arrogance; instead, it's about cultivating a deep sense of self-respect and believing in your capabilities. This process requires active participation, self-reflection, and a willingness to challenge limiting beliefs.

One of the first steps in cultivating self-esteem is *identifying your strengths.* We often focus on our weaknesses, dwelling on our perceived flaws and shortcomings. However, shifting the focus to our strengths can be transformative. Take some time for quiet reflection. Consider your skills, talents, and positive attributes. What are you good at? What do you enjoy doing? What are you proud of accomplishing? Write these down; create a list you can refer to whenever self-doubt creeps in. This isn't about boasting; it's about acknowledging your inherent capabilities and celebrating your unique gifts.

For example, perhaps you excel at problem-solving, are a compassionate listener, or have a knack for creative writing. These are not trivial attributes; they are valuable assets that contribute to your overall worth. Acknowledge them, celebrate them, and use them to build your self-confidence. The more you recognize and utilize your strengths, the more confident and self-assured you will become.

Another vital component of building self-esteem is *celebrating your achievements, both big and small.* We often undervalue our accomplishments, dismissing them as insignificant or simply "luck." However, every achievement, no matter how small, is a testament to your efforts, dedication, and perseverance. Take time to acknowledge your successes, no matter how minor they may seem. Did you finally finish that project you'd been putting off? Did you overcome a personal challenge? Did you show kindness to someone in need? These are all achievements worth celebrating.

Keep a journal dedicated to your accomplishments. Write down your successes, big or small, and reflect on the effort and perseverance required to achieve them. This practice will reinforce your sense of accomplishment and build your self-esteem over time. Celebrating your successes not only boosts your confidence but also motivates you to continue striving for your goals. It creates a positive feedback loop, encouraging further growth and achievement. Setting realistic and achievable goals is equally important in building self-esteem. Setting overly ambitious goals can lead to disappointment and frustration, eroding your self-confidence. Start with small, manageable goals that you can realistically achieve. As you achieve these goals, you'll build momentum, creating a sense of accomplishment and self-efficacy. As your confidence grows, you can gradually increase the difficulty of your goals. Break down larger goals into smaller, more manageable steps. This approach prevents overwhelm and allows you to celebrate each small victory along the way.

For instance, if your goal is to write a novel, you might start with a smaller goal, like writing a chapter per week. Or if your goal is to improve your fitness, you might start with a daily walk, gradually increasing the duration and intensity of your workouts. The key is to celebrate each milestone, reinforcing your belief in your ability to achieve your goals.

Self-acceptance, as discussed earlier, is intrinsically linked to self-esteem. Without accepting your imperfections and flaws, it's difficult to truly believe in your worth. Self-acceptance doesn't mean ignoring areas for improvement. It means recognizing that you are a complex individual with both strengths and weaknesses, and that your imperfections are part of what makes you unique. Embrace your quirks, your vulnerabilities, and your less-than-perfect qualities. They are part of your story, shaping your character and making you who you are. The practice of self-compassion is essential in cultivating self-esteem. Treat yourself with the same kindness, understanding, and forgiveness that you would offer a loved one. When faced with setbacks or failures, avoid self-criticism and instead offer yourself words of encouragement and support. Acknowledge your mistakes without dwelling on them; learn from them and move forward. Self-compassion is about recognizing your humanity and accepting that everyone makes mistakes.

The energy healing modalities discussed earlier can be instrumental in building self-esteem and self-worth. Reiki, for instance, can help release stagnant energy that may be blocking your self-acceptance and hindering your self-esteem. Focusing Reiki energy on your crown chakra, associated with connection to your higher self and spiritual awareness, can promote feelings of self-worth and confidence. Similarly, focusing on the solar plexus chakra, the seat of personal power, can empower you to believe in yourself and your abilities.

Numerology can provide further insight. Your numerological profile can reveal your inherent strengths and potential challenges related to self-esteem. For example, if your life path number suggests a tendency toward self-doubt, you can develop strategies to counter this pattern. This could involve focusing on affirmations, visualization exercises, or practicing self-compassion techniques. By understanding your numerological predispositions, you can approach your self-esteem journey with increased self-awareness and targeted strategies. Astrology also offers a valuable perspective. Your birth chart highlights personality traits and potential challenges related to self-worth. Understanding your planetary placements can guide you in identifying areas where you might struggle with self-esteem and develop strategies to build your confidence. For example, if you have a strong Saturn influence in your chart, you might have a tendency toward perfectionism or self-criticism. Recognizing this pattern allows you to develop coping mechanisms and build greater self-acceptance.

Crystal healing complements these modalities. Crystals can amplify intentions and energy flow. Citrine, the crystal of abundance and prosperity, can boost self-esteem and confidence by amplifying feelings of self-worth and empowerment. Tiger eye, known for its strength and courage, can help overcome self-doubt and promote self-belief. Using these crystals in conjunction with other self-esteem building practices can enhance the overall effectiveness of the process.

The journey toward cultivating self-esteem and self-worth is a *continuous process*, requiring consistent effort and self-reflection. There will be times when self-doubt resurfaces, when you question your capabilities or worth. But through consistent practice of self-compassion, setting realistic goals, celebrating achievements, and harnessing the power of energy healing modalities, you can build a strong foundation of self-esteem and self-love, paving the way for a more fulfilling and empowered life. Remember, your inherent worth is immeasurable, and your journey toward self-acceptance and self-love is a testament to your strength and resilience. Embrace the process, celebrate your progress, and continue to nurture your beautiful and unique self.Embracing self-compassion and self-love is a transformative journey, but it's not solely an internal process. It's deeply intertwined with how we nurture our physical and emotional well-being. Neglecting our physical and emotional needs creates a fertile ground for self-criticism and undermines our capacity for self-acceptance. Just as we wouldn't expect a plant to thrive without water and sunlight, we cannot expect to flourish emotionally and spiritually without tending to our fundamental needs.

The first step in nurturing these needs is *recognizing them*. Often, we are so busy attending to the demands of others – family, work, social obligations – that we forget to prioritize our own well-being. We push ourselves to the brink of exhaustion, ignoring warning signs of burnout and neglecting our physical and emotional health. This leads to a vicious cycle: exhaustion fuels self-criticism, self-criticism fuels more neglect, and the cycle continues, leaving us feeling depleted and disconnected from ourselves.

Let's start with the physical. Our bodies are incredible vessels, capable of incredible things. But they require proper nourishment, rest, and movement to function optimally. This isn't about achieving some unattainable ideal of perfection; it's about showing respect for your body and recognizing its needs. Are you getting enough sleep? Most adults need 7-9 hours of quality sleep each night. Chronic sleep deprivation has a detrimental impact on mood, cognitive function, and overall well-being, making self-compassion significantly harder. If you struggle with sleep, explore techniques like mindfulness meditation before bed, creating a relaxing bedtime routine, or seeking professional help if necessary.

What about your diet? Are you nourishing your body with wholesome foods, providing it with the fuel it needs to function at its best? A diet rich in fruits, vegetables, and whole grains provides the essential vitamins and minerals for optimal health. Conversely, a diet high in processed foods, sugar, and unhealthy fats can leave you feeling sluggish, irritable, and prone to illness, which impacts your self-esteem negatively. This isn't about restrictive dieting; it's about making conscious choices to support your physical well-being. Small changes, like swapping sugary drinks for water, adding more vegetables to your meals, or choosing whole grains over refined carbohydrates, can have a profound impact on how you feel both physically and emotionally.

Movement is another crucial aspect of physical self-care. Regular physical activity not only improves physical health but also releases endorphins, which have mood-boosting effects. You don't need to become a marathon runner; even short bursts of activity, such as a brisk walk, a yoga session, or a dance class, can make a difference. Find an activity you enjoy and incorporate it into your routine. The key is consistency, even if it's just for 15-20 minutes a day. This could be as simple as taking a walk during your lunch break, climbing stairs instead of using an elevator, or doing some stretching exercises at home. Remember, the goal is not to punish your body but to nourish and celebrate it.

Now let's turn to the emotional. Emotional well-being is just as crucial as physical well-being. Our emotions are powerful forces that shape our thoughts, behaviors, and overall experiences. Ignoring or suppressing our emotions can lead to stress, anxiety, and depression. Creating space for emotional self-care allows you to process and understand your emotions, fostering greater self-awareness and self-acceptance. Start by identifying your emotional triggers. What situations, people, or thoughts evoke strong emotional responses in you? Once you understand your triggers, you can develop strategies for managing your emotional responses.

Mindfulness practices, such as meditation and deep breathing exercises, are valuable tools for managing emotions. These techniques help you to become more aware of your emotions without judgment, allowing you to observe them without getting carried away by them. Mindfulness allows you to create a space between the stimulus and your emotional response, offering you a chance to choose how you respond rather than reacting impulsively. Even a few minutes of meditation each day can have a profoundly calming effect, reducing stress and promoting emotional balance.

Journaling is another powerful tool for emotional self-care. Writing down your thoughts and feelings can help you process them, gain clarity, and identify patterns in your emotional experiences. It allows you to externalize your internal world, providing a sense of release and perspective. It's not about writing perfectly formed sentences or creating a masterpiece; it's about expressing what's inside you, without judgment.

Connecting with others who support you is crucial. Building strong relationships with friends, family, or a supportive community fosters a sense of belonging and reduces feelings of isolation. It's vital to nurture these relationships, actively participating and investing in them. However, it is just as important to recognize when relationships are detrimental to your well-being. Learning to set healthy boundaries, and walking away from toxic connections, is a fundamental act of self-love.

Creative expression is another form of emotional self-care. Engaging in creative activities, such as painting, drawing, writing, music, or dance, provides an outlet for self-expression and emotional release. It's a way to channel energy, explore your feelings, and discover new aspects of yourself. These activities don't need to be masterpieces; the process itself is therapeutic. The act of creation allows for emotional processing and a deeper connection to oneself.

Setting boundaries is a critical aspect of self-care. It's about protecting your energy and time by saying no to requests or situations that drain you. It's about prioritizing your well-being and setting limits on what you're willing to tolerate. This may involve saying no to extra work projects, declining social invitations that don't align with your energy levels, or communicating your needs clearly to others. Setting boundaries empowers you to take control of your life, protect your emotional well-being, and foster respect from others.

Spending time in nature is also a powerful way to nurture both your physical and emotional well-being. Studies have shown that spending time outdoors reduces stress, improves mood, and boosts creativity. It connects you to something larger than yourself, reminding you of your place in the world, and fosters a sense of peace and tranquility. A simple walk in a park, a hike in the woods, or even sitting on your porch and observing nature can have a profound impact on your overall well-being.

Remember, self-care is not selfish; it's an act of self-love and respect. It's about prioritizing your well-being, both physical and emotional, so you can live a life that is fulfilling, meaningful, and aligned with your values. By nurturing your physical and emotional needs, you create a fertile ground for self-compassion to flourish, leading you on a path of greater self-acceptance and self-love. The journey is continuous, requiring consistent effort and self-awareness, but the rewards are immeasurable. The stronger and healthier you become, both physically and emotionally, the more capable you are of embracing the love and compassion you deserve.

Chapter 11: Setting Intentions and Goals

Defining your vision for the future is akin to charting a course across a starlit ocean. You have the compass of your values, the sails of your intentions, and the vast expanse of potential before you. But before you can set sail, you must first know your destination. What is the vision you hold for your life, not just in the immediate future, but in the years to come? This isn't about setting rigid expectations; it's about cultivating a clear and compelling image of what you want to create.

Begin by taking some quiet time for *reflection*. Find a peaceful space where you can be undisturbed. Light a candle, play some calming music, or simply sit in nature. Allow yourself to drift into a state of stillness, letting go of the daily anxieties and pressures that often cloud your vision. In this space of tranquility, begin to explore the deeper desires of your heart. What truly matters to you? What kind of life do you envision for yourself?

Consider all aspects of your being – your physical, emotional, mental, and spiritual well-being. What does a thriving, fulfilling life look like for you in each of these areas? Do you envision a life filled with adventure and travel? A life dedicated to creative pursuits? A life of service to others? Perhaps it's a harmonious blend of all these elements. There are no right or wrong answers; this is your personal vision, shaped by your unique values and aspirations. Once you have a sense of your overall vision, it's time to break it down into more manageable goals. Rather than striving for one grand aspiration, focus on smaller, more achievable steps. These goals should be SMART – Specific, Measurable, Achievable, Relevant, and Time-bound. For example, instead of saying "I want to be healthier," a SMART goal might be, "I will walk for 30 minutes three times a week for the next three months."

This process of breaking down your vision into smaller, achievable steps will make your journey feel less overwhelming and more empowering. It will provide you with a sense of accomplishment as you achieve each milestone, motivating you to continue moving towards your larger vision. Remember, consistency is key. Even small, consistent efforts will bring you closer to your desired outcome than sporadic bursts of intense activity.

Incorporate your understanding of energy work into your goal setting. Imagine your goals as seeds you are planting within your energy field. Visualize them taking root, growing strong, and blossoming into fruition. Use affirmations to reinforce your intentions, speaking them aloud with conviction and feeling. The power of positive affirmations, combined with the energy of intention, can significantly enhance your ability to manifest your goals. Consider the role of your chakras in this process. Each chakra represents a different aspect of your being, and aligning them can enhance your ability to manifest your goals. For example, if your goal is related to abundance, focus on your sacral chakra (located below the navel) and visualize its energy flowing freely. If your goal is related to creativity, focus on your solar plexus chakra (located above the navel) and visualize its energy radiating outward. By aligning your chakras and directing your energy toward your goals, you can create a powerful synergy that supports your intentions.

Crystals can also serve as powerful allies in your journey. Choose crystals that resonate with your goals and intentions. For example, citrine is associated with abundance and prosperity, amethyst with spiritual awareness and intuition, and carnelian with courage and creativity. Hold the chosen crystals during your meditation or visualization practices, allowing their energy to amplify your intentions.

Numerology can also shed light on the path toward your goals. Calculate your life path number, destiny number, and other relevant numerological aspects to understand your natural talents and potential challenges. This information can help you tailor your goals and strategies to align with your unique energetic blueprint.

Astrology can offer further insights into your journey. Consider your birth chart and the current planetary transits to understand the energetic influences affecting your life. This knowledge can help you time your actions strategically, taking advantage of periods of heightened energy and navigating potential obstacles with greater awareness.

Remember, the journey towards achieving your goals is not always a linear one. *There will be moments of challenge and setbacks.* Embrace these experiences as opportunities for growth and learning. Review your goals regularly, making adjustments as needed, and celebrate your successes along the way. Stay focused on your vision, and trust in the universe's support. Your commitment, combined with the power of intention, energy work, and the wisdom of ancient practices, will guide you towards creating the future you desire.

As you navigate this process, remember that your vision for the future is not static. It's a living, breathing entity that evolves and expands as you grow and learn. Be open to new possibilities and allow your vision to evolve alongside your personal growth. The journey of self-discovery is an ongoing one, and your vision for the future will continue to unfold with each step you take.

The process of defining your vision and setting intentions is not a solitary endeavor. Engage with a supportive community of like-minded individuals, sharing your progress, celebrating your successes, and seeking guidance when needed. Connect with others who share your values and inspire you to strive for your greatest potential. Their encouragement and support can make a significant difference in your journey.

Furthermore, remember to infuse this process with self-compassion and kindness. Do not judge yourself harshly if you falter or encounter obstacles. Acknowledge your efforts, learn from your mistakes, and continue to move forward with unwavering determination. The journey is as important as the destination, and the lessons you learn along the way will enrich your life immeasurably.

Consider creating a vision board to visually represent your aspirations. Gather images, quotes, and symbols that embody your vision for the future. Arrange them on a board and place it in a prominent location where you'll see it daily. This visual reminder will help keep your goals top-of-mind and reinforce your intentions. This act of creation itself can be a powerful form of self-expression and emotional processing, further solidifying your commitment to your vision.

Regularly revisit your vision board, reflecting on your progress and adjusting your goals as needed. This practice serves as a potent reminder of your aspirations, keeping you focused and motivated. Consider adding new elements to your board as your vision evolves and expands, reflecting the ongoing dynamic nature of your journey.

Finally, cultivate a deep sense of gratitude for all that you have already achieved. Acknowledging your past successes will help build your confidence and fuel your drive to achieve your future goals. This practice of gratitude enhances your positive energy, creating a more fertile ground for manifestation. By combining gratitude with intention, you create a powerful synergy that accelerates your progress toward realizing your dreams.

Remember that the universe is abundant, and there is more than enough for everyone to achieve their aspirations. Believe in your ability to manifest your desires, trust in the process, and celebrate each step of your journey toward the magnificent future you are creating. The path ahead may be winding and challenging, but with unwavering intention and self-belief, you can and will reach your desired destination. The journey is the reward, and the self-discovery and growth you experience along the way are gifts in themselves, far exceeding the mere attainment of your goals. Embrace the entire process with open arms and an open heart, and watch as your vision for the future blossoms into reality.Now that you've established a vibrant vision for your future, a luminous tapestry woven from your deepest desires and aspirations, it's time to bring it to life. This isn't simply about wishing upon a star; it's about translating that celestial vision into tangible, achievable steps. Think of your overarching vision as a magnificent mountain peak, breathtaking in its majesty. Reaching the summit requires not a single, Herculean leap, but a series of carefully planned ascents, each step building upon the last.

Let's begin by dissecting those grand aspirations into smaller, more manageable chunks. This is where the art of intention-setting meets practical action. Remember the SMART principle we discussed earlier? Specific, Measurable, Achievable, Relevant, and Time-bound. This framework is your scaffolding, providing structure and support as you build your path to success.

Let's illustrate this with some examples. Imagine your grand vision includes "achieving financial freedom." This is a broad goal, potentially overwhelming in its scope. Let's break it down:

Specific: Instead of "financial freedom," let's define it as "paying off my credit card debt and saving $10,000." This is much clearer and more focused.

Measurable: We can track progress weekly or monthly, noting the amount of debt paid and the amount saved. This provides concrete evidence of advancement.

Achievable: Based on your current income and expenses, is $10,000 achievable within a reasonable timeframe, say, a year? If not, adjust the amount accordingly. Remember, progress, not perfection, is the key here.

Relevant: Does this goal align with your overall vision and values? If financial freedom is truly a core element of your ideal life, then the answer is yes.

Time-bound: Set a deadline. Instead of an open-ended timeframe, aim for a specific date— for instance, to achieve your $10,000 savings and debt elimination goal by December 31st, 2024.

Now, let's break this down further into actionable steps:

1. **Create a detailed budget:** Track all income and expenses meticulously. This is crucial for identifying areas where you can cut back and reallocate funds.

2. **Identify areas for reduction:** Where can you trim expenses? Can you reduce dining out, subscriptions, or entertainment costs? Every small saving adds up.

3. **Explore additional income streams:** Can you take on freelance work, sell unused items, or invest in a side hustle? Supplementing your income significantly accelerates your progress.

4. **Automate savings:** Set up automatic transfers from your checking account to your savings account each pay period. This ensures consistent savings without requiring constant willpower.

5. **Review and adjust monthly:** Regularly assess your progress, celebrating your milestones and adjusting your strategy as needed. Life throws curveballs; flexibility is key.

Let's consider another example: "Improving my physical health." This expansive vision also requires a structured approach.

Specific: Instead of "improving health," aim for "losing 15 pounds and running a 5k." Concrete goals provide clear direction.

Measurable: Track your weight weekly and monitor your running progress, perhaps using a fitness tracker.

Achievable: Is losing 15 pounds and running a 5k within a reasonable timeframe, say, six months? Adjust as needed to make it achievable for your current fitness level.

Relevant: Does this goal align with your vision of a healthier, more energetic you?

Time-bound: Set a deadline for achieving your weight loss and running goal, perhaps by the end of summer.

Actionable steps might include:

1. **Consult a healthcare professional:** Get a personalized fitness plan, ensuring your approach is safe and effective.
2. **Create a balanced meal plan:** Focus on nutrient-rich foods, prioritizing whole grains, fruits, vegetables, and lean proteins.
3. **Establish a consistent workout routine:** Include both cardiovascular and strength training exercises in your schedule.
4. **Track your progress:** Monitor your weight, running time, and overall fitness level.
5. **Find an exercise buddy:** Enlist support to enhance motivation and accountability.

Now, let's integrate the energy work principles we've discussed. Visualize the energy flowing freely through your chakras as you take each step. Imagine your sacral chakra, the center of abundance, actively supporting your financial goals. Visualize the energy of your root chakra, grounding you and providing stability as you build a healthier lifestyle. Use affirmations: "I am abundantly wealthy," "I am healthy and strong," repeating them with conviction. Select crystals that resonate with your intentions – citrine for abundance, amethyst for clarity, carnelian for energy and vitality. Hold them while meditating on your goals.

Your numerology and astrological charts can provide further insight. Understanding your life path number and current planetary transits can inform your strategic timing, identifying periods when your efforts are most likely to bear fruit. Are there astrological aspects supporting creativity when pursuing your artistic ambitions? Does your numerology suggest specific periods of increased financial opportunity? Use these insights to refine your planning and maximize your chances of success.

Remember, setbacks are inevitable. Treat them not as failures but as valuable learning opportunities. Adjust your strategy, reaffirm your intentions, and continue moving forward. This is a journey of growth, and the lessons learned along the way are just as important as the destination. Celebrate your achievements, no matter how small, and maintain a positive, grateful attitude. The universe conspires with those who actively create their dreams. Trust in your abilities, trust in the process, and watch as your vision unfolds, a vibrant masterpiece painted stroke by stroke, step by step. The journey itself is a testament to your dedication and strength, and the rewards — both tangible and intangible — will far exceed your initial expectations. Embrace the journey, and the summit will inevitably be yours. The path to manifesting our deepest desires is rarely a straight line. Obstacles, detours, and unexpected roadblocks are as much a part of the journey as the triumphs and celebrations. Embracing this reality, understanding the nature of these challenges, and equipping ourselves with the tools to navigate them is crucial for maintaining momentum and ultimately achieving our goals. Let's explore some common obstacles and develop strategies for overcoming them.

One of the most significant hurdles is *self-doubt*. That insidious voice whispering negativity, questioning our abilities, and planting seeds of fear. This inner critic can manifest in various ways, from procrastination and avoidance to outright self-sabotage. Recognizing this inner voice as a separate entity, not the true reflection of your capabilities, is the first step. Challenge its pronouncements. Instead of accepting its limiting beliefs, counter them with affirmations and positive self-talk. Remember past successes, however small, and acknowledge your inherent strength and resilience. Journaling can be an invaluable tool here; writing down your fears and then reframing them into positive statements can significantly shift your perspective.

Another significant obstacle is a *lack of clarity*. While we've discussed setting SMART goals, maintaining unwavering clarity throughout the process is essential. Life's complexities can easily cloud our vision, causing us to stray from our intended path. Regularly review your intentions. Reconnect with the emotional energy that initially fueled your desires. Meditate on your goals, visualizing their realization and feeling the associated joy and satisfaction. The act of revisiting your goals, reinforcing their significance, strengthens your resolve and keeps you focused amidst life's distractions. Utilize your crystals for this; hold your intention-setting stones, grounding yourself in their energy, and re-center your mind on your aspirations.

External factors also play a significant role. Unexpected life events, from illness to financial setbacks, can disrupt even the most meticulously planned trajectory. Learning to adapt and adjust is crucial. Flexibility, not rigidity, is the hallmark of a successful manifestation journey. When faced with unexpected challenges, view them not as roadblocks but as opportunities for recalibration. Re-evaluate your goals, making adjustments as needed to align with your new circumstances. Remember, the journey is as much about growth and adaptation as it is about achieving the specific outcome.

Maintaining motivation over an extended period is another common challenge. Initial enthusiasm can wane as the journey progresses. That is why building a strong support system is paramount. Surround yourself with positive, like-minded individuals who encourage and uplift you. This could be a group of friends, family members, or a supportive community. Sharing your goals and challenges with others can provide valuable insights, encouragement, and accountability. Consider finding a mentor or coach who can offer guidance and support, helping you navigate obstacles and stay focused.

Accountability partners can provide structured support. Regular check-ins, sharing your progress, and discussing challenges can keep you motivated and on track. The act of reporting your achievements, however small, provides a sense of accomplishment and strengthens your commitment. Celebrating milestones, no matter how insignificant they may seem, is essential to maintain positive momentum. Acknowledge your progress and appreciate your efforts. This positive reinforcement strengthens your belief in your ability to achieve your goals. Setbacks are inevitable; they are not failures but valuable learning opportunities. They provide insights into areas that need improvement and adjustment. Don't let setbacks derail your entire plan. Instead, use them as feedback. Analyze what went wrong, identify areas for improvement, and adjust your strategy accordingly. Maintaining a positive attitude throughout this process is crucial. Focus on your strengths, embrace your resilience, and remember that progress, not perfection, is the key.

Numerology can offer valuable insights into periods of heightened energy and opportunity. Understanding your life path number and the numerological vibrations surrounding your goals can help you identify opportune moments for action and periods when it's wise to conserve your energy. Astrology, too, can reveal auspicious times for initiating new projects or tackling challenging aspects of your goals. By paying attention to these celestial cues, you can synchronize your actions with the universe's natural rhythms, enhancing the likelihood of success.

The chakra system provides a powerful framework for understanding and managing the energetic aspects of goal attainment. Visualize the energy flowing smoothly through your chakras as you work towards your objectives. For instance, a clear throat chakra is essential for confident communication and effective action, while a strong solar plexus chakra fosters self-assurance and determination. Work on balancing and strengthening your chakras through meditation, visualization, and energy healing practices like Reiki. Crystal healing can also be incorporated; specific crystals can enhance the energy of particular chakras, thereby supporting your goal-achieving efforts. Amethyst promotes clarity, while carnelian boosts energy and vitality. Citrine enhances abundance, and green aventurine supports growth and prosperity.

Affirmations are potent tools for reinforcing positive beliefs and overcoming limiting thoughts. Repeat positive statements that align with your goals, such as "I am confident and capable," "I am attracting abundance into my life," or "I am making consistent progress toward my goals." Say these affirmations aloud, visualize the embodiment of these qualities, and feel the energy shift within you. Repeat them daily, embedding them into your subconscious mind and paving the way for positive change.

Remember, the path to achieving your intentions is a journey of self-discovery and growth. It's not always easy, but it is always rewarding. By embracing the challenges, learning from setbacks, and cultivating a supportive environment, you can maintain your motivation and achieve your goals with grace and resilience. The universe is abundant and supportive, ready to assist you in manifesting your heart's desires. Trust in the process, trust in yourself, and watch your visions unfold. The journey itself is a testament to your strength, and the ultimate reward is not merely the achievement of your goals, but the profound personal growth you experience along the way. This transformative journey will leave you stronger, wiser, and more deeply connected to your own inner power and the boundless potential of the universe.Measuring progress isn't simply about ticking off boxes on a to-do list; it's about understanding the subtle shifts in your energy, the deepening of your connection to your intentions, and the evolving wisdom gained along the way. This holistic approach requires a multi-faceted assessment, going beyond the purely material to encompass the energetic and spiritual dimensions of your journey.

One effective method is to maintain a detailed journal. Don't just record your daily activities; delve into the emotional landscape of your experience. Note down the moments of doubt, the surges of inspiration, the challenges overcome, and the small victories celebrated. This detailed record serves as a living testament to your progress, allowing you to see the patterns and trends that might otherwise go unnoticed. Consider incorporating your numerological insights into your journaling. Note the numerological significance of dates related to key milestones or challenges, perhaps revealing hidden synchronicities and guiding your understanding of energetic flows.

Beyond the written word, consider incorporating visual representations of your progress. Create a vision board, a physical manifestation of your goals, incorporating images, quotes, and symbols that resonate with your aspirations. As you progress, add new elements to the board, visually representing your achievements and reaffirming your commitment. Alternatively, you could create a progress chart, tracking your daily or weekly progress in a visual format. This offers a tangible representation of your journey, making your accomplishments more visible and rewarding.

Remember the power of introspection. Regular meditation sessions can provide valuable insights into your progress. As you quiet your mind, pay attention to the subtle shifts in your energy and emotional state. Notice any resistance or blockages that might be hindering your progress. Use this time to reconnect with your intentions, reaffirming your commitment and re-energizing your focus. Incorporate crystal healing into your meditation practice. Hold a clear quartz crystal, known for its amplification properties, to enhance your clarity and connection to your higher self, allowing you to more readily discern any obstacles or areas needing attention.

Another powerful tool is self-assessment through the lens of your chakras. Are you feeling grounded and stable (root chakra)? Are you experiencing creativity and passion (sacral chakra)? Is your self-esteem flourishing (solar plexus chakra)? Is your communication clear and assertive (throat chakra)? Is your connection to your intuition strong (third eye chakra)? Is your connection to the divine effortless (crown chakra)? Any imbalances or blockages in your chakras might be indicative of areas needing attention in your pursuit of your goals. Address these imbalances through specific chakra balancing exercises, such as yoga, meditation, or energy healing practices. Remember to utilize corresponding chakra stones to support your efforts. For instance, red jasper for grounding, carnelian for passion, and lapis lazuli for communication.

Engage in regular self-reflection by asking yourself key questions: What progress have I made? What obstacles have I encountered? What adjustments are necessary? What lessons have I learned? Honesty and self-compassion are essential in this process. Don't judge yourself harshly for setbacks; view them as opportunities for growth and learning. Each challenge overcome strengthens your resilience and deepens your understanding of yourself and your journey. Embrace the lessons, make necessary adjustments, and move forward with renewed determination.

Regularly review your goals, ensuring they still align with your current values and aspirations.

Life is fluid, and your goals may naturally evolve over time. Don't be afraid to adjust your goals or your approach as needed. Flexibility and adaptability are crucial attributes in navigating the complexities of life and achieving your intentions. Use astrology and numerology to guide your adjustments. Identify periods of heightened energy and opportunity, aligning your actions with the natural rhythms of the universe. Pay attention to astrological transits and planetary alignments that might impact your progress, and use numerological insights to understand the vibrational energy surrounding your goals.

Your support system plays a vital role in measuring progress and adjusting your approach. Share your progress and challenges with your accountability partners, friends, family, or mentor. Their feedback, encouragement, and insights can provide invaluable support and perspective. Celebrate milestones along the way, acknowledging both the large and small achievements. These celebrations reinforce your sense of accomplishment and maintain your motivation.

Consider incorporating regular Reiki sessions into your routine. Reiki promotes energetic balance and healing, supporting you in overcoming obstacles and maintaining a positive energy flow. A Reiki practitioner can also help you identify any energy blockages that may be hindering your progress, and they can assist in clearing these blockages to facilitate a smoother and more efficient journey toward your goals.

Adjustments are an integral part of the journey. Don't view adjustments as failures, but as opportunities for course correction. If you find yourself consistently facing obstacles in one area, re-evaluate your strategy. Consider breaking down larger goals into smaller, more manageable steps. This allows for a more gradual and less overwhelming approach, enabling you to celebrate frequent achievements and maintain a strong sense of accomplishment.

Pay close attention to your intuition. Your inner wisdom often provides guidance on when to adjust your approach or even your goals. Learn to trust your gut feelings, as these intuitive nudges often hold valuable clues about your journey's path. Practice mindfulness and meditation to strengthen your connection to your inner voice and enhance your intuitive abilities.

Remember, the journey is as significant as the destination. Embrace the process, learn from each experience, and celebrate your growth along the way. The journey itself is a testament to your strength, resilience, and unwavering commitment to your well-being. Trust in the universal flow and your innate ability to manifest your desires. The universe supports your journey, offering guidance and assistance along the way. Maintain a positive attitude, trust in your inner wisdom, and allow yourself to be guided by the ever-flowing currents of the cosmic healing code. Your journey is unique and powerful; embrace it fully.Celebrating successes, both big and small, is an essential component of a fulfilling journey towards self-healing and goal attainment. It's not simply about reaching the finish line; it's about savoring the journey and acknowledging the steps taken along the way. Each milestone, each hurdle cleared, is a testament to your commitment and resilience, deserving of recognition and celebration.

One powerful way to celebrate successes is through ritual. Create a personal ritual that marks your accomplishments. This could be as simple as lighting a candle and taking a moment of quiet reflection, expressing gratitude for your progress. It could also involve something more elaborate, like a celebratory bath infused with essential oils that resonate with your goals, perhaps lavender for relaxation or rosemary for invigoration. The key is to make the ritual personal and meaningful, reflecting your unique preferences and energy.

Consider the power of sound in celebrating your milestones. Chanting affirmations, playing uplifting music, or even simply humming a joyful tune can shift your energy and amplify your feelings of accomplishment. The vibrations of sound resonate deeply within your being, reinforcing feelings of joy and gratitude, and enhancing the overall positive impact of celebrating your successes. Experiment with different sounds and frequencies, finding what resonates most powerfully with your unique energetic signature.

Another rewarding way to celebrate is through acts of self-care. Treat yourself to something you enjoy—a massage, a relaxing soak in a bath, a delicious meal, or a quiet evening spent pursuing a hobby. Self-care is not a luxury; it's a necessity, particularly when navigating the transformative journey of self-healing. By nurturing yourself, you replenish your energy and reinforce your commitment to your well-being.

The visual representation of your accomplishments also holds significant power. Create a "success board," similar to a vision board but dedicated solely to celebrating your achievements. Include photos, notes, or mementos representing your milestones. This visual record serves as a powerful reminder of your progress, strengthening your sense of accomplishment and motivating you to continue moving forward.

Share your successes with your support system. Communicate your achievements with loved ones, friends, mentors, or accountability partners. Their joy in your success will amplify your own, creating a positive feedback loop that reinforces your motivation and commitment. Sharing your journey also allows others to benefit from your experiences and insights, strengthening the collective energy of support and growth.

Incorporate the principles of numerology into your celebrations. Calculate the numerological value of your accomplishments, reflecting on the vibrational energy associated with the resulting number. This can offer further insights into the significance of your achievements and their impact on your overall journey. For example, a number seven might signify introspection and spiritual growth, while a number eleven might represent intuition and spiritual awakening. Understanding the numerological significance of your accomplishments adds another layer of depth and meaning to your celebrations.

Astrology can also offer guidance in timing your celebrations. Identify astrologically auspicious periods for celebrating your achievements, aligning your celebrations with the natural energetic flow of the universe. This can further enhance the positive impact of your celebrations, creating a powerful synergy between your personal efforts and the cosmic energies at play.

Remember that acknowledging milestones isn't just about the big wins; it's also about celebrating the small victories along the way. These small achievements are often the building blocks of larger successes, and recognizing them reinforces your commitment and builds momentum. Acknowledge the small steps, the daily acts of self-care, the consistent effort, and the small breakthroughs—they all contribute to the bigger picture.

Engage in acts of gratitude. Express gratitude for your accomplishments and the lessons learned along the way. This practice shifts your focus to the positive aspects of your journey, fostering a sense of appreciation and reinforcing your motivation. Consider keeping a gratitude journal, specifically noting down the milestones and successes you've achieved, along with the lessons learned.

Consider creating a personalized reward system. Reward yourself for reaching specific milestones. This doesn't necessarily have to involve material rewards, though those can be effective motivators. Rewards could include extra self-care time, a special treat, or a fun activity. The key is to choose rewards that align with your values and preferences. Incorporate the use of crystals into your celebrations. Different crystals resonate with different energies. Choose crystals that align with your accomplishments and intentions, amplifying the positive energy and reinforcing your sense of accomplishment. For example, Citrine, known for its abundance and manifestation properties, can be used to celebrate financial achievements, while Amethyst, linked to spiritual growth and peace, might be suitable for celebrating milestones related to spiritual development.

Remember the importance of self-compassion. Don't get caught up in comparing your journey to others. Everyone's path is unique, and celebrating your own progress is crucial, regardless of external comparisons. Celebrate your achievements with kindness and self-acceptance, understanding that setbacks are a natural part of any transformative journey. Your celebrations should be authentic expressions of your joy and gratitude. Don't feel pressured to conform to any specific expectations. Let your celebrations reflect your personality and values. It's about honoring your journey and recognizing the effort and commitment you've invested in your well-being.

Celebrate the lessons learned, even from setbacks. View challenges not as failures but as opportunities for growth and learning. Reflect on what you've learned from these experiences and incorporate those lessons into your future endeavors. This perspective shifts the focus from disappointment to a constructive learning experience, reinforcing your resilience and adaptability.

Through mindful celebration, you not only acknowledge your progress but also deepen your connection to your intentions. The act of celebrating reinforces your commitment and empowers you to continue moving forward with renewed energy and purpose. Celebrate your achievements with intention, gratitude, and joy. This mindful approach amplifies the positive impact of your celebrations, fostering a cycle of positive reinforcement that supports your continued growth and well-being. The universe celebrates your victories with you; allow yourself to feel the joy and embrace the abundance of your accomplishments. Remember, the journey of self-discovery and holistic healing is a marathon, not a sprint. There will be moments of doubt, challenges to overcome, and adjustments to be made. But through consistent effort, self-compassion, and mindful celebration, you will steadily move towards achieving your goals and experiencing the transformative power of the cosmic healing code. **Embrace the journey, cherish the milestones, and celebrate your remarkable progress. You are worthy of your own celebration. And the universe rejoices in your success.**

Chapter 12: Building Supportive Relationships

Building supportive relationships is a cornerstone of holistic well-being. Just as we nurture our physical and spiritual selves, we must also cultivate healthy connections with others. These relationships *provide a vital source of energy, support, and emotional sustenance, enriching our lives and contributing to our overall sense of fulfillment.* However, not all relationships are created equal. Identifying truly healthy relationships requires discernment and self-awareness, an understanding of our own needs and boundaries, and a recognition of the qualities that foster growth and mutual respect.

One of the most fundamental characteristics of a healthy relationship is **mutual respect**. This goes beyond simple politeness; it involves a deep appreciation for the other person's individuality, beliefs, and values, even if they differ from our own. In a respectful relationship, there is a willingness to listen actively and empathetically, to understand different perspectives, and to engage in constructive dialogue even when disagreements arise. There's an absence of judgment, criticism, or attempts to control or manipulate the other person. Respect manifests in valuing the other person's time, thoughts, and feelings, demonstrated through consistent consideration and thoughtful actions. It's about acknowledging their inherent worth and treating them with kindness and compassion, regardless of the situation. A lack of respect, on the other hand, often manifests as belittling comments, dismissive behavior, or constant criticism, eroding the foundation of the relationship and leaving one or both parties feeling diminished.

Support is another essential element of a healthy relationship. This involves being there for the other person during both good times and bad, offering encouragement, understanding, and practical help when needed. Support isn't about fixing the other person's problems but rather providing a safe and empathetic space for them to process their experiences and find their own solutions. It means celebrating their successes and offering comfort during times of struggle, without judgment or pressure. This could involve simply listening attentively, offering a shoulder to cry on, providing practical assistance, or simply being present and offering unwavering support. True support is unconditional, offering strength during challenging times and celebrating triumphs without reservation. It's about fostering a sense of security and trust, knowing that you can rely on the other person to be there for you, whatever life may throw your way.

Open and honest communication is the lifeblood of any healthy relationship. This involves expressing your thoughts and feelings clearly and respectfully, even when difficult conversations are necessary. It also involves actively listening to the other person, seeking to understand their perspective, and responding with empathy and consideration. Healthy communication avoids passive-aggressiveness, manipulation, or the withholding of information. Instead, it encourages open dialogue and the ability to address conflict constructively, resolving disagreements through understanding and compromise. Clear and honest communication ensures that expectations are managed, needs are met, and issues are addressed effectively. It is essential to build a foundation of trust and transparency so that the relationship can evolve in harmony and mutual understanding. This can also involve seeking external support from a qualified therapist if necessary.

Boundaries are crucial in maintaining healthy relationships. This means having a clear understanding of your own limits and communicating them effectively to others. Boundaries protect your emotional, physical, and mental well-being, preventing others from overstepping and causing harm. Healthy boundaries can involve setting limits on time commitment, managing expectations for emotional support, defining acceptable communication styles, or asserting your physical boundaries. Establishing and maintaining healthy boundaries is not selfish but rather self-respecting and essential for personal well-being. They help define the limits of acceptable behavior within the relationship, preventing emotional, mental, or physical exhaustion. Respecting each other's boundaries is vital to the success of any healthy relationship.

Emotional connection is fundamental to a fulfilling relationship. This involves feeling genuinely seen, heard, and understood by the other person. Emotional connection fosters empathy, trust, and intimacy, leading to a deeper sense of connection and belonging. It's not just about physical intimacy, although that can be a part of it, but it also deeply involves understanding each other's emotional landscape. This means sharing vulnerabilities, expressing emotions openly, and offering emotional support without judgment. It involves cultivating trust and a sense of security, allowing for open and honest expression of emotions. A strong emotional connection is the bedrock of a lasting and meaningful relationship. This connection manifests in shared laughter, mutual vulnerability, and a shared understanding of each other's emotional needs.

In the context of holistic wellness, recognizing the energetic exchange within relationships is essential. Just as we are connected to the universal energy field, we are also connected energetically to the people in our lives. Healthy relationships involve a balanced exchange of positive energy, creating a mutually beneficial dynamic. Conversely, unhealthy relationships can drain our energy, leaving us feeling depleted and exhausted. By paying attention to how we feel in the presence of others, we can gain insights into the quality of the energetic exchange and make informed choices about the relationships we nurture. Using energy healing modalities, such as Reiki, can help cleanse and balance our energy field, mitigating the impact of negative relationships and strengthening our ability to create and maintain healthy ones. Crystal healing can also be utilized to support energetic balance, selecting crystals such as rose quartz for fostering compassion and love, or amethyst for promoting inner peace and emotional healing within our relationships.

Identifying healthy relationships requires self-reflection and honest assessment. Ask yourself: Do I feel respected, supported, and understood in this relationship? Is there open and honest communication? Are my boundaries respected? Do I feel emotionally fulfilled? Do I feel energized or drained after interacting with this person? If the answer to most of these questions is yes, it is likely a healthy relationship. If not, you may need to reconsider the dynamics of the relationship or take steps to establish healthier boundaries and communication patterns. Remember, you deserve to be in relationships that nourish your soul and enhance your well-being. Prioritizing your emotional and energetic well-being within your relationships will lead to deeper, more fulfilling connections that contribute positively to your holistic journey of self-discovery. It is crucial to remember that setting boundaries and communicating your needs are essential for fostering mutually respectful and enriching relationships.

The journey towards building healthy supportive relationships is an ongoing process. It involves *conscious effort, self-awareness, and a willingness to work through challenges.* By nurturing these relationships, we create a supportive network that enhances our holistic well-being, providing emotional sustenance and a sense of belonging. This support system acts as a powerful catalyst for personal growth and helps us navigate the complexities of life with greater resilience and grace. Through attentive self-care, mindful communication, and a commitment to mutual respect, we can cultivate relationships that enhance our lives and contribute to our overall well-being, enriching our journey towards holistic healing. The energetic balance within these relationships contributes to our overall energetic health, creating a harmonious flow of energy that supports both our personal growth and the growth of our relationships. It's a reciprocal exchange, where we give and receive support, love, and understanding, creating a stronger, more fulfilling life. Remember that healthy relationships are not static; they require continuous nurturing and attention, just like any other aspect of holistic well-being. It's a journey of growth and mutual understanding, requiring consistent effort and commitment. But the rewards—a deeper sense of connection, belonging, and support—are immeasurable.Communicating effectively is the cornerstone of any strong relationship, and this is especially true within the framework of holistic well-being. Our relationships are energetic exchanges, and clear, honest communication is the conduit through which this energy flows. When communication falters, the flow becomes stagnant, leading to misunderstandings, resentment, and ultimately, energetic imbalances. Mastering effective communication isn't about winning arguments or always getting your way; it's about creating a space where everyone feels heard, understood, and respected. This fosters a positive energetic exchange, strengthening the bonds between individuals and contributing to overall well-being.

One of the most crucial skills in effective communication is active listening. This goes far beyond simply hearing the words the other person is saying. Active listening involves fully engaging with the speaker, both verbally and nonverbally. It means paying close attention to their words, their tone of voice, and their body language. It requires putting aside your own thoughts and judgments to truly understand their perspective. Show your attentiveness through nonverbal cues: maintain eye contact (without staring intensely), nod occasionally to show you're following along, and use verbal affirmations like "I understand," or "Tell me more." Ask clarifying questions to ensure you're comprehending their message accurately. Avoid interrupting, even if you strongly disagree. Instead, wait for them to finish before responding. Reflect back what you've heard to confirm your understanding, for instance, "So, it sounds like you're feeling frustrated because..." This validates their feelings and ensures they feel heard and understood. Active listening, when practiced consistently, creates a safe space for vulnerability and trust, fostering a deeper emotional connection. Energetically, this creates a harmonious flow, strengthening the positive energy exchange within the relationship.

Equally important is **assertive communication**. This involves expressing your needs and opinions clearly and respectfully, without being aggressive or passive. Assertiveness is about finding the balance between expressing your truth and respecting the other person's feelings. It's about standing up for yourself without putting others down. Passive communication, on the other hand, often leads to resentment and suppressed emotions, creating energetic blockages. Aggressive communication, conversely, can damage relationships and create an environment of fear and tension. Assertive communication involves using "I" statements to express your feelings and needs without blaming or accusing the other person. For example, instead of saying, "You always leave the dishes dirty," try, "I feel frustrated when the dishes are left unwashed, as it adds to my workload." This approach focuses on your feelings and needs, rather than placing blame, encouraging a more constructive dialogue. Assertive communication requires practice and self-awareness, but the payoff is a healthier, more balanced relationship where everyone feels respected and heard. It cultivates emotional maturity and strengthens energetic boundaries, ensuring that your energy is not depleted by unmet needs or unspoken resentments.

Constructively expressing emotions is another vital aspect of effective communication. Emotions are a natural part of the human experience, and suppressing them can lead to various problems, both physically and emotionally. When you suppress your emotions, you create energetic blockages that can manifest as physical ailments or emotional distress. Instead, learn to identify and express your emotions in a healthy and constructive manner. This doesn't mean unleashing a torrent of anger or negativity. It means expressing your feelings in a calm and respectful way, using "I" statements and focusing on the specific situation. For instance, instead of yelling, "This is unacceptable!", try, "I feel hurt and disappointed when...". Clearly articulate the reason behind your emotion. This clarity helps the other person understand your perspective without feeling attacked. Allowing space for the other person to express their emotions is equally crucial. Create a safe space for open dialogue where both parties feel comfortable expressing their feelings without fear of judgment. The energetic exchange in such an environment becomes positive and mutually beneficial. By expressing your emotions constructively, you're creating an environment of emotional safety and building trust, thus fostering a stronger and more fulfilling relationship.

Nonverbal communication plays a significant role in how our messages are received. Body language, tone of voice, and facial expressions can often speak louder than words. Pay attention to your own nonverbal cues and those of the other person. Are your body language and tone aligned with your words? If not, the disconnect might be causing confusion and misinterpretations. Maintaining eye contact, using open and welcoming body posture, and matching your tone to your message helps ensure your message is received clearly and effectively. Conversely, crossed arms, averted gaze, or a harsh tone can convey defensiveness or hostility. Observe the other person's body language as well; it can provide valuable insights into their emotional state and level of engagement. This mindful awareness enhances communication and strengthens the energetic connection between you and the other person.

Conflict is inevitable in any relationship, but how you handle conflict determines the health and longevity of that connection. Effective communication is vital in navigating disagreements. Avoid accusatory language and personal attacks; focus on the issue at hand, not the person. Use "I" statements to express your concerns and actively listen to the other person's perspective. Look for common ground and areas of agreement. If the conflict escalates, take a break to cool down before resuming the conversation. Consider seeking mediation from a neutral third party if you're struggling to resolve the issue independently. Remember, conflict resolution is an opportunity for growth and deeper understanding. Approaching conflicts with a focus on mutual respect and clear communication strengthens the energetic bonds within your relationships, transforming potential negativity into a catalyst for increased intimacy and trust. The key is to address conflict constructively, not to avoid it altogether.

Finally, remember that effective communication is a skill that can be learned and improved upon. It takes practice, patience, and a willingness to be vulnerable. Pay attention to your communication patterns, and seek feedback from trusted friends or a therapist if needed. Consider taking a communication skills workshop or reading books on the subject. The effort you put into improving your communication skills will significantly impact the quality of your relationships and contribute substantially to your overall well-being. By cultivating effective communication, you're not only strengthening your relationships but also enhancing your energetic field, creating a more harmonious and fulfilling life. The investment in your communication skills is an investment in your holistic health, a cornerstone of building strong, supportive, and energetically balanced relationships. Remember, effective communication is a continuous journey, not a destination, requiring ongoing self-reflection and refinement.Setting healthy boundaries is an act of self-love, a declaration of self-respect that reverberates through every aspect of your being, profoundly impacting your relationships and overall well-being. It's about recognizing your limits, understanding your needs, and respectfully communicating them to others. This isn't about being selfish; it's about safeguarding your energy, preventing burnout, and ensuring your emotional well-being isn't compromised. Think of your energy as a precious resource, one that needs to be nurtured and protected. When you consistently overextend yourself, neglecting your own needs to accommodate others, you deplete this vital energy, leaving yourself vulnerable to stress, anxiety, and resentment.

Learning to say "no" is a critical component of setting healthy boundaries. Many of us are conditioned to please others, fearing rejection or conflict if we decline requests. This ingrained tendency often stems from childhood conditioning or a deep-seated need for external validation. However, consistently agreeing to things that drain your energy or compromise your values creates an energetic imbalance, leaving you feeling depleted and resentful. The ability to say "no" is not a sign of selfishness; it's an act of self-preservation. It's about prioritizing your own well-being and recognizing that your time, energy, and emotional resources are finite.

Imagine your energy field as a beautiful, shimmering aura, radiating outwards. Every interaction, every decision, affects the vibrancy and strength of this aura. When you say "yes" to something that doesn't align with your values or drains your energy, you create a small tear or weakening in this field. Over time, these small tears accumulate, diminishing the overall strength and vibrancy of your aura, leaving you vulnerable to negative energies and emotional distress. Conversely, when you set healthy boundaries and say "no" to things that deplete you, you strengthen your aura, creating a protective barrier against negativity. This protective shield allows your energy to flow freely, enhancing your overall well-being and strengthening your relationships.

The process of setting boundaries starts with self-awareness. Take time for introspection, exploring your values, needs, and limits. What activities drain your energy? What situations leave you feeling stressed or overwhelmed? What are your non-negotiables? Journaling, meditation, or spending time in nature can be helpful in this process. Pay attention to your physical and emotional responses. Your body often provides subtle cues—a tightening in your chest, a headache, a feeling of unease—that signal when a boundary has been crossed. Learn to recognize these signals as important messages from your body, guiding you towards self-preservation.

Once you understand your boundaries, communicating them effectively is crucial. This involves assertive communication, expressing your needs clearly and respectfully, without being aggressive or passive. Practice using "I" statements, focusing on your feelings and needs without blaming others. For example, instead of saying, "You always make me late," try, "I feel stressed when we're constantly running behind schedule, because it makes me feel rushed and overwhelmed." This approach is less accusatory and more likely to encourage a constructive conversation.

Remember, setting boundaries isn't about controlling others; it's about taking control of your own life and protecting your energy. It's about communicating your needs and expectations so that others can understand and respect them. Don't expect immediate compliance; it often takes time for others to adjust to new boundaries. Be prepared to reiterate your boundaries as needed, and be consistent in upholding them. Inconsistency weakens your boundaries, making them less effective over time.

Let's explore some practical examples. Imagine a friend consistently calls you at inconvenient times, interrupting your work or family time. A healthy boundary might be to explain, "I appreciate you calling, but I'm usually busy during work hours. Could we schedule a time to chat later in the evening?" This clearly communicates your need for time and respect while offering an alternative solution. Or, perhaps a family member frequently asks you for favors that you don't have the time or energy to fulfill. You might say, "I care about you, but I'm currently overloaded with responsibilities. I'm not able to assist you with this right now." This is a kind but firm assertion of your limits.

In romantic relationships, boundaries are particularly crucial. It's essential to communicate your needs regarding physical intimacy, emotional support, and personal space. For example, you might establish a boundary around your personal time, stating, "I need some time alone each day to recharge. It's important for my well-being." Or, if you're uncomfortable with certain forms of physical affection, you might say, "I love you, but I'm not comfortable with that level of physical touch. Could we find ways to express our affection that feel more comfortable for both of us?" These clear statements protect your emotional and physical well-being while fostering deeper intimacy built on mutual respect.

In professional settings, healthy boundaries are equally vital. Overworking or being constantly available can lead to burnout and resentment. Setting clear boundaries regarding your workload, availability, and communication expectations is essential for your professional and personal well-being. This might involve politely declining extra assignments when your plate is already full or setting specific hours for responding to emails. For example, "I'm happy to help, but I'm currently working on a tight deadline. Could we discuss this next week?" or "I respond to emails between 9 am and 5 pm. I'll get back to you during those hours." These simple yet firm statements protect your time and prevent you from becoming overextended.

It's crucial to remember that saying "no" doesn't necessarily mean ending a relationship or sacrificing your friendships. It's about creating a sustainable dynamic where everyone's needs are respected. When you set healthy boundaries, you're actually strengthening your relationships by fostering mutual respect and ensuring the relationships are built on a foundation of balance and reciprocity. It empowers your relationships, allowing for genuine connection and preventing resentment from festering.

Setting healthy boundaries and saying "no" might initially feel uncomfortable, especially if you're used to people-pleasing. However, it's a transformative process that enhances your self-esteem, protects your energy, and improves the quality of your relationships. It's a journey that requires practice and patience, but the rewards—a life filled with more energy, less stress, and healthier, more fulfilling relationships—are immeasurable. Remember, saying "no" to things that deplete you allows you to say "yes" to the things that truly matter, allowing your energy to flow freely, enhancing your well-being and enriching your life. It's a powerful act of self-care, a key to unlocking a more authentic and fulfilling life journey. Embrace the power of "no" as a pathway to a more balanced and joyful existence. This is your journey towards self-mastery, a vital step in creating the life you truly desire. Through mindful boundary setting, you not only protect yourself but also invite healthier, more fulfilling interactions, creating a ripple effect of positive energy that extends to all aspects of your life.Conflict is an inevitable part of any relationship, regardless of how close or harmonious it may seem. Disagreements arise from differing perspectives, unmet needs, or misunderstandings. However, the way we navigate these conflicts significantly impacts the health and longevity of our connections. Instead of viewing conflict as a threat to our relationships, we can reframe it as an opportunity for growth, understanding, and deeper connection. The key lies in resolving conflicts constructively, fostering mutual respect, and enhancing communication.

One of the foundational elements of constructive conflict resolution is active listening. This goes beyond simply hearing what the other person is saying; it involves truly understanding their perspective, empathizing with their feelings, and acknowledging their point of view, even if you don't agree with it. Imagine a scenario where you and your partner disagree about how to spend your weekend. Active listening would involve attentively listening to your partner's proposal, asking clarifying questions to ensure you fully grasp their reasoning, and acknowledging their feelings without interrupting. For instance, you might say, "I understand you're feeling frustrated because you had hoped we'd spend the weekend relaxing at home. Let me hear more about why that's important to you." This approach demonstrates respect and validation, creating a safe space for open communication.

Equally important is the art of expressing your own needs and feelings clearly and respectfully. This involves using "I" statements, focusing on your emotions and experiences without blaming or accusing the other person. Instead of saying, "You always make me feel ignored," you could say, "I feel ignored when our conversations are constantly interrupted, and I would appreciate it if we could find a way to focus on each other during our time together." This approach avoids defensiveness, allowing for a more productive discussion. Remember, the goal is not to win the argument, but to find a mutually acceptable solution that addresses the concerns of both parties.

Another vital aspect of constructive conflict resolution is empathy. Trying to understand the other person's perspective, even if you disagree with it, can be challenging. However, practicing empathy helps de-escalate conflict and fosters mutual respect. Ask yourself: "What are their underlying needs and concerns? What might be motivating their behavior?" This approach helps move beyond surface-level disagreements and address the root cause of the conflict. Let's say a friend consistently cancels plans at the last minute. Instead of immediately becoming frustrated, try to understand the underlying reasons. Are they overwhelmed with work? Are they experiencing personal difficulties? Approaching the situation with empathy allows for a more compassionate and understanding response.

Finding common ground is crucial in resolving conflicts constructively. Despite differences in perspectives, there are often shared goals or values. Identifying these commonalities can provide a bridge for understanding and collaboration. In the example of the weekend plans, both partners might value spending quality time together, but disagree on the best way to achieve that. Acknowledging this shared value can help find a compromise that satisfies both individuals. Perhaps you can spend Saturday relaxing at home and dedicate Sunday to an activity you both enjoy. Identifying common ground creates a sense of unity and helps move the conversation towards finding a solution.

Compromise is often the key to resolving conflicts amicably. It involves finding a mutually acceptable solution that addresses the needs of all parties involved. This may not always be a perfect solution for everyone, but it's a practical way to move forward and maintain a healthy relationship. It requires a willingness to give and take, acknowledging that neither party will always get everything they want. Consider the scenario of two siblings arguing over a toy. A constructive compromise might involve sharing the toy for a specific time or taking turns playing with it. The compromise may not satisfy each sibling perfectly, but it allows them to resolve the conflict and continue their relationship without significant damage.

In some cases, seeking external assistance may be beneficial. Mediators or therapists can offer objective guidance, helping parties communicate more effectively and find mutually acceptable solutions. These professionals create a safe space where individuals feel comfortable expressing their feelings and needs, without fear of judgment. They can provide valuable tools and strategies for constructive communication, conflict resolution, and relationship building. This is especially helpful in situations where the conflict is long-standing or involves intense emotions.

Preventing future conflicts involves proactive communication and establishing clear expectations. Regular check-ins and open dialogues can help prevent small disagreements from escalating into major conflicts. This requires honesty and transparency, where each party openly shares their needs and concerns. It also involves setting clear boundaries and expectations, defining acceptable behavior and addressing any potential issues early on. Regular communication fosters mutual understanding and empathy, reducing the likelihood of conflict arising in the future.

After conflict resolution, it's important to reflect on the process and learn from the experience. Analyzing what triggered the conflict, how it was handled, and the lessons learned is crucial for future relationship growth. This process can strengthen the bond, demonstrating mutual respect and a shared commitment to the relationship. For example, following the weekend planning dispute, the couple might discuss what they learned about each other's preferences and find ways to incorporate these into their future plans. This reflective practice turns the conflict into a valuable learning opportunity.

Constructive conflict resolution isn't a one-time event; it's a continuous process requiring dedication and commitment from all parties involved. It's about fostering mutual respect, understanding, and empathy, and acknowledging that disagreements are a normal part of any relationship. By embracing these strategies, we can transform conflict into an opportunity for growth, creating deeper connections and fostering healthier, more resilient relationships that withstand the test of time. Through mindful communication and a commitment to understanding, we can navigate disagreements, learn from each other, and emerge with stronger bonds and deeper appreciation for one another. The process itself builds resilience and strengthens the relationship, fostering a deeper sense of connection and trust. This journey towards harmonious conflict resolution is a continuous act of self-improvement and relationship building, paving the way for a more fulfilling and meaningful life.Building a supportive community is not merely a social endeavor; it's a crucial element of holistic well-being, deeply intertwined with our spiritual and energetic growth. The individuals we surround ourselves with significantly influence our emotional, mental, and even physical health. Just as nourishing food fuels our bodies, positive relationships nourish our souls, providing a bedrock of support during challenging times and celebrating triumphs with unwavering enthusiasm. This supportive network acts as a powerful energetic amplifier, magnifying our intentions and bolstering our capacity for self-healing.

Imagine your energy field as a delicate ecosystem. Negative interactions, toxic relationships, and draining energies can disrupt this ecosystem, leading to imbalances that manifest as physical ailments, emotional distress, or spiritual stagnation. Conversely, a supportive community acts as a protective shield, deflecting negative energies and nurturing the positive ones. The collective energy of supportive individuals can elevate our vibrational frequency, creating a resonant field that facilitates healing and growth. This is where the synergy of energy healing modalities like Reiki, crystal healing, and numerology becomes particularly relevant.

Reiki, with its focus on universal life force energy, can be profoundly enhanced through the presence of supportive individuals. When we share Reiki with loved ones or receive it within a nurturing group setting, the energy flow becomes amplified, creating a powerful healing vortex. The intention of healing is magnified, and the recipient experiences a deeper sense of connection and well-being. This collective healing extends beyond the immediate participants, creating a ripple effect that touches the broader community.

Crystals, with their unique vibrational properties, also play a significant role in enhancing the energy of a supportive community. Certain crystals, like amethyst or rose quartz, are known for their ability to promote peace, harmony, and emotional balance. Using these crystals during group meditations or gatherings can create a harmonious energy field, enhancing the collective healing and fostering a deeper sense of connection among participants. The combined energy of the crystals and the intention of the group creates a synergistic effect that transcends the individual capabilities of each person.

Numerology, with its focus on the vibrational essence of numbers, can also provide insights into building a supportive community. Understanding the numerological significance of relationships can help us identify individuals who resonate with our energy and support our growth. By aligning ourselves with those whose life path numbers complement our own, we can cultivate stronger bonds that foster mutual growth and understanding. This understanding can help us navigate potential conflicts with greater ease and compassion, preventing energy drain and fostering positive connections.

The chakra system provides another framework for understanding the importance of a supportive community. Each chakra corresponds to specific aspects of our being, and imbalances in these energy centers can manifest as physical or emotional problems. A supportive community helps us maintain a healthy chakra system by providing emotional support, fostering self-acceptance, and promoting overall well-being. For instance, a strong root chakra, linked to feelings of security and grounding, is nurtured by supportive relationships that offer a sense of belonging and stability. Similarly, a balanced heart chakra, associated with love and compassion, thrives in an environment of genuine connection and empathy.

Building a supportive community requires conscious effort and intention. It's not merely about accumulating acquaintances; it's about cultivating genuine, meaningful relationships with individuals who share our values and support our growth. This involves actively seeking out individuals who resonate with our energy, fostering open communication, and offering genuine support in return. Participating in group activities, workshops, or spiritual gatherings can provide valuable opportunities to connect with like-minded individuals and expand our supportive network.

One powerful method for cultivating a supportive community is through shared experiences. Engaging in activities that promote personal growth, such as yoga retreats, meditation workshops, or volunteer work, creates opportunities to connect with others on a deeper level.

Shared experiences foster a sense of camaraderie and understanding, laying the foundation for lasting friendships and mutual support. The energy shared during these activities becomes a binding force, strengthening the bonds between individuals.

Active listening is paramount in building any strong relationship, and this is particularly true within a supportive community. It requires moving beyond simple hearing to truly understanding and empathizing with the experiences and perspectives of others. This creates a safe space where individuals feel comfortable sharing their vulnerabilities and seeking support without judgment. Active listening is a powerful energy exchange, reinforcing the bonds of trust and fostering deeper connection.

Furthermore, the *willingness to offer support and understanding unconditionally is essential*. This involves providing encouragement during difficult times, celebrating successes without envy, and offering a non-judgmental ear when needed. This reciprocal exchange of energy fosters a resilient community where individuals feel empowered to share their challenges and seek support without fear of judgment. This reciprocal energy creates a cycle of positive reinforcement that strengthens the collective well-being of the community. Understanding personal boundaries is equally crucial. While a supportive community promotes closeness and connection, it's vital to maintain healthy boundaries to prevent energy drain or exploitation. This means setting clear limits on what we're willing to give and receive, and respectfully communicating those boundaries to others. This creates a sustainable environment where each individual can thrive without feeling overwhelmed or depleted. Setting boundaries is an act of self-preservation that ensures the longevity and health of the community as a whole.

Beyond personal relationships, aligning with organizations or groups that share your values and goals can expand your supportive network. Joining a book club, a spiritual group, or a volunteer organization provides opportunities to connect with like-minded individuals and contribute to something larger than yourself. This alignment of values creates a synergistic effect, magnifying the positive energy and enhancing the collective sense of purpose. Ultimately, building a supportive community is a journey of self-discovery and reciprocal growth. It's about consciously cultivating relationships that nurture our soul and amplify our positive energy. It's about creating a network of individuals who uplift, inspire, and support our journey towards holistic well-being. This intentional approach to community building will not only enrich your personal life but will also contribute to a more harmonious and compassionate world. The rewards extend far beyond personal well-being, creating a ripple effect of positivity that influences the lives of others. Through mindful effort and compassionate intention, we can cultivate a supportive community that fosters growth, strengthens our resilience, and enhances our overall well-being, leaving a lasting positive impact on the world around us.

Chapter 13: Living a Purposeful Life

The journey towards holistic well-being isn't just about external practices; it's a deeply personal exploration of your inner landscape. Building a strong foundation for a fulfilling life requires understanding your unique purpose and aligning your actions with your core values. This is the compass that guides you through life's complexities, providing direction and meaning amidst the inevitable challenges. Without this inner clarity, external practices, however powerful, can feel like navigating a ship without a map, leaving you adrift in a sea of uncertainty.

Identifying your life purpose is akin to uncovering a hidden treasure map, revealing a path tailored specifically to you. It's not a destination, but a dynamic, evolving process of self-discovery that unfolds throughout life. It's about understanding what truly resonates with your soul, what ignites your passion, and what leaves you feeling deeply fulfilled. This isn't a single, fixed answer; it's a journey of continuous refinement and growth. Your purpose may shift and evolve as you grow and experience new facets of life.

One powerful method for uncovering your life purpose is through *deep introspection and self-reflection*. Take some quiet time, free from distractions, to delve into your inner world. Journaling can be a potent tool here. Ask yourself profound questions: What truly excites me? What activities make me lose track of time? What are my unique talents and skills? What impact do I want to leave on the world? What causes are close to my heart? Don't censor your answers; allow your intuition to guide you. Write freely, without judgment, exploring the depths of your aspirations and desires. Let your subconscious mind reveal the hidden pathways that lead to your true calling.

Consider incorporating meditation into your self-reflection practice. Find a comfortable position, close your eyes, and focus on your breath. Allow your thoughts to flow freely without judgment, observing them without getting carried away. As your mind settles, gently ask yourself those same probing questions. Often, the answers emerge not through conscious thought but through subtle intuitive whispers. Meditative introspection creates space for your inner wisdom to emerge, leading you toward a clearer understanding of your life purpose. Beyond introspection, engage in activities that awaken your curiosity and passion. Experiment with different hobbies, volunteer for causes you care about, or explore new learning opportunities. Observe your responses to these experiences. Which activities leave you feeling energized and fulfilled, and which leave you drained and uninspired? These experiences provide valuable clues about your intrinsic motivations and passions, revealing hidden pathways towards your purpose. Don't be afraid to step outside your comfort zone. Often, the greatest discoveries are made when we embrace the unknown.

Identifying your core values is equally critical. Values are the guiding principles that shape your decisions and actions. They are the moral compass that steers your life. They are deeply personal and may differ from the values of others. Understanding your core values is crucial for aligning your actions with your purpose, ensuring that your life's work is congruent with your deepest beliefs and aspirations.

Several exercises can help you identify your core values. One effective method is to create a list of qualities that you admire in others. What characteristics do you find inspiring or admirable in individuals you respect? These often reflect the values you hold dear, often unconsciously. Once you have your list, reflect on which qualities are most important to you. Which ones resonate most deeply with your soul? These are the cornerstones of your personal value system.

Another powerful exercise is to visualize your ideal life. Close your eyes and imagine your life ten years from now, living a life that is completely fulfilling and aligned with your purpose. What aspects of this ideal life stand out? What are the relationships, achievements, and experiences that define it? The characteristics that shape this vision often reflect your core values.

Once you've identified your core values, consider how they align with your life choices. Are your daily actions and decisions consistent with these values? If not, identify areas where adjustments are needed. This may involve setting new boundaries, changing careers, altering relationships, or making significant lifestyle shifts. This alignment isn't always easy, but it's essential for a truly purposeful life.

Remember that your values and purpose are deeply intertwined. Your purpose reveals what you're here to do, while your values dictate how you do it. They work in harmony, shaping a path that is both meaningful and authentic. For example, if your core value is compassion, your purpose might involve working with vulnerable populations, volunteering at an animal shelter, or pursuing a career in healthcare. If your core value is creativity, your purpose could involve writing, painting, composing music, or designing innovative products.

Aligning your life choices with your purpose and values is a continuous process, not a one-time event. As you grow and evolve, your understanding of your purpose and values may deepen and shift. This is a natural part of life's journey. Regular self-reflection and reassessment of your goals will keep you on the path of authenticity and fulfillment. The synergy between your purpose, values, and the energy healing modalities discussed earlier is significant. Reiki can enhance your ability to connect with your inner wisdom, providing a pathway for your intuition to guide you. Crystal healing can help amplify your intentions and enhance your connection to your purpose. The vibrational frequencies of certain crystals can reinforce your commitment to your values and empower you to make conscious choices aligned with your life's purpose. Numerology can shed light on your life path, providing insights into your inherent talents and aptitudes, helping you discover and align with your unique purpose. Understanding the numerology of your name and birthdate can uncover hidden patterns and guide you toward a deeper understanding of yourself and your life's journey.

The chakra system offers another framework for understanding the connection between purpose, values, and well-being. A balanced chakra system is essential for a fulfilling life. Your purpose is often linked to the activation and balance of certain chakras. For example, a strong root chakra provides a sense of security and stability, enabling you to pursue your purpose with confidence and groundedness. A balanced heart chakra fosters compassionate action, aligning your purpose with your values. An open throat chakra empowers you to communicate your purpose effectively and inspires you to express your authentic self. By actively working with your chakra system through meditation, energy healing, or other practices, you can enhance your ability to live a truly purposeful life.

The path to living a purposeful life is not always straightforward. There will be moments of doubt, setbacks, and challenges. But by consistently connecting with your inner wisdom, aligning your actions with your values, and embracing the support of your community and energy practices, you can navigate these challenges with grace and resilience. Remember that the journey itself is part of the process; the exploration, the learning, and the growth are all integral aspects of discovering and living your authentic purpose. This journey is a lifelong adventure, an unfolding tapestry of self-discovery and profound fulfillment. Embrace the process, trust your intuition, and enjoy the incredible journey of living a life truly aligned with your soul's purpose.Understanding your strengths and talents is crucial to living a purposeful life. It's about recognizing the unique gifts you bring to the world, those inherent abilities that make you uniquely you. These aren't just about skills learned; they're about innate aptitudes, passions, and the things you excel at effortlessly, almost as if guided by an inner compass. Identifying these strengths provides a powerful foundation for creating a life that is both fulfilling and meaningful. It allows you to leverage your natural abilities, creating a life that feels effortless and aligned with your soul's purpose.

One effective way to identify your strengths is through introspection. Take some time for quiet contemplation, perhaps in nature or a peaceful space, free from distractions. Journaling can be an invaluable tool here. Ask yourself probing questions: What tasks do I accomplish with ease and efficiency? What activities do I consistently find myself drawn to, even if they are challenging? What feedback have I received from others about my abilities, where they consistently praise my performance or approach?

Go beyond simple skills. Consider the qualities you possess. Are you a natural problem-solver, adept at finding creative solutions? Do you excel at collaboration, seamlessly bringing people together to achieve a common goal? Are you a meticulous detail-oriented individual, or do you excel at big-picture thinking and strategy? These intrinsic qualities are often overlooked but are foundational to your overall success and fulfillment. Are you empathetic and compassionate, naturally drawn to helping others? Or are you a natural leader, inspiring those around you with your vision and confidence? Understanding these qualities helps you identify work environments and roles that perfectly suit your personality and capabilities.

Don't limit yourself to your professional life. Explore your strengths in your personal relationships, hobbies, and volunteer work. What makes you shine in your personal life? What role do you naturally take on when assisting friends or family? Are you a skilled listener, a patient caregiver, a mediator, or a source of unwavering support? These personal strengths often reflect deeply ingrained traits that can be effectively utilized in your professional life as well, potentially opening up opportunities you might not have considered.
Consider seeking external feedback. Ask trusted friends, family members, or colleagues for their honest opinions on your strengths. They often see our abilities and talents more clearly than we do ourselves, offering valuable perspectives and insights that we may have overlooked. Look for recurring themes in their feedback; these may highlight talents you didn't fully recognize.

Beyond self-reflection and external feedback, consider using various tools to identify your strengths and talents. Personality tests, such as the Myers-Briggs Type Indicator (MBTI) or StrengthsFinder, can offer valuable insights into your personality type and inherent strengths. While these tests shouldn't be the sole basis for self-discovery, they can provide a helpful framework for further exploration and understanding.

Once you've identified your strengths and talents, the next step is to leverage them to their full potential. This involves exploring how you can integrate these abilities into your work, personal relationships, and overall life purpose. Are there career paths or entrepreneurial ventures that allow you to use your strengths every day? Are there volunteer opportunities or community projects where you can make a significant contribution using your unique gifts? Consider how you can combine your various strengths to create a synergistic effect. For example, if you are both a skilled writer and a compassionate listener, you might consider a career in journalism or counseling, combining your writing ability with your ability to connect with people. This combination unleashes far more power than relying on either skill individually.

Moreover, explore how your strengths can contribute to a larger purpose. What is the positive impact you want to make on the world? How can your abilities help others and contribute to a cause that is close to your heart? Connecting your strengths with a larger purpose imbues your work with deeper meaning and fulfillment.

This process is not merely about identifying what you're good at; it's about understanding what you *love* doing, where your skills seamlessly intertwine with your passions. This intersection is where true fulfillment lies. When your strengths align with your values and life purpose, you experience a sense of flow, a natural ease and enthusiasm for your daily activities. This alignment reduces stress and increases overall well-being.

Remember that your strengths and talents can evolve over time. As you grow and learn, your abilities will develop, and new talents may emerge. Regular self-reflection and exploration are crucial to maintaining awareness of your strengths and to identify emerging capabilities. Using the tools of energy healing can further enhance your understanding of your strengths. Reiki, for example, can facilitate a deeper connection to your intuition, guiding you towards activities and pursuits that naturally align with your inherent talents. Crystal healing can amplify your focus and enhance your confidence, empowering you to utilize your strengths fully. Specific crystals can aid in unlocking creative potential or bolstering self-belief, depending on your needs.

Numerology offers another perspective. Analyzing your numerological profile, particularly your life path number, can reveal hidden talents and aptitudes, providing insights into your natural inclinations. It could highlight areas where you might excel unexpectedly, opening up opportunities you had not considered. Your birthdate and name, when analyzed through numerological lenses, may unveil hidden aspects of your personality and inherent capabilities.

Understanding your chakra system also proves beneficial. Each chakra is associated with specific energies and qualities. Identifying your dominant chakras can illuminate your strengths and areas for development. A strong root chakra might indicate strong grounding and resilience, while a vibrant solar plexus chakra might reveal confidence and leadership potential. Working with your chakras through meditation, energy healing, or other practices can unlock and enhance your inherent gifts.

The journey of identifying and utilizing your strengths is an ongoing process, not a destination. Be patient with yourself, celebrate your achievements, and embrace the continuous growth and development that comes with self-discovery. By recognizing and nurturing your unique talents, you pave the way towards a life filled with purpose, fulfillment, and profound meaning. The universe has gifted you with specific abilities; it's time to discover and embrace them. This is the key to unlocking a life lived authentically, a life where your inherent gifts shine brightly, illuminating not only your path but also the lives of those around you. Having identified your inherent strengths and talents, the next crucial step in living a purposeful life is setting goals that truly resonate with your core values and life's mission. This isn't about chasing arbitrary achievements; it's about aligning your actions with your deepest sense of self. It's about creating a roadmap that leads you towards a life of genuine fulfillment, a life where your daily activities reflect your authentic self.

Setting goals aligned with your purpose requires introspection and a clear understanding of your values. What truly matters to you? What principles guide your decisions and shape your interactions with the world? Are you driven by a desire to create, to connect, to serve, to learn, or to lead? Understanding your values provides the bedrock upon which you can build meaningful goals.

Consider creating a values clarification exercise. Take a quiet moment, perhaps amidst nature's embrace or in a peaceful space conducive to introspection. Write down a list of ten words or phrases that represent your core values. These could include things like creativity, compassion, integrity, freedom, growth, or community. Reflect on why these values are important to you. How do they shape your decisions and interactions? How do they manifest in your daily life? Are there instances where your actions have aligned with these values, and conversely, times where they have fallen short? Understanding this alignment (or misalignment) is crucial for goal setting.

Once you've identified your core values, begin to brainstorm goals that directly reflect those values. These goals should feel intrinsically motivating, drawing you forward not out of obligation but out of a deep-seated desire for alignment and fulfillment. For example, if creativity is a core value, your goals might include writing a novel, painting a series of landscapes, composing music, starting a blog, or even designing a new wardrobe. These goals are not simply tasks; they are expressions of your inner self.

If connection is a paramount value, your goals might involve volunteering at a local organization, strengthening your relationships with loved ones, joining a community group, or mentoring someone in need. If service is your guiding principle, you might dedicate yourself to fundraising for a cause you believe in, volunteering at a hospital or shelter, or even starting a non-profit organization. If learning is a priority, consider enrolling in a class, pursuing a degree, attending workshops, traveling to new places, or dedicating time to mastering a new skill. The possibilities are vast and as unique as you are.

Your goals shouldn't be solely focused on external validation or societal expectations. They should be intrinsically rewarding, providing a sense of accomplishment and inner peace. This is where the power of intention-setting comes into play. Before setting a goal, visualize yourself achieving it. Feel the emotions associated with that success. Let your imagination paint a vibrant picture of the positive impact that achieving this goal will have on your life and those around you. This visualization technique, infused with the intention of achieving the goal, greatly enhances the likelihood of success.

Remember, your goals should be SMART: Specific, Measurable, Achievable, Relevant, and Time-bound. A vague goal, such as "be healthier," is far less effective than a specific, measurable goal, such as "lose ten pounds in three months by walking for thirty minutes three times a week and following a balanced diet." The specificity and measurability provide clarity and direction, making the goal more manageable and ultimately, more attainable. Relevance ensures your goals align with your values and life purpose, while the time-bound element adds a sense of urgency and accountability.

When setting goals, consider employing the wisdom of your energetic body. Reiki can assist in clarifying your intentions and strengthening your commitment to your goals. Visualize your goals as energy flowing through your chakras, fueling your progress and facilitating a sense of alignment and empowerment. Use crystals that resonate with your intention—amethyst for spiritual growth, citrine for manifestation, or carnelian for courage and action.

Numerology can also provide insights into your goal-setting journey. Analyzing your numerological profile, particularly your life path number, can reveal your inherent talents and aptitudes, illuminating paths that lead to fulfilling achievements. It can also offer warnings of potential challenges and illuminate strategies to overcome them. Understanding the numerological energy associated with your chosen goals can provide a deeper understanding of the opportunities and potential obstacles you may encounter along the way.

Astrology, too, offers guidance. Understanding your natal chart and current planetary transits can illuminate optimal times for setting intentions and initiating actions toward your goals. By harmonizing your actions with celestial energies, you can maximize your potential for success.

Your chakra system is a vital component of your energetic roadmap. Ensure that your goals are in alignment with the overall balance of your chakra system. If you are experiencing imbalances in specific chakras, address them through meditation, energy healing, or other practices before setting goals, ensuring that the foundation of your energetic system is optimally supporting your progress.

Break down larger goals into smaller, more manageable steps. This helps prevent overwhelm and maintains momentum. Celebrate your achievements along the way, no matter how small they may seem. Acknowledge your progress and celebrate your victories—this reinforces positive momentum and strengthens your commitment to achieving your larger aspirations. Regular self-reflection is crucial. Review your goals regularly, adjusting them as needed to reflect your evolving priorities and circumstances. Life is a dynamic journey, and your goals should adapt accordingly, mirroring the continuous evolution of your self-understanding and personal growth.

Remember, this is not a race. This is a journey of self-discovery and fulfillment. Be patient with yourself, embrace the process, and celebrate your progress. By setting goals that align with your purpose and values, you are creating a life that is both meaningful and deeply fulfilling, a life that authentically reflects your unique gifts and talents, and a life where every step aligns with your soul's true calling. The journey may have its challenges, but the destination—a life lived authentically and with purpose—is well worth the effort. Trust in the universe's guidance, and trust in your own inherent ability to create the life you are destined to live.The path to a purposeful life isn't merely about introspection and goal-setting; it's about taking action and making a tangible difference in the world. Identifying your talents and aligning your goals with your values is only half the battle. The true power lies in translating your intentions into meaningful actions that resonate with your soul's purpose.

This isn't about grand gestures or sweeping changes; it's about consistent, small actions that collectively create a ripple effect of positive change, both in your own life and the lives of others.

Consider the energy you are putting into the world. Just as Reiki channels healing energy, your actions channel your life force, your unique contribution to the universe's tapestry. Every act of kindness, every creative endeavor, every act of service, is a powerful expression of your energy and a contribution to the collective well-being. This contribution isn't simply about doing good; it's about aligning your energy with your purpose, creating a synergistic relationship between your inner world and the external reality you are shaping.

Let's explore this concept through the lens of your chakras. Your root chakra, grounded in security and stability, can be strengthened by actions that provide a sense of security for yourself and others. This could involve financial planning, creating a safe and comfortable home, or contributing to organizations that provide shelter and basic needs. Your sacral chakra, associated with creativity and emotional expression, thrives on actions that foster connection and joy. This might involve engaging in creative pursuits, nurturing relationships, or participating in activities that bring you pleasure and fulfillment.

Your solar plexus chakra, related to self-esteem and personal power, is nourished by actions that assert your strength and confidence. This could involve taking on challenges, speaking your truth, setting boundaries, or pursuing your ambitions with unwavering determination. Your heart chakra, the center of compassion and love, flourishes through acts of kindness, generosity, and empathy. This might involve volunteering your time, donating to charity, expressing gratitude, or simply offering a listening ear to someone in need.

Your throat chakra, the center of communication and self-expression, is energized by authentic communication and the pursuit of knowledge. This involves speaking your truth, expressing your creativity, pursuing educational opportunities, or engaging in meaningful conversations that expand your understanding and contribute to the collective wisdom. Your third eye chakra, associated with intuition and insight, is awakened by acts of introspection, meditation, and spiritual exploration. This could include engaging in spiritual practices, spending time in nature, or pursuing activities that deepen your connection with your inner wisdom. Finally, your crown chakra, representing connection to the divine and universal consciousness, is nourished through actions that foster spiritual growth, service to humanity, and a deep sense of interconnectedness. This might involve meditation, prayer, acts of service to the community or world, and a dedication to living a life of purpose.

The actions you take should not be driven by external validation or societal expectations. They should be authentic expressions of your inner values, aligning with your personal truth and serving as a conduit for your unique energy. This is where the power of numerology comes into play. Your life path number, calculated from your birthdate, reveals your inherent talents and life purpose. Understanding this number can provide invaluable insights into the types of actions that will resonate most deeply with your soul's purpose. For example, a life path number associated with creativity might indicate that artistic endeavors are crucial for your fulfillment, while a number linked to service might suggest that acts of compassion and helping others are essential for your journey.

Astrology can further illuminate the timing and nature of your actions. By aligning your actions with favorable planetary transits, you can amplify the positive energy and enhance the impact of your efforts. Understanding your astrological chart can reveal periods of heightened energy and opportunity, enabling you to optimize your contributions and maximize their effect. Remember, the universe is always working in your favor, but aligning your actions with celestial energies can help you ride the waves of opportunity with grace and intention.

The importance of crystal healing shouldn't be overlooked. Certain crystals resonate with specific chakras and intentions, amplifying your energy and facilitating the manifestation of your goals. For instance, carnelian can enhance courage and action, aiding you in taking the necessary steps to fulfill your purpose. Amethyst can amplify spiritual growth, encouraging introspection and deepening your connection to your inner guidance. Citrine can enhance manifestation, supporting your ability to bring your vision into reality. By strategically using crystals, you can enhance the energetic flow supporting your actions.

Consider volunteering at a local charity, mentoring a young person, or donating to a cause that resonates with your values. These acts of service are not only beneficial to others, but they also contribute to your own spiritual growth and sense of purpose. If creativity is your calling, consider writing a book, painting a series of landscapes, composing music, starting a blog, or developing a new product. Let your unique talents flow freely, sharing your gifts with the world. If your passion lies in learning, embark on a new educational endeavor, travel to new places, or master a new skill. The journey of learning is an ongoing process that fuels your personal growth and empowers you to make a greater contribution. If leadership is your strength, lead initiatives in your community or workplace, inspiring others and shaping a more positive future. The possibilities are vast and limited only by your imagination and willingness to take action.

Remember to break down larger goals into smaller, more manageable steps. Avoid overwhelm by focusing on one step at a time and celebrate every achievement along the way. This reinforces positive momentum and keeps you motivated on your journey. Regular self-reflection is essential; review your progress, adjust your course as needed, and always stay aligned with your authentic self. Your life purpose is an ongoing journey, a continuous evolution of self-discovery and meaningful action.

Finally, remember the interconnectedness of all things. Your actions, however small they may seem, have a ripple effect, impacting not only your life but also the lives of those around you and ultimately the world at large. By living a purposeful life and taking meaningful action, you are not only fulfilling your own potential but also contributing to the greater good, creating a world that is more compassionate, beautiful, and harmonious. This is the true essence of living a life aligned with your soul's purpose—a life of both personal fulfillment and meaningful contribution. Embrace the journey, trust your intuition, and let your actions become a testament to the power of living a life deeply connected to your purpose.Living with intention and gratitude is not merely a philosophical concept; it's the very bedrock upon which a purposeful life is built. It's the fertile ground from which meaningful actions sprout and flourish. Imagine your life as a garden. Without intention, your garden becomes a chaotic tangle of weeds and untended growth. Without gratitude, even the most vibrant blooms fail to bring true joy. Intention provides the design, the careful planning of what you wish to cultivate. Gratitude is the sunlight and rain, nourishing the growth and celebrating the beauty that unfolds.

To live with intention is to approach each day with a conscious awareness of your goals and values. It's about aligning your actions with your deepest aspirations. This requires a level of self-awareness that goes beyond simply knowing what you want; it requires understanding *why* you want it. What are the deeper motivations driving your desires? Are they rooted in your core values, or are they influenced by external pressures and societal expectations? Take, for example, the desire for financial success. Many pursue wealth driven by a desire for security, a valid and understandable motivation often rooted in the root chakra. However, if this pursuit overshadows other aspects of life—relationships, health, personal fulfillment—it becomes unbalanced. Intentional living involves examining this motivation: Is financial success a means to an end, a stepping stone to greater freedom and the ability to pursue other passions? Or is it an end in itself, a substitute for genuine fulfillment? The answer shapes how you pursue it. An intentional approach would involve planning, creating a realistic budget, seeking financial education, and possibly supplementing income through a creative endeavor, ensuring a balance that doesn't compromise other areas of your being.

This intentional approach extends to all aspects of your life. Consider your relationships. Intentional connection involves nurturing them through conscious effort, actively listening, and expressing appreciation. It's about setting healthy boundaries, prioritizing quality time, and engaging in meaningful interactions. This is not just about maintaining relationships; it's about deepening them, fostering growth, and mutual support. Are you truly present and engaged, or are you merely going through the motions? Intention demands mindfulness and conscious presence.

Furthermore, intention is deeply connected to your chakras. By consciously directing your energy towards specific goals aligned with your values, you strengthen and balance your chakra system. For instance, if you're working on strengthening your willpower (solar plexus chakra), you might set an intention to overcome a specific procrastination habit by breaking down a large task into smaller, more manageable steps. Each small victory fuels your self-esteem and confidence, leading to a healthier, more energized solar plexus.

The practice of gratitude complements intention, forming a powerful synergy that amplifies the positive energy you radiate. Gratitude is not merely a passive acknowledgment of blessings; it's an active practice that shifts your perspective, allowing you to appreciate the abundance in your life, regardless of your circumstances. It fosters contentment and inner peace, creating a positive feedback loop that further enhances your intentionality.
Start by keeping a gratitude journal. Each day, jot down at least three things you are grateful for, however small. These could be simple things: a sunny day, a delicious meal, a kind word from a friend. As you consistently practice gratitude, you begin to notice more things to appreciate, fostering a more positive outlook. The very act of writing down these blessings reinforces the feeling of appreciation, shifting your focus from lack to abundance.

This practice is particularly potent when combined with crystal healing. Certain crystals amplify feelings of gratitude and abundance. Rose quartz, known for its heart-opening properties, promotes feelings of love and appreciation. Citrine, a crystal of abundance, enhances positivity and attracts good fortune. By holding these crystals while reflecting on your blessings, you amplify the positive energy and deepen your feeling of gratitude. Imagine meditating with rose quartz, focusing on specific people or situations in your life for which you're grateful; visualize the energy of gratitude flowing from the crystal, infusing your being with a sense of appreciation and love.

Furthermore, numerology and astrology can guide your practice of intention and gratitude. Your life path number reveals your inherent talents and motivations, allowing you to set intentions that resonate with your true self. Understanding your astrological chart can help you identify auspicious times for setting intentions and expressing gratitude, ensuring that your actions are aligned with celestial energies.

Let's say your numerology indicates a strong connection to creativity, and your astrological chart shows a period of heightened creativity. You might set an intention to express your creativity through a specific project, say writing a short story or painting a landscape. As you work on this project, practice gratitude for the talents and opportunities that allow you to engage in this creative expression. By combining these practices, you leverage cosmic energies to amplify your creative process, achieving a profound sense of fulfillment.

However, the power of intention and gratitude lies not only in the grand gestures but also in the everyday moments. Express gratitude to your barista for making your coffee, acknowledge the kindness of a stranger, appreciate the beauty of a sunset. These small acts of gratitude, performed with intention, weave a tapestry of positivity that enriches your life and the lives of those around you. This is not about forced positivity but about cultivating an attitude of appreciation, noticing the simple joys that often go unnoticed.

Imagine starting your day by expressing gratitude for your health, your home, your loved ones. As you go through your day, consciously choose actions that align with your values and purpose, constantly mindful of the impact you're making. Before bed, revisit these moments, reinforcing the positive energy and deepening your sense of gratitude. This cyclical process reinforces intentionality and gratitude, fostering a positive feedback loop that enhances your overall well-being and creates a more purposeful and fulfilling life. It's a continuous practice, an ongoing journey of self-discovery, allowing you to cultivate a life that truly resonates with your soul. Remember that the universe is always working in your favor, and gratitude helps you recognize the abundance it provides, making you more receptive to the blessings on your path. This conscious living, balanced by both intention and gratitude, is the path to a deeply fulfilling and purposeful life.

Chapter 14: Integrating Holistic Wellness into Your Everyday Life

Integrating holistic wellness into your daily life isn't about a drastic overnight overhaul; *it's a gentle, iterative process, a blossoming rather than a sudden explosion.* Think of it as tending a garden—you wouldn't expect a fully flourishing landscape to appear overnight. It requires consistent nurturing, patient observation, and a willingness to adapt to the ever-changing seasons of life. Sustainable change requires a shift in mindset, moving from a place of striving for perfection to embracing progress and self-compassion. This journey is unique to each individual, acknowledging that what works for one may not work for another. The key lies in finding practices that resonate deeply with your soul and integrating them seamlessly into the fabric of your daily existence.

One of the most crucial aspects of sustainable change is *setting realistic goals.* Avoid overwhelming yourself with ambitious targets that are ultimately unsustainable. Instead, begin with small, manageable steps. If your intention is to incorporate daily meditation, for instance, don't start with an hour-long session. Begin with five minutes, focusing on your breath, and gradually increase the duration as you feel comfortable. Similarly, if you aim to improve your diet, don't abruptly eliminate all processed foods. Instead, start by replacing one unhealthy snack with a healthier alternative each day. These small victories, consistently repeated, build momentum and foster a sense of accomplishment that motivates you to continue on your path.

Self-compassion is paramount throughout this process. There will be days when you falter, days when your intentions fall short. This is not a sign of failure but an opportunity for growth. Acknowledge your imperfections with kindness and understanding. Remember that setbacks are inevitable, and they don't negate the progress you've already made. Instead of beating yourself up over a missed meditation session or an indulgent meal, gently redirect your focus back to your intentions, renewing your commitment with renewed vigor. This self-compassion extends to your interactions with your body, nurturing it with conscious care rather than judgment.

Alongside realistic goals and self-compassion, consistency is vital. Sustainable changes require ongoing effort, not just sporadic bursts of enthusiasm. Incorporate your holistic practices into your daily routine, making them as much a part of your day as brushing your teeth or making your morning coffee. This consistent engagement, even if it's just for a few minutes each day, cultivates a deeper connection with your inner self and strengthens your commitment to your well-being. For example, if you want to incorporate crystal healing into your life, designate a specific time each day – perhaps while you're drinking your tea or before going to bed – to hold a specific crystal and focus on its energy. This routine helps to embed the practice into your daily life.

To further support your sustainable change, seek out a supportive community or mentor. Sharing your journey with others who are on a similar path can provide encouragement, accountability, and a sense of belonging. A mentor, whether a friend, family member, or holistic wellness practitioner, can offer guidance, support, and personalized insights, helping you to navigate any challenges that arise. This network of support can be invaluable when facing obstacles or moments of self-doubt, offering encouragement and reminders of your strengths. Connecting with others who understand your journey can transform isolated struggles into shared experiences of growth.

Consider incorporating techniques that enhance your self-awareness. Journaling, for example, provides a space to reflect on your progress, identify areas needing attention, and track your emotional and energetic shifts. This self-reflective process helps to clarify your intentions, highlight patterns of behavior, and identify potential roadblocks along the way. Regularly reviewing your journal entries can provide valuable insights, allowing you to adjust your approach as needed, keeping your practices relevant and effective. It's an ongoing dialogue with yourself, fostering introspection and self-understanding.

Another valuable tool is mindfulness meditation. Even short sessions can help you to become more attuned to your body's signals, recognizing patterns of stress, tension, and emotional reactivity. This heightened awareness allows you to make more conscious choices, responding to challenges with greater clarity and composure. Mindfulness empowers you to recognize what triggers imbalances and adjust your lifestyle accordingly.

The integration of numerology and astrology into your sustainable lifestyle can offer further guidance and support. By understanding your numerological profile, you can gain insights into your natural strengths and potential challenges, informing your goal-setting and providing a framework for self-acceptance and growth. Likewise, understanding your astrological chart can help you identify periods of heightened energy and receptivity, aligning your actions with cosmic rhythms for enhanced effectiveness. For example, if your numerology suggests a predisposition towards creativity, set intentions that support this inherent talent, such as regularly practicing a creative hobby or pursuing creative projects.

Additionally, chakra work, combined with crystal healing, can provide a pathway to sustainable change by addressing energetic blockages that may be hindering your progress. Each chakra is associated with specific aspects of well-being, and imbalances in these energy centers can manifest as physical, emotional, or mental symptoms. By working with crystals attuned to each chakra, you can gently encourage the flow of energy, promoting balance and healing. For instance, if you're feeling overwhelmed and stressed (solar plexus chakra imbalance), you might use crystals like citrine or carnelian to help revitalize and restore balance to this energy center.

The process of integrating holistic wellness into your everyday life is not a race but a marathon. Embrace the journey with patience, self-compassion, and a willingness to learn and grow. By incorporating sustainable practices that align with your values and resonate with your soul, you can cultivate a life that is not only healthier and more balanced but also deeply fulfilling and purposeful. Remember that true, lasting change is a gradual process that unfolds over time, not a sudden transformation. Celebrate your progress, learn from your setbacks, and continue to nurture your well-being with consistent effort and unwavering self-love. The journey itself is a testament to your commitment to living a more authentic and holistic life. And remember, the universe is your ally in this journey; trust the process and allow yourself to be guided by your intuition. The rewards of this holistic approach far outweigh the challenges, leading you toward a richer, more vibrant, and truly fulfilling existence. This transformation is not merely a change in lifestyle, but a fundamental shift in your relationship with yourself and the world around you – a journey of continuous growth and self-discovery, guided by the wisdom of your inner self and the wisdom of the universe. Maintaining a consistent holistic wellness practice requires more than just initial enthusiasm; it demands a strategic approach to overcome inevitable challenges and sustain motivation over time. Think of it like training for a marathon: the initial burst of energy is crucial, but enduring stamina requires careful planning and consistent effort. This journey is deeply personal, and the methods that work for one individual may not resonate with another. The key is to discover strategies that truly align with your unique personality, lifestyle, and spiritual path.

One common obstacle is the tendency to set unrealistic expectations. We often fall into the trap of believing that a complete transformation should occur overnight. This is a recipe for disappointment and burnout. Instead, begin by identifying one or two practices you genuinely wish to integrate into your life. Perhaps it's a daily 10-minute meditation session, a commitment to incorporating more whole foods into your diet, or a regular practice of energy healing techniques. Start small, celebrate each milestone, and gradually add more practices as you build a solid foundation. This incremental approach fosters a sense of accomplishment and prevents overwhelming feelings of pressure.

Another crucial element is self-compassion. This isn't about self-indulgence, but rather about cultivating a gentle, understanding approach to yourself, acknowledging that you will inevitably experience setbacks. There will be days when you miss your meditation, succumb to a less-than-healthy meal, or feel completely drained of energy. When this occurs, avoid self-criticism. Instead, acknowledge the lapse with kindness, forgive yourself, and gently redirect your focus back to your intentions. Self-compassion is a crucial ingredient in creating sustainable change because it acknowledges the inherent imperfections of the human experience. It's about treating yourself with the same care and understanding you would offer a dear friend facing similar challenges.

To maintain motivation, consider incorporating elements of gamification into your wellness routine. This could involve tracking your progress using a journal, a dedicated app, or even a simple chart. Visually witnessing your progress can be a powerful motivator. Reward yourself for achieving milestones—not with unhealthy treats, but with activities that nurture your well-being, such as a relaxing bath, a massage, or time spent in nature. These small rewards reinforce positive habits and provide a sense of accomplishment that fuels your continued commitment.

Building a supportive community is invaluable. Sharing your journey with others who are also committed to holistic wellness can provide accountability, encouragement, and a sense of shared purpose. This could involve joining a meditation group, attending workshops, connecting with like-minded individuals online, or simply sharing your experiences with a trusted friend or family member. The collective energy of a supportive community can strengthen your resolve and provide a space for sharing challenges and celebrating victories.

Visual reminders can be exceptionally effective. Place inspiring quotes, images of your desired outcome (perhaps a picture of yourself feeling energized and healthy), or crystals that resonate with your intentions in prominent locations around your home or workspace. These visual cues serve as subtle reminders of your commitment and can help to maintain your focus. The constant presence of these reminders can help to integrate your wellness practices more seamlessly into your daily routine.

Incorporating the principles of numerology and astrology can further enhance your motivation and provide a deeper understanding of your unique path. Understanding your numerological profile can highlight your inherent strengths and challenges, providing insights into your natural tendencies and informing your goal-setting process. Astrology can help you to align your wellness practices with cyclical rhythms and periods of heightened energy. For example, you might schedule more demanding practices during periods of increased planetary energy, while allowing for more rest and relaxation during periods of lower energy.

Harnessing the power of intention setting can be a remarkably effective tool for maintaining momentum. Each morning, or before beginning your daily wellness practices, consciously set your intentions for the day. Visualize yourself achieving your goals, feeling the positive energy associated with those accomplishments. This act of consciously aligning your energy with your intentions creates a powerful synergy that enhances your motivation and facilitates success.

Flexibility is key. Life is unpredictable, and there will be times when your well-planned routine needs adjustment. Be kind to yourself when unexpected events disrupt your schedule. Instead of viewing these disruptions as failures, see them as opportunities to adapt and adjust your approach. Flexibility allows you to maintain your commitment without becoming rigid or overly structured. It's about maintaining the overall spirit of your commitment, even if the specific details change.

Regular self-reflection is vital for maintaining both consistency and motivation. Journaling can be a profound tool for tracking your progress, identifying challenges, and celebrating successes. This self-reflective process allows you to gain clarity, understand your patterns, and adjust your approach as needed. It's a conversation with your inner self, a space to observe your emotional and energetic shifts, and to honor the journey of self-discovery. Finally, remember that maintaining a holistic wellness practice is not a race, but a lifelong journey. There will be moments of doubt, challenges to overcome, and times when you question your progress. Embrace these moments as integral parts of the process, learning from them and growing stronger with each experience. The commitment to self-care and holistic wellness is a testament to your self-love and dedication to a more fulfilling and vibrant life. It's a journey of self-discovery, a path towards deeper connection with your inner self and the universal energies that surround you. And the rewards – a deeper sense of self-awareness, enhanced physical and emotional well-being, and a greater sense of peace and purpose – are immeasurable. Embrace the journey, celebrate your progress, and trust in the power of your own inherent resilience and the unwavering support of the universe. The path to holistic wellness, while deeply rewarding, is not always a solitary journey. Even the most self-sufficient individuals can benefit from seeking guidance and support along the way. Just as a skilled navigator utilizes charts and compasses, we too can leverage the expertise and wisdom of others to navigate the complexities of our inner landscapes. This doesn't signify weakness, but rather a recognition of the inherent value in collaborative growth and the power of shared experience.

Consider the analogy of a musician learning a complex instrument. While self-teaching is possible, a skilled teacher can provide invaluable insights, correct technique, and offer tailored feedback, accelerating the learning process and preventing the development of ingrained bad habits. Similarly, in our journey towards holistic wellness, seeking guidance from experienced practitioners can significantly enhance our progress and deepen our understanding.

Numerous professionals can offer valuable support. Reiki masters, for example, can provide energy healing sessions, clearing energetic blockages and promoting a sense of balance and well-being. Their expertise in channeling universal life force energy can facilitate profound healing on physical, emotional, and spiritual levels. Similarly, experienced astrologers can interpret your birth chart, offering insights into your personality, life path, and karmic patterns. This understanding can inform your wellness practices, guiding you towards activities and approaches that align with your unique energetic signature. Numerology experts, by analyzing the numerical vibrations associated with your name and birthdate, can reveal further insights into your strengths, weaknesses, and life purpose, enabling you to tailor your wellness practices to your inherent nature.

Crystal healers, with their deep knowledge of the vibrational properties of different crystals, can help you select crystals that resonate with your specific needs and intentions. These crystals can be used in meditation, energy healing sessions, or simply placed around your home to enhance the overall energy field. Furthermore, certified yoga instructors, meditation teachers, and nutritionists can provide specialized guidance and support, offering tailored programs to address your individual needs and goals.

Beyond individual practitioners, support groups and communities can play a vital role in maintaining motivation and fostering a sense of shared purpose. Joining a meditation group, a Reiki circle, or an online forum dedicated to holistic wellness can provide a sense of belonging and shared experience. Sharing your journey with like-minded individuals allows you to connect with others who understand the challenges and rewards of the path, offering mutual support, encouragement, and accountability. The collective energy within these groups can be incredibly empowering, creating a synergistic effect that strengthens individual resolve.

Finding appropriate support can be as simple as conducting an online search for practitioners in your area. Websites, social media groups, and online directories can help you locate individuals specializing in different modalities. When searching for practitioners, pay attention to their credentials, experience, and testimonials. Read reviews, browse their websites, and if possible, schedule a brief consultation before committing to a longer-term engagement. Trust your intuition; if a practitioner doesn't feel right for you, don't hesitate to seek someone else.

Remember, seeking support is not an admission of failure; rather, it is a demonstration of self-awareness and a commitment to continuous growth. It's a recognition that we all require guidance and support at different points on our journey. The path to holistic wellness is rarely linear; there will be moments of doubt, setbacks, and periods of intense self-reflection. A supportive network acts as a buffer against these challenges, offering encouragement, understanding, and the strength needed to navigate difficult times.

Furthermore, don't underestimate the value of seeking support from friends and family who understand and respect your commitment to holistic wellness. These individuals may not possess the specialized knowledge of trained practitioners, but their unwavering love and support can be incredibly powerful. Sharing your experiences with trusted loved ones can provide a sense of validation, emotional release, and a safe space to explore your thoughts and feelings. Remember to be clear about your needs and boundaries, ensuring that your interactions with loved ones are supportive and nurturing rather than critical or judgmental. In addition to professional and personal support, consider exploring online resources and communities. Numerous websites, blogs, and forums are dedicated to holistic wellness, offering articles, advice, and opportunities to connect with like-minded individuals. These resources can provide valuable information, enhance your understanding of different modalities, and foster a sense of connection with a wider community of individuals on a similar path. Remember to be discerning when selecting online resources, ensuring that the information is accurate, reliable, and sourced from reputable sources.

The integration of holistic wellness practices into your daily life is a continuous process of learning, adapting, and refining your approach. This journey is deeply personal, and there is no one-size-fits-all solution. Embracing the support available to you – whether from professional practitioners, supportive communities, or trusted loved ones – significantly enhances your chances of success and deepens your overall experience. This collaborative approach fosters a sense of shared responsibility, creating a powerful network that nourishes both your personal growth and the collective journey towards holistic well-being. Remember that seeking support is not a sign of weakness, but rather a testament to your commitment to your own self-care and the pursuit of a truly fulfilling and vibrant life.

The tools and techniques discussed throughout this book—Reiki, numerology, astrology, chakra work, and crystal healing—are powerful instruments for personal transformation, but their effectiveness is greatly amplified when combined with the support of others. Consider the synergistic power of a group Reiki session, where the combined energy of multiple practitioners creates a powerful healing field. This collective energy is significantly stronger than the energy of a single practitioner, demonstrating the power of collaboration in achieving holistic wellness. Similarly, discussing astrological insights with a group can lead to a deeper understanding of individual experiences and the interconnectedness of life itself.

Building a supportive community doesn't necessarily require joining large organizations or attending numerous workshops. It could be as simple as sharing your experiences and practices with a close friend or family member. The key is to establish a connection with individuals who respect and understand your commitment to self-care. This could be a daily check-in with a friend, sharing your meditation experiences, or discussing your progress in incorporating healthy eating habits. The simple act of sharing your journey can significantly boost your motivation and provide a sense of accountability.

Furthermore, remember that support isn't always about receiving advice or guidance; it can also be about offering support to others. Sharing your knowledge and experiences with others who are also embarking on their holistic wellness journey can be a remarkably rewarding experience. This act of giving can strengthen your own commitment, deepen your understanding, and create a virtuous cycle of mutual support and growth. By supporting others, you not only enhance their journey, but you also reinforce your own commitment to holistic wellness.

In conclusion, integrating holistic wellness into your everyday life is a journey of self-discovery, personal growth, and continuous learning. While the practices and techniques explored in this book offer a roadmap for transformation, remember that your journey is unique. Seek support when needed, utilize the available resources, and embrace the power of community to maximize your potential and achieve a truly fulfilling and balanced life.

Remember that the support you seek and the support you offer are integral parts of this transformative journey. Embrace both, and you will discover a profound depth of strength and resilience within yourself and within the supportive network you cultivate. The path to holistic wellness is a marathon, not a sprint. There will be days filled with vibrant energy and effortless flow, where the practices feel intuitive and the results are palpable. Then there will be days when the energy feels sluggish, the motivation wanes, and the path ahead seems shrouded in fog. This is perfectly normal. The ebb and flow of energy is a fundamental aspect of life itself, and acknowledging this inherent rhythm is crucial to maintaining a compassionate and understanding approach to your journey.

Instead of viewing these challenging moments as failures, reframe them as opportunities for growth. Each stumble, each setback, each moment of doubt, offers valuable lessons that shape and refine your understanding of yourself and your path. Embrace these moments with self-compassion, recognizing that they are an integral part of the unfolding process. Journaling can be a powerful tool here, allowing you to process your emotions, reflect on your experiences, and gain a deeper understanding of your inner landscape.

Self-compassion is not self-indulgence; it is a recognition of your inherent worthiness and a commitment to treating yourself with the same kindness and understanding you would offer a cherished friend. When faced with challenges, speak to yourself with the same gentleness and encouragement you would offer someone you love. Avoid self-criticism and harsh judgment; instead, focus on self-acceptance and self-forgiveness.

Celebrate the small victories. Did you manage to meditate for five minutes today, even when your mind was racing? That's a triumph! Did you choose a nourishing meal over processed junk food? That's a significant step towards holistic wellness. Did you take a moment to connect with nature, even if it was just a brief walk around the block? That's a powerful act of self-care.

Keep a progress journal, not just to track your practices, but to document your feelings, insights, and celebrations. Record your daily experiences, noting both your triumphs and your challenges. Reflect on the lessons learned and the shifts in your perspective. Reviewing this journal periodically can provide a powerful reminder of how far you've come and the consistent progress you've made.

Consider creating a visual representation of your progress. This could be a mood board, a vision board, a collage, or even a simple chart tracking your daily practices. Seeing your progress visually can be incredibly motivating, reinforcing your commitment and reminding you of the positive changes you've implemented. This visual reminder can be particularly useful during those moments when doubt creeps in or motivation falters.
Reward yourself for your efforts. These rewards don't have to be extravagant; they can be simple gestures of self-care that nourish your body, mind, and spirit. A long bath with essential oils, a relaxing massage, a quiet evening spent reading a favorite book, or a peaceful walk in nature – these are all powerful ways to celebrate your achievements and acknowledge your commitment to self-care.

Remember that holistic wellness is a lifelong journey, not a destination. There is no finish line; it's a continuous process of growth, learning, and self-discovery. Embrace the ongoing nature of this path, recognizing that there will always be new challenges, new opportunities, and new levels of self-understanding to explore.

The tools and techniques you've learned – Reiki, numerology, astrology, chakra work, and crystal healing – are not merely practices; they are companions on your journey. They are instruments of self-discovery, helping you to understand your energetic landscape, identify your strengths and weaknesses, and cultivate a deeper connection with your inner self. Each practice offers unique insights, enriching your understanding of your body, mind, and spirit. Reiki can help you to clear energetic blockages, promoting a sense of balance and well-being. Numerology can provide insights into your life path and purpose, guiding you towards activities that align with your inherent nature. Astrology can help you to understand your personality and karmic patterns, informing your choices and actions. Chakra work can help you to balance your energy centers, promoting emotional, physical, and spiritual harmony. Crystal healing can enhance your energy field, promoting healing and well-being.

These modalities, when integrated into your daily life, create a powerful synergy, amplifying their individual effects and contributing to a holistic approach to self-care. The more consistently you engage with these practices, the more attuned you become to your own energy and the subtle shifts within your being.

Remember to be patient with yourself. The process of integrating holistic wellness into your daily life takes time, effort, and dedication. There will be days when you feel overwhelmed, frustrated, or discouraged. But perseverance is key. Keep practicing, keep learning, keep growing, and remember to celebrate every step along the way.

Consider the metaphor of a gardener nurturing a delicate plant. The gardener doesn't expect immediate blooms; they understand that growth takes time, nourishment, and consistent care. Similarly, your journey towards holistic wellness requires patience, nurturing, and consistent effort. Celebrate the small buds of progress, knowing that they will eventually blossom into something beautiful and profound.

The essence of holistic wellness lies not just in the practices themselves, but in the cultivation of a mindful and compassionate approach to your life. It's about listening to your body, honoring your emotions, and fostering a deep connection with your inner self. It's about embracing your imperfections, celebrating your strengths, and recognizing that you are worthy of love, acceptance, and unwavering self-compassion.

As you continue on your journey, remember that you are not alone. You have access to a wealth of resources – practitioners, support groups, online communities, and personal connections – to guide and support you along the way. Embrace these resources, allowing them to enrich your experience and deepen your understanding of holistic wellness.

Celebrate your progress, acknowledge your challenges, and embrace the ongoing nature of your journey. The path to holistic wellness is a continuous process of growth, self-discovery, and self-acceptance. Embrace the journey, and you will discover a profound sense of well-being and fulfillment that extends far beyond the physical realm. The journey itself is the reward, a testament to your dedication, your resilience, and your unwavering commitment to a life of purpose, joy, and profound inner peace. The celebration is not merely at the end; it is woven into the very fabric of the journey itself.The journey towards holistic wellness is a deeply personal one, a unique tapestry woven from the threads of your individual experiences, beliefs, and aspirations. There's no single, prescribed path; rather, it's a continuous unfolding, a dance between self-discovery and self-acceptance. Embrace the imperfections, the stumbles, and the moments of doubt, for they are all integral parts of the beautiful, intricate design of your life.

Think of your body as a finely tuned instrument, capable of producing harmonious melodies when its strings are properly aligned. Each of the practices—Reiki, numerology, astrology, chakra work, and crystal healing—acts as a skilled tuner, gently adjusting and refining the vibrational frequencies within you. Reiki, with its gentle energy flows, clears blockages and promotes a sense of deep relaxation, allowing the body's natural healing mechanisms to flourish. Numerology unveils the hidden patterns and energies embedded within your birth date, offering insights into your life path and the unique gifts you bring to the world. Astrology illuminates the celestial influences shaping your personality and life experiences, providing a framework for understanding your strengths, challenges, and karmic patterns. Chakra work, the balancing of your energy centers, is akin to tuning the individual notes of your instrument. Each chakra resonates with specific aspects of your being—physical, emotional, mental, and spiritual—and when they are in harmony, your entire being vibrates with a sense of balance and well-being. The vibrant colors and energies of crystals further amplify this process, acting as powerful conduits of healing energy, supporting the chakras in their quest for equilibrium.

Remember, this is not simply about mastering techniques; it's about cultivating a deeper connection with your inner self, a profound understanding of your own energetic landscape. It's about listening to the whispers of your intuition, honoring the wisdom of your body, and nurturing the spirit that resides within. Imagine yourself as a conductor of an orchestra, each instrument representing a facet of your being—your physical body, your emotions, your intellect, your spirit. Your role is to harmonize these elements, to create a symphony of well-being that resonates through every aspect of your life.

Self-compassion is the unwavering conductor's baton, guiding you with kindness and understanding through the sometimes discordant notes of life. When challenges arise, and they inevitably will, approach them with gentle curiosity, seeking the lessons embedded within. Avoid harsh self-criticism; instead, treat yourself with the same empathy and support you would offer a close friend facing a similar struggle. Journaling becomes your confidante, a safe space to explore your emotions, process your experiences, and gain a clearer perspective on your journey.

The practice of self-reflection is crucial. Take time each day, perhaps during your morning meditation or evening journaling, to reflect on your progress. Acknowledge your achievements, however small they may seem, and celebrate the steps you've taken towards holistic well-being. Did you manage to incorporate a few minutes of mindful breathing into your day? Did you choose a nourishing meal over a less healthy option? Did you spend a few moments connecting with nature? Each of these acts, seemingly insignificant on their own, contributes to the larger tapestry of your well-being.

Visualize your progress, creating a tangible representation of your journey. A vision board, a mood board, or a simple chart tracking your daily practices can serve as a powerful reminder of how far you've come and the positive changes you've implemented. This visual representation can be especially helpful during times of doubt or discouragement, providing a tangible testament to your commitment and perseverance.

Celebrate your milestones with acts of self-care—a relaxing bath, a rejuvenating massage, a quiet evening spent reading, or a peaceful walk in nature. These are not merely rewards; they are essential components of your journey, nourishing your body, mind, and spirit. They are acts of self-love, affirming your commitment to your well-being and acknowledging the effort you've invested in your growth.

Integrate these practices into your daily routine, making them an integral part of your life. Start small, perhaps incorporating just one or two practices at a time. Consistency is key; even a few minutes of dedicated practice each day can have a profound impact on your overall well-being. Gradually incorporate more practices as you feel comfortable and confident in your abilities.

The tools you've learned—Reiki, numerology, astrology, chakra work, and crystal healing—are not merely techniques; they are powerful allies on your path to holistic wellness. They are instruments of self-discovery, helping you to uncover your hidden strengths, address your challenges, and cultivate a deeper connection with your inner self. Each modality offers unique insights, enriching your understanding of your complex and multifaceted nature. Consider the synergy between these practices. Reiki can clear energetic blockages, creating a receptive environment for the other modalities to work their magic. Numerology can reveal your life path and purpose, guiding you towards activities and relationships that align with your true nature. Astrology can provide insight into your personality and karmic patterns, helping you to navigate life's challenges with greater awareness and understanding. Chakra work can balance your energy centers, promoting emotional, physical, and spiritual harmony. Crystal healing can amplify the healing energy of the other modalities, enhancing your overall sense of well-being.

As you integrate these practices into your daily life, you'll become increasingly attuned to the subtle energies within and around you. You'll develop a deeper understanding of your body's needs, your emotions, and your spiritual aspirations. You'll cultivate a greater sense of self-awareness, allowing you to navigate life's challenges with greater ease and grace. Embrace the imperfections inherent in the journey. There will be days when you feel overwhelmed, frustrated, or discouraged. There will be times when your energy feels low, your motivation wanes, and the path ahead seems unclear. These moments are opportunities for growth, chances to learn from your mistakes, and develop greater self-compassion.

View setbacks not as failures but as valuable lessons, integral components of the learning process. Journaling can be invaluable during these times, providing a safe space to explore your emotions, process your experiences, and gain a deeper understanding of your inner world.

Remember, holistic wellness is a lifelong journey, a continuous process of growth, learning, and self-discovery. There's no finish line, no ultimate destination; it's a path of continuous exploration and evolution. Embrace the ongoing nature of this journey, accepting the ebbs and flows of energy, the moments of triumph and the periods of challenge. Celebrate the small victories, acknowledge the lessons learned from setbacks, and cultivate unwavering self-compassion throughout the process. The reward lies not solely in the destination but in the richness and growth experienced along the way. Embrace the journey; the transformation is the destination.

Chapter 15: Continuing Your Cosmic Healing Journey

Now, as we approach the culmination of our year-long journey, let's pause and reflect. **Let's take a moment to celebrate the incredible transformation you've undergone, the remarkable progress you've made on your path toward holistic well-being.** This isn't merely about ticking off boxes on a checklist; it's about recognizing the profound shifts in your perspective, your energy, and your connection to yourself and the universe.

This process of self-assessment isn't about judgment or criticism; it's an act of loving self-inquiry, a chance to honor the dedication and effort you've invested in your growth. It's about acknowledging your triumphs, however small they may seem, and identifying areas where you can continue to nurture and expand your well-being. Think of it as a gentle check-in with your inner self, a loving conversation between you and the wiser, more empowered version of yourself you've become.

Begin by creating a peaceful and quiet space for reflection. Light a candle, play soothing music, or sit amidst the comforting embrace of nature. Allow yourself to fully relax, releasing any tension or stress that may be lingering in your body. Breathe deeply, feeling the rhythm of your breath, connecting with the present moment. This space of tranquility is your sanctuary, a sacred place where you can connect with your inner wisdom.

Now, let your thoughts gently drift back over the past year. Recall the daily practices you've undertaken—the Reiki sessions, the numerological explorations, the astrological insights, the chakra balancing, and the crystal healings. Remember the moments of connection, the breakthroughs, and the times you felt a deep sense of peace and harmony. Let these memories fill you with a sense of gratitude and accomplishment.

Consider the changes you've witnessed in your physical, emotional, and spiritual well-being.

Have you noticed an increase in your energy levels? Do you find yourself feeling more grounded and centered? Have you experienced a shift in your emotional landscape, a greater capacity for resilience and self-compassion? Has your spiritual awareness deepened, revealing a richer connection to the universe?

Journaling can be an invaluable tool during this self-assessment process. Write down your observations, your reflections, and your feelings. Don't censor yourself; allow your thoughts and emotions to flow freely onto the page. This process of writing is not only cathartic but also helps you to organize and clarify your thoughts, facilitating deeper self-understanding. Perhaps you've noticed a significant improvement in your sleep patterns, a reduction in stress levels, or a heightened sense of clarity and focus. These are all signs of progress, tangible evidence of the positive impact of your dedication to holistic wellness. Celebrate these victories, acknowledging the effort and commitment that led to these positive changes.

However, also acknowledge that there may be areas where you feel you could have made more progress. This isn't about self-criticism; it's about identifying areas where you can focus your energies in the coming year. Perhaps you struggled with consistency in your daily practices, or you found certain modalities more challenging than others. These insights are invaluable, providing a roadmap for future growth.

For example, you might have found the daily Reiki practice incredibly beneficial for stress reduction, but you may have struggled to maintain a regular schedule for chakra balancing. This recognition isn't a failure; it's an opportunity. Perhaps you need to adjust your approach to chakra work, finding ways to integrate it more seamlessly into your daily life. Maybe you need to explore different techniques, find a supportive community, or simply adjust your expectations to achieve sustainable consistency.

Remember, the journey of holistic wellness is not a linear progression; it's a winding path with its share of twists and turns. There will be days when you feel on top of the world, and there will be days when you feel challenged, discouraged, or overwhelmed. Both are perfectly normal parts of the process.

If you've experienced setbacks or challenges, don't allow them to diminish the progress you've already made. Instead, view them as opportunities for learning and growth. What lessons can you extract from these experiences? How can you apply these learnings to navigate future challenges with greater resilience and grace?

Now, consider your numerological insights. Has your understanding of your life path number deepened, providing clarity on your purpose and direction? Have you used this understanding to guide your choices and actions, aligning yourself with your true nature and potential? Similarly, how has your understanding of your astrological chart enhanced your self-awareness? Has it helped you navigate relationships, career decisions, or personal challenges with greater insight?

Reflect on the synergy between the different modalities. How have Reiki, numerology, astrology, chakra work, and crystal healing complemented and supported one another? Have you noticed how one practice enhances the effectiveness of others? For instance, a Reiki session might have cleared energetic blockages, making you more receptive to the insights gained through numerology or astrology.

As you delve deeper into this self-assessment, you may discover themes or patterns emerging from your experiences. These recurring themes offer valuable insights into your strengths, your challenges, and your areas for growth. By recognizing these patterns, you can develop a clearer understanding of your individual needs and develop a more targeted approach to your holistic wellness journey.

This process of reflection is not just about looking back; it's also about looking forward. What are your goals for the coming year? How can you build upon the foundation you've already established? What new practices might you explore? What adjustments might you make to your existing routines to foster even greater well-being?

Perhaps you'll deepen your exploration of Reiki, becoming proficient in advanced techniques. Or maybe you'll explore other energy healing modalities, such as Pranic Healing or Therapeutic Touch. You might delve deeper into the study of astrology, learning to interpret birth charts with greater precision and understanding. Or you may embark on a journey of crystal healing, expanding your knowledge of different crystals and their properties. You may even delve into the world of sound healing, or explore the many forms of meditation. Remember, the journey of holistic wellness is a lifelong endeavor, a continuous process of learning, growth, and self-discovery. There's no endpoint, no ultimate destination. Embrace the ongoing nature of this journey, celebrating your achievements, learning from your challenges, and cultivating unwavering self-compassion along the way.

The transformation you've experienced isn't just about acquiring new skills or techniques; it's about cultivating a deeper connection with yourself, a profound understanding of your inner landscape, and a powerful sense of self-empowerment. It's about learning to listen to your intuition, honor your body's wisdom, and nurture the vibrant spirit that resides within you. This is the true essence of the Cosmic Healing Code. Now that we've reflected on the past year's journey, a vibrant landscape of self-discovery unfolds before us. It's time to cultivate new intentions, seeds of growth that will blossom into an even more radiant version of ourselves. This isn't about striving for perfection; it's about embracing the ongoing evolution of our holistic well-being. Think of it as charting a course for the next leg of our voyage, guided by the wisdom we've gained and the potential we've yet to unlock.

Let's begin by identifying areas where you feel a gentle pull, a whisper of curiosity or a yearning for deeper exploration. Perhaps your Reiki practice has blossomed, and you find yourself drawn to the intricacies of advanced techniques like distant healing or karuna Reiki. Maybe the subtle energies of crystals have captivated your imagination, prompting you to delve into the rich world of crystal grids or explore the vibrational properties of specific stones tailored to specific needs or intentions.

Consider your numerological profile. Have you fully embraced the insights it offers? Perhaps you've only scratched the surface of understanding your life path number or your soul urge number. Now is the time to delve deeper, exploring the nuances of your numerological blueprint to uncover hidden potentials and align your actions with your unique destiny. This deeper understanding can provide clarity on career paths, relationship dynamics, and even health choices. For example, if your life path number suggests a creative calling, you might set an intention to dedicate more time to artistic expression, perhaps through painting, writing, or music, allowing that creative energy to flow freely.

And what about your astrological chart? It's a celestial map of your soul, rich with insights into your strengths, challenges, and karmic patterns. Perhaps you're ready to explore the intricacies of planetary transits, gaining a deeper understanding of how cosmic energies impact your life. This might involve learning about astrological forecasting, enabling you to navigate life's challenges with greater awareness and grace. Or maybe you'll explore the art of synastry, gaining deeper understanding of your relationship dynamics with loved ones. Understanding your astrological predispositions allows you to make conscious choices aligned with your cosmic blueprint.

Our chakra system, the energetic powerhouse within, deserves continued attention. Perhaps you've mastered balancing your root and crown chakras, but you sense an energetic imbalance in your solar plexus or heart chakra. This could manifest as issues with self-esteem, emotional vulnerability, or difficulty expressing your needs. Setting intentions to heal these areas involves specific practices, like breathwork, visualization, or targeted crystal healing to facilitate energy flow. You might set the intention to practice heart chakra meditations daily, utilizing rose quartz to amplify the healing process, or perhaps incorporate yoga postures to open and strengthen the heart center.

Imagine your intentions as radiant beams of light, focused and purposeful, illuminating the path towards your holistic well-being. Write them down in a journal, making them specific, measurable, achievable, relevant, and time-bound (SMART goals). For instance, instead of setting a vague intention like "improve my energy levels," aim for something more precise, like "increase my energy levels by practicing 15 minutes of daily Qi Gong three times per week for the next three months."

Once you've identified your intentions, visualize yourself achieving them. Feel the energy of these goals resonating within you. Engage all your senses; what will you see, hear, feel, smell, and taste as you achieve these intentions? This visualization process anchors your intentions into your subconscious mind, imbuing them with power and momentum.

Now, let's consider the integration of these different modalities. How can you synergistically blend Reiki, numerology, astrology, chakra work, and crystal healing to create a holistic approach to your continued growth? For instance, a Reiki session could prepare your energy field for a deeper numerological exploration, revealing hidden patterns and enhancing your understanding of your life path. Or you might utilize crystal healing to balance specific chakras highlighted in your astrological chart, creating a personalized energetic alignment.

Remember, there is no "one size fits all" approach to holistic healing. The beauty of this journey is the opportunity to personalize your practices and create a unique path that aligns with your individual needs and preferences. Embrace experimentation, exploring different techniques and modalities until you find what resonates most deeply with your soul. Beyond the specific modalities, cultivating self-compassion is essential for continued growth. Acknowledge that there will be days when your motivation wanes, when you feel overwhelmed or discouraged. These are natural parts of the process. Treat yourself with kindness, understanding, and forgiveness. Celebrate your progress, no matter how small it may seem, and remember that every step forward, no matter how tentative, is a significant achievement on your path.

Setting intentions is not a one-time event; it's an ongoing dialogue with yourself, a process of refinement and adaptation. Regularly revisit your intentions, assessing your progress and making adjustments as needed. Allow yourself the flexibility to adjust your path, to explore new avenues of growth and to adapt to the ebb and flow of life. Remember, your journey of holistic wellness is a continuous unfolding, a vibrant tapestry woven with self-discovery, growth, and self-love.

As you embark on this new phase of your journey, remember the power of community. Connecting with like-minded individuals who share your passion for holistic wellness can provide invaluable support, inspiration, and encouragement. Sharing your experiences, challenges, and triumphs with others can create a sense of belonging and mutual understanding.

Perhaps you'll consider joining a Reiki circle, attending a crystal healing workshop, or participating in an astrology study group. These shared experiences can amplify your growth, providing a supportive environment for exploring new techniques and deepening your understanding of the modalities.

The final piece of the puzzle is to maintain a deep connection with your intuition. Trust your inner guidance, your innate wisdom. Pay attention to the subtle nudges and whispers from your inner self. They are your compass, guiding you towards the path that is uniquely yours. This is not just about setting intentions, but listening to the subtle cues from your body and your soul. These cues are essential for making adjustments to your intentions and ensuring that they remain aligned with your truest self. Learn to differentiate between fear-based thoughts and intuition-led guidance.

So, as you embark on the next chapter of your cosmic healing journey, remember that this is a journey of self-discovery, self-empowerment, and deep connection with the universe. Embrace the challenges, celebrate the triumphs, and above all, cherish the continuous unfolding of your holistic well-being. The power to heal, to grow, and to thrive resides within you. Now, go forth and create the life that is truly meant to be yours. The path to holistic wellness is not a sprint; it's a marathon, a continuous journey of self-discovery and growth. While setting intentions and exploring different modalities are crucial steps, the true power lies in consistently integrating these practices into your daily life. Think of your daily routine as the fertile ground where the seeds of your intentions can sprout, blossom, and bear fruit. Consistency is the key, fostering a rhythm of self-care that nourishes your mind, body, and spirit.

This isn't about creating an inflexible, rigid schedule that feels restrictive and burdensome. Instead, envision a flexible framework, a gentle guide that supports your evolving needs. Start small. Perhaps dedicate just five minutes each morning to a grounding meditation, focusing on your breath and connecting with the present moment. Or, choose one crystal that resonates with your current intention, carrying it with you throughout the day as a tangible reminder of your commitment to self-healing.

The benefits of daily practice are profound and multifaceted. Regular Reiki self-healing sessions, even brief ones, can subtly yet powerfully shift your energetic field, clearing blockages and promoting a sense of calm and centeredness. This consistent energy work helps to maintain a state of balance, preventing energy depletion and promoting a sense of overall well-being. You might notice a significant difference in your stress levels, sleep quality, and overall vitality as a result of this consistent practice. Try incorporating short Reiki sessions before sleep, allowing the gentle energy to wash over you and prepare you for a restful night.

Similarly, incorporating numerology into your daily life can provide daily insights and guidance. Perhaps you could take a moment each morning to reflect on the energy of the current day, considering its numerical significance and how it might influence your actions and interactions. This might involve looking up the numerological significance of the current date, focusing on its vibrations and energies for the day. This simple ritual can infuse your day with intention and awareness.

The wisdom of astrology offers daily guidance as well. You can begin your day by briefly consulting your daily horoscope, considering any planetary influences that might affect your mood or energy levels. This doesn't mean rigidly adhering to astrological predictions; rather, it provides a framework for self-awareness, helping you navigate potential challenges with greater grace and understanding. This awareness allows for proactive adjustments to your schedule and approach to potential situations. For example, if a challenging planetary aspect is indicated, you could plan for extra self-care or prioritize tasks that require less mental or emotional exertion.

Your chakra system, the energetic core of your being, benefits immensely from daily attention. Even a few minutes of focused breathwork, visualization, or specific yoga poses can make a significant difference in balancing your energy centers. You can target a different chakra each day, creating a weekly cycle of energetic nourishment. This consistent practice can address imbalances and prevent energetic blockages from accumulating, promoting a sense of flow and vitality.

Crystal healing, too, can be incorporated into your daily routine with minimal effort. Keep a selection of crystals readily available, choosing one or two to work with based on your current needs or intentions. Hold them in your hands, meditate with them, or simply place them near you as a source of supportive energy throughout the day. The consistent presence of these crystals can act as a constant reminder of your commitment to healing and promote a sense of serenity and well-being.

The beauty of these daily practices is their adaptability. They can be integrated seamlessly into your existing routine, requiring minimal time commitment yet delivering substantial rewards. The key is consistency. Make these practices a non-negotiable part of your day, a commitment to yourself and your well-being.

Maintaining momentum can be challenging, particularly during times of stress or emotional upheaval. It's during these periods that your daily practices become even more crucial. When life throws curveballs, your routine acts as an anchor, providing a sense of stability and grounding. However, it's important to remember that flexibility is key. If your schedule changes, adapt your practices accordingly. It's better to engage in shorter, more frequent practices than to abandon them altogether.

If you find yourself struggling to maintain your routine, consider what might be hindering your progress. Is it a lack of time, a lack of motivation, or something else entirely? Identifying the root cause enables you to implement targeted strategies for overcoming challenges. For instance, if time is a constraint, explore shorter, more efficient practices. If motivation lags, try setting smaller, more achievable goals. Perhaps you could start with just 5 minutes of daily meditation instead of 30 minutes and gradually increase the duration as you build consistency.

Cultivating self-compassion is paramount. There will be days when you miss a practice, or when your dedication falters. This is perfectly normal. Rather than berating yourself, treat yourself with kindness and understanding. Acknowledge your imperfections, forgive yourself, and gently redirect your focus back to your chosen path. Celebrate every small victory, every step you take towards your goals.

Remember that building a sustainable holistic wellness practice is a process. It requires patience, perseverance, and a deep commitment to self-care. Don't be discouraged by setbacks. Instead, view them as opportunities for growth and learning. Continuously evaluate your progress, making adjustments to your routine as needed. This self-reflection will help you refine your practices and create a sustainable holistic wellness approach that aligns perfectly with your individual needs and preferences.

It's also vital to remember the power of intention. Your daily practices aren't merely mechanical repetitions; they're acts of conscious creation. By approaching your routines with mindful awareness, you amplify their healing power. Imagine the energy you're channeling, the intentions you're manifesting, and the positive impact you're creating within yourself.

Building a supportive community can also significantly contribute to maintaining your daily practices. Sharing your experiences, challenges, and successes with like-minded individuals creates a sense of belonging and mutual support. This shared journey can provide encouragement and inspiration during moments of doubt or discouragement. Consider joining a local group, attending workshops, or connecting with others online who share your passion for holistic wellness. This sense of community can significantly boost your motivation and commitment.

Furthermore, remember to listen to your intuition. Your body and soul offer valuable guidance; pay attention to subtle cues and adjust your practices accordingly. Perhaps your energy levels are low, indicating a need for more rest or relaxation. Or, you might feel drawn to a specific modality or practice, suggesting a deeper exploration is in order. Trust your inner wisdom and allow your journey to unfold organically.

Your daily practices are not merely rituals; they are acts of self-love, self-care, and profound connection with your inner self and the universe. They are the building blocks of a vibrant, fulfilling life, grounded in holistic well-being. Embrace the journey, trust the process, and celebrate the transformative power of consistency. The path to holistic wellness is a lifelong endeavor, and each day offers a new opportunity to nurture your mind, body, and spirit. Go forth, and create a life of vibrant health, joy, and profound inner peace. The journey inward is a deeply personal one, and while the structured practices outlined thus far provide a strong foundation, true mastery lies in weaving these techniques into the very fabric of your daily existence. Imagine your life as a vibrant tapestry, with each thread representing a different healing modality. The richer the tapestry, the more vibrant and resilient your life becomes.

The key is not to force these threads together, but to gently and organically integrate them, allowing them to intertwine naturally.

This isn't about adding more to your already full plate; it's about transforming your existing routines into opportunities for healing and self-discovery. Instead of viewing these practices as additional tasks, consider them acts of self-love, moments of mindful connection with yourself and the universe. This subtle shift in perspective can make all the difference in sustaining your commitment to your holistic wellness journey.

Let's explore practical ways to integrate energy healing into your everyday life, transforming mundane activities into avenues for self-care and transformation. For instance, consider your morning routine. Instead of rushing through the motions, transform this time into a sacred ritual, infusing it with intention and energy work.

Begin your day with a few minutes of mindful breathing, focusing on the sensation of each inhale and exhale. Visualize a golden light filling your body, clearing any stagnant energy and replacing it with vibrant, life-giving force. This simple act can set the tone for the entire day, ensuring you begin with a sense of calm and centeredness.

As you shower, imagine the water washing away not only physical impurities but also emotional and energetic blockages. Visualize the water carrying away any stress, negativity, or anxieties you may be carrying, leaving you feeling refreshed and renewed. This simple visualization can transform a mundane task into a powerful cleansing ritual.

While you're getting dressed, choose a crystal that resonates with your intention for the day. Perhaps you need clarity, focus, or emotional grounding. Select a crystal that aligns with your specific need, holding it in your hand as you dress, allowing its energy to infuse your day. Amethyst for clarity, Carnelian for courage, or Clear Quartz for amplification—the choice is yours, guided by your intuition.

Throughout your workday, take short breaks for mindful moments. Even a few minutes of deep breathing or a brief Reiki self-treatment can significantly reduce stress and restore your energy levels. Imagine the healing energy flowing through you, replenishing your vitality and restoring your equilibrium.

During lunch, take a moment to connect with nature, even if it's just by looking out the window and appreciating the beauty of the natural world. Nature's energy can be incredibly grounding and restorative, helping to balance your chakras and reconnect you to the Earth's life force. If possible, take a walk outside, allowing the fresh air and sunlight to rejuvenate your spirit.

In the evening, as you prepare for bed, perform a short Reiki session, allowing the gentle energy to wash over you, preparing your mind and body for a restful night's sleep. Visualize the energy flowing through your body, releasing tension and promoting a sense of deep relaxation. This nightly ritual can significantly improve the quality of your sleep and leave you feeling refreshed and revitalized in the morning.

Numerology can be seamlessly woven into your daily life by paying attention to the numerical significance of dates and times. Observe the recurring numbers you encounter throughout the day and reflect on their potential message. This conscious observation can offer subtle guidance and insights into the energies at play.

Similarly, astrology can provide daily perspectives. Consider the planetary influences on your day and reflect on how these energies might impact your mood and interactions. This doesn't mean adhering rigidly to astrological predictions, but rather using this knowledge to navigate challenges with greater awareness and grace.

Integrating chakra work into your daily life can be done through conscious movement and mindful awareness. Incorporate yoga poses that target specific chakras, or spend a few minutes each day visualizing and focusing on each energy center. This simple practice can significantly enhance your energy flow and overall well-being.

Crystal healing can be effortlessly incorporated by placing crystals around your living space. Strategically placing crystals in different areas of your home can enhance the energy flow and promote a sense of harmony and balance. For example, amethyst in your bedroom can promote restful sleep, while citrine in your living room can enhance positivity and joy. Beyond these specific suggestions, the key to integrating energy healing into your daily life is to cultivate a sense of mindful awareness. Approach each activity with intention, paying attention to your physical sensations, emotions, and energy flow. This consistent state of awareness can subtly yet powerfully transform your entire life into a continuous healing journey.

Remember, the path to holistic wellness is not a destination but a journey. There will be days when you feel more connected to your energy and others where you feel more challenged. Embrace these fluctuations as integral parts of your growth, and approach each day with compassion and understanding for yourself.

Don't be discouraged by occasional lapses in your routine. Life is unpredictable, and there will be times when your energy levels are low, or you face unexpected challenges. The beauty of these holistic practices is their adaptability. If you miss a day or two, simply resume your routine without self-criticism. Consistency is key, not perfection.

Celebrate your successes, no matter how small. Acknowledge your progress and appreciate the positive changes you are experiencing. This positive reinforcement will help maintain your motivation and commitment to your holistic wellness journey.

Create a supportive environment that fosters your self-care practices. This might involve surrounding yourself with supportive friends and family, seeking guidance from experienced practitioners, or joining online communities dedicated to holistic wellness. Sharing your experiences can strengthen your resolve and provide a sense of connection with like-minded individuals.

Finally, listen to your body. If you feel drawn towards a particular modality or practice, explore it further. Your intuition is your most powerful guide on this journey. Trust your inner wisdom, and allow your path to unfold organically. Your commitment to self-care is an act of profound self-love, paving the way for a life of vibrancy, joy, and deep inner peace.

Embrace the journey, and watch as your life transforms into a testament to the power of holistic well-being. The journey doesn't end with the completion of this year-long exploration; rather, it marks the beginning of a lifelong commitment to self-discovery and holistic well-being. Think of this year as laying the foundation, building a solid structure upon which you can continue to construct your personal sanctuary of inner peace and vibrant health. The practices you've learned – Reiki, numerology, astrology, crystal healing, and chakra work – are not merely techniques to be applied for a set period; they are tools, instruments in your ongoing symphony of self-care and personal growth.

Imagine your life as a garden. The seeds you've planted this past year are now beginning to sprout. Some may be tender seedlings, needing gentle nurturing and consistent attention. Others may be stronger, more resilient, flourishing even with minimal care. But all require ongoing tending, a continuous commitment to providing the right conditions for growth. Just as a gardener regularly waters, weeds, and fertilizes their plants, you must consistently nurture your inner landscape, tending to your energetic, emotional, and spiritual well-being. This means continuing with your daily practices, even if it's only for a few minutes each day. The consistency, the ritualistic aspect, is more significant than the duration. A few minutes of mindful breathing, a quick Reiki self-treatment, or a moment spent meditating on your chakras can make a world of difference in your overall energy and well-being. The key is to integrate these practices organically into your daily life, weaving them into the fabric of your existence rather than viewing them as separate, additional tasks.

Consider your routines. Do you commute? Use that time for mindful listening to calming music or a guided meditation. Waiting in line? Use that time to focus on your breath, or silently repeat an affirmation of self-love and gratitude. Even the mundane activities of washing dishes or folding laundry can become opportunities for mindfulness, bringing awareness to the present moment and appreciating the simple acts of daily life.

The integration of numerology and astrology doesn't necessitate complex calculations or elaborate charts. Observe the numbers you encounter throughout your day. Do you frequently see the number 11? Reflect on its potential meaning, considering its association with intuition and spiritual awakening. Pay attention to the daily astrological transits. Are the planets influencing your energy in a particular way? Use this awareness to navigate challenges with greater understanding and compassion for yourself and others.

As your understanding of your chakras deepens, explore different ways to balance and harmonize them. Continue your yoga practice, adding new poses that specifically target certain energy centers. Experiment with different crystals, placing them strategically near your chakras to amplify their energy. Pay attention to your intuition, and allow it to guide you in your choices. The body is always communicating; learn to listen to its subtle whispers, the signals it sends through energy shifts, physical sensations, and emotional fluctuations.

Crystal healing offers an ongoing opportunity for exploration. Expand your collection, researching the properties of different crystals and discovering which ones resonate with you. Use crystals in different ways – holding them during meditation, placing them in your living space, wearing them as jewelry. Experiment and discover what works best for you. The power of Reiki extends far beyond personal self-healing. Consider sharing the gift of Reiki with others. Volunteer at a hospice, offer treatments to friends and family, or even explore the possibility of becoming a certified Reiki practitioner. The act of giving is incredibly healing, both for the giver and the receiver.

As you progress on your journey, you'll naturally gravitate towards certain modalities more than others. Don't fight this; allow your interests to guide you. Explore advanced techniques within your preferred practices. Consider taking workshops, attending retreats, or seeking guidance from experienced teachers and mentors. The beauty of this holistic approach lies in its adaptability and the potential for ongoing learning and growth.

Remember that setbacks are inevitable. There will be days when you feel overwhelmed, discouraged, or disconnected from your inner peace. This is part of the process. Don't judge yourself harshly; simply acknowledge these moments, accept them with compassion, and gently redirect your attention back to your practices. The key is consistency, not perfection. Celebrate your successes, no matter how small. Acknowledge your progress, and appreciate the positive changes you've made.

Create a supportive community. Share your experiences with friends, family, or online communities dedicated to holistic well-being. Connect with like-minded individuals who understand and support your journey. Sharing your experiences and learning from others can deepen your understanding and strengthen your commitment to your holistic path. Beyond the specific techniques, cultivate a sense of mindful awareness in all aspects of your life. Approach each activity with intention, paying attention to your physical sensations, emotions, and energy flow. This continuous state of presence can transform mundane tasks into opportunities for healing and self-discovery. Living mindfully, with intention and awareness, transforms life itself into a sacred practice.

This is not just about physical health, but about a deep, abiding sense of inner peace and joy. It's about connecting with your spirit, understanding your purpose, and living a life that is both meaningful and fulfilling. The practices you've learned are keys to unlocking this potential, guiding you towards a life brimming with vitality, resilience, and an unwavering connection to the boundless energy of the universe. Embrace this lifelong journey, trusting in your inner wisdom and the transformative power of holistic well-being. Your future self will thank you for it. The journey continues, always evolving, always unfolding, always revealing new depths of self-discovery and understanding. The path is your own, unique and personal, guided by your intuition and powered by your unwavering commitment to your well-being. This commitment is an act of profound self-love, an investment in your present and future happiness, a testament to the extraordinary power you hold within. Continue to explore, to learn, to grow, and to embrace the extraordinary journey of a lifetime spent nurturing your holistic well-being. The universe supports you; now support yourself. I love you and I am proud of you!

A Comprehensive List of Crystals and Their Properties:

Amethyst – Calming, protection, spiritual awareness, enhances intuition and psychic abilities.

Clear Quartz – Amplifies energy, clarity of mind, master healer, programmable for any intention.

Rose Quartz – Love, compassion, emotional healing, heart chakra balancing.

Black Tourmaline – Protection, grounding, shields against negative energy and EMFs.

Citrine – Abundance, confidence, creativity, energizes personal will.

Selenite – Cleansing, spiritual connection, clears blockages, purifies space and other crystals.

Lapis Lazuli – Wisdom, truth, enhances intellectual ability and spiritual insight.

Obsidian – Deep healing, psychic protection, releases emotional blockages.

Tiger's Eye – Confidence, courage, protection, balances emotional extremes.

Carnelian – Vitality, motivation, creativity, supports reproductive and sacral chakra energy.

Smoky Quartz – Grounding, detoxification, releases fear and anxiety.

Aventurine – Luck, prosperity, heart healing, emotional recovery.

Hematite – Stability, grounding, improves focus, transforms negativity into positivity.

Fluorite – Mental clarity, protection from EMFs, balances spiritual energy.

Moonstone – Divine feminine energy, intuition, emotional balance, fertility.

Labradorite – Transformation, psychic abilities, protects aura, spiritual awakening.

Blue Lace Agate – Peace, communication, soothes anxiety and clears throat chakra.

Malachite – Emotional release, transformation, absorbs negative energies.

Garnet – Passion, strength, grounding, revitalizes energy and love.

Chrysocolla – Communication, feminine empowerment, emotional release.

Turquoise – Protection, healing, communication, ancient spiritual ally.

Howlite – Calm, sleep support, reduces anger and stress.

Amazonite – Harmony, truth, courage, balances masculine and feminine energies.

Pyrite – Abundance, protection, energy boost, shields from negativity.

Kyanite – Alignment, communication, never needs cleansing.

Celestite – Angelic communication, peace, supports dream recall and meditation.

Chakra Balancing Exercises

Root Chakra (Muladhara) – Grounding & Stability:

Grounding Meditation – Visualize roots growing from your spine into the earth.

Walking Barefoot in Nature – Connects your body to Earth's frequency.

Yoga Poses – Mountain pose (Tadasana), Warrior I, Squats.

Eat Earthy Foods – Root vegetables like carrots, beets, and potatoes.

Affirmations – "I am safe. I am grounded. I am secure."

Red Color Visualization – Imagine red light spinning at the base of your spine.

Use Crystals – Red Jasper, Hematite, Smoky Quartz.

Drumming or Low-Frequency Sounds – Promotes grounding energy.

Sacral Chakra (Svadhisthana) – Creativity & Emotions:

Hip-Opening Yoga – Pigeon pose, Bound Angle, Cobra.

Creative Expression – Painting, dancing, writing, singing.

Water Immersion – Swimming, bathing, or listening to flowing water.

Sensory Exploration – Savor tastes, scents, and textures mindfully.

Affirmations – "I am creative. I embrace pleasure and joy."

Orange Visualization – Orange energy in the pelvic region.

Use Crystals – Carnelian, Sunstone, Orange Calcite.

Practice Flowing Movement – Belly dancing, tai chi.

Solar Plexus Chakra (Manipura) – Confidence & Willpower:

Core-Strengthening Yoga – Boat pose, Plank, Bow.

Sunbathing or Fire Gazing – Energizes the solar chakra.

Goal Setting & Action Steps – Build personal power and follow-through.

Affirmations – "I am strong. I am confident. I am in control."

Yellow Visualization – Bright yellow light at your navel.

Use Crystals – Citrine, Tiger's Eye, Yellow Jasper.

Digestive Health Focus – Eat warm, yellow foods like bananas and turmeric tea.

Breath of Fire (Kapalabhati Pranayama) – Energizes the solar plexus.

Heart Chakra (Anahata) – Love & Compassion:

Heart-Opening Yoga – Camel pose, Cobra, Bridge, Fish pose.

Loving-Kindness Meditation (Metta) – Send love to yourself and others.

Practice Forgiveness – Journal or speak forgiveness to free energy.

Affirmations – "I love and accept myself. I give and receive love freely."

Green Visualization – Emerald green light glowing from your chest.

Use Crystals – Rose Quartz, Green Aventurine, Rhodonite.

Acts of Kindness – Volunteer, compliment someone, show appreciation.

Emotional Release Techniques – Cry, laugh, hug, or express love.

Throat Chakra (Vishuddha) — Communication & Truth:

Vocal Toning or Chanting 'HAM' — Clears and activates the throat chakra.

Journaling or Speaking Your Truth — Honest expression releases blockage.

Sing or Recite Poetry — Use your voice creatively.

Affirmations — "I speak my truth with clarity and love."

Blue Visualization — Sky-blue light spinning in your throat.

Use Crystals — Lapis Lazuli, Blue Lace Agate, Aquamarine.

Hydration — Drink water and herbal teas regularly.

Neck and Shoulder Yoga Stretches — Releases tension in the vocal channel.

Third Eye Chakra (Ajna) — Intuition & Insight:

Meditation with Focus on Third Eye — Gently place attention between your eyebrows.

Mindful Observation — Watch the sky, nature, or candle flame.

Visualization Practice — Visualize outcomes or scenarios vividly.

Affirmations — "I trust my intuition. I see clearly."

Indigo Visualization — Deep indigo light at your forehead.

Use Crystals — Amethyst, Fluorite, Labradorite.

Practice Dream Journaling — Record and reflect on intuitive insights.

Reduce Screen Time — Detox from visual clutter and overstimulation.

Crown Chakra (Sahasrara) – Spiritual Connection:

Silent Meditation – Focus on being and consciousness beyond thought.

Prayer or Communion with Higher Self – Ask for guidance or connection.

Visualization of White or Violet Light – Flowing from the top of your head upward.

Affirmations – "I am connected to divine wisdom. I am one with all."

Use Crystals – Selenite, Clear Quartz, Lepidolite.

Practice Gratitude – Deepen your connection to the universe.

Spiritual Reading or Chanting 'OM' – Uplift the spirit through wisdom and vibration.

Crown-Opening Yoga Poses – Headstand, Lotus, Corpse Pose (Savasana).

Reiki Self-Treatment Guide

Step-by-Step Instructions to Channel Universal Energy for Self-Healing

Step 1: Prepare the Space and Your Mind

- **Find a quiet space** where you won't be disturbed for 20–30 minutes.

- Sit or lie down comfortably.

- **Optional:** Light a candle, burn incense, or play calming music.

- **Set an intention**, such as:
  "I allow healing energy to flow through me for my highest good."

Step 2: Activate Reiki Energy

- Place your hands together in **Gassho (prayer position)** at your heart.

- Take a few deep breaths and mentally say:
  "I now activate Reiki."

- Some practitioners visualize light flowing through their crown into their hands.

Step 3: Scan Your Body (Byosen Scan)

- Slowly move your hands above your body (a few inches away) to **feel for areas of tension, heat, or discomfort**.

- Trust your intuition – your hands may feel pulled to specific spots.

Step 4: Reiki Hand Positions

Perform each hand position for **2–5 minutes**. Let your intuition guide you to stay longer where needed.

➤ Head Positions

1. **Eyes/Forehead** – Palms gently over the eyes or third eye.

2. **Temples** – One hand on each side of your head.

3. **Crown** – Hands hovering above or resting on the top of your head.

4. **Back of Head** – One hand at the base of the skull, one near the top.

➤ **Upper Body**

5. **Throat** – Hands lightly placed over the neck (do not apply pressure).

6. **Heart** – One hand on the heart, one on the upper chest.

7. **Solar Plexus** – Hands on your upper abdomen.

8. **Sacral Area** – Below the navel (creative/emotional center).

9. **Root/Lower Abdomen** – Hands near the pelvic area.

➤ **Back of the Body (Optional if lying down)**

10. **Shoulders** – Hands on top or just above shoulders.

11. **Lower Back** – Rest hands on each side of the spine.

12. **Tailbone/Base of Spine** – Hands at the bottom of your back.

Step 5: Close the Session

- Place hands back in Gassho.

- Say silently: *"Thank you, Reiki, for this healing."*

- Sit quietly for a few minutes.

- Drink a glass of water and reflect on how you feel.

Tips for Best Results

- Practice **daily** for consistency and deep healing.

- Don't worry if you don't "feel" energy at first—it works regardless.

- Be **patient, gentle, and open** to emotional release or insights.

Astrological Correspondences for Chakra Healing

Root Chakra (Muladhara):

- **Zodiac Signs:** Capricorn, Taurus

- **Planetary Rulers:** Saturn, Earth

- **Healing Themes:**
  Grounding, physical safety, survival, connection to the body, security.
  Supports healing of: fear, instability, anxiety, lack of trust in the material world.

Sacral Chakra (Svadhisthana):

- **Zodiac Signs:** Cancer, Scorpio, Pisces

- **Planetary Rulers:** Moon, Pluto, Neptune

- **Healing Themes:**
  Emotional flow, sexuality, intimacy, pleasure, creativity.
  Supports healing of: emotional repression, guilt, fear of change, creative blockages.

Solar Plexus Chakra (Manipura):

- **Zodiac Signs:** Aries, Leo, Sagittarius

- **Planetary Rulers:** Mars, Sun, Jupiter

- **Healing Themes:**
  Personal power, confidence, self-worth, ambition, decision-making.
  Supports healing of: low self-esteem, fear of judgment, lack of direction, anger.

Heart Chakra (Anahata):

- **Zodiac Signs:** Libra, Taurus

- **Planetary Rulers:** Venus

- **Healing Themes:**
Love, compassion, emotional balance, forgiveness, relationships.
Supports healing of: heartbreak, grief, resentment, isolation, co-dependence.

Throat Chakra (Vishuddha):

- **Zodiac Signs:** Gemini, Virgo

- **Planetary Rulers:** Mercury

- **Healing Themes:**
Communication, truth, self-expression, inner voice, authenticity.
Supports healing of: fear of speaking, dishonesty, repression, shame around words.

Third Eye Chakra (Ajna):

- **Zodiac Signs:** Sagittarius, Aquarius

- **Planetary Rulers:** Jupiter, Uranus

- **Healing Themes:**
Intuition, vision, insight, clarity, perception.
Supports healing of: confusion, skepticism, lack of focus, blocked inner guidance.

Crown Chakra (Sahasrara):

- **Zodiac Signs:** Pisces, Aquarius

- **Planetary Rulers:** Neptune, Uranus

- **Healing Themes:**
Divine consciousness, spiritual connection, enlightenment, higher self.
Supports healing of: spiritual disconnection, apathy, fear of the unknown, ego-attachment.

Final Reflection: The Light Within

As you come to the final page of this journey, know that this is not the end—it is a beginning. You have moved through sacred teachings, cosmic wisdom, and ancient energy codes that have lived in the collective consciousness for thousands of years. Now, they live in you.

Whether you are just starting to explore energy healing or deepening an already awakened path, remember this: **you are your own healer**. Every technique you've learned, every chakra you've opened, every vibration you've aligned with—these are now tools within your soul's medicine bag.

Close your eyes. Inhale deeply. Feel the earth beneath you and the sky above you. Let the energies you've awakened rise gently through each chakra, like sunlight moving through stained glass. You are grounded. You are radiant. You are limitless.

Let this knowledge guide you. Let your intuition be your compass. Let love be your language.

Made in United States
Cleveland, OH
24 May 2025

17194479R00162